The Bright Lights

The Bright Lights

A Theatre Life

Marian Seldes

Illustrated with photographs

Limelight Editions   New York

First Limelight Edition, March 1984

Copyright © 1978 by Marian Seldes
All rights reserved under International and Pan-American
Copyright Conventions. Published in the United States by
Proscenium Publishers Inc., New York, and simultaneously
in Canada by Fitzhenry & Whiteside Limited, Toronto.
Originally published by Houghton Mifflin Company

ISBN 0–87910–001–X

Manufactured in the United States of America

Library of Congress Cataloging in Publication Data

Seldes, Marian.
The bright lights.

1. Seldes, Marian. 2. Actors—United States—Biography.
I. Title.
[PN2287.S346A32   1984]   792'.028'0924 [B]
83-24402

I am writing for myself and strangers.
This is the only way that I can do it. Everybody is a real one to me, everybody is like
someone else too to me. No one of them that
I know can want to know it and so I write
for myself and strangers.

— Gertrude Stein

Illustrations

1

I knew.

Tim and I would walk home from school, have dinner, do our homework and take our baths, and by eight o'clock we would go to our rooms.

"Good-night, my only brother." He was my only brother and that was our first endlessly repeated joke. He might not even hear me, lying on his bed, arms around his radio as he listened in the dark. The horns from the boats on the East River and my parents' laughter were the sounds that accompanied the perfect time of each evening.

The light switch was by the door in my room at the top of the house. The moment I turned it off and moved to the bed, the play would begin: A long mirror caught my reflection, the street light making it dim, and the always white long nightgown became a costume in some dream. I understood that what I was seeing was myself, but my feeling was that it was a creature observed from a greater distance than the length of the room, who moved differently and looked unreal. Someone was in the room with me. I watched, fascinated. Was still. Moved again. Spoke. No echo. Someone who was surely me, but not me.

In the stillness there was no fear. I tried to make the moment last and expand the instant of glimpsing the mirrored figure into a time for a play of my own imagining to begin.

As long as we lived on Henderson Place I waited for the evening to come, for the play to happen. As I repeated the ritual, I came to know that I was going to be an actress.

The Christmas Pageant took place in the theatre at the Dalton School. The first year we were there Tim, who was two grades ahead of me, played one of the Kings on the stage. My first part was as one of three angels posed in an arched alcove in the main hallway outside the doors of the theatre. Bright spotlights focused on us, hotter and brighter than the sun. We wore costumes of royal blue felt, with gold waistbands fastened on the inside with safety pins, strips of gold oilcloth binding our necks and waists. We knelt motionless until the audience had walked by and we heard the sounds of the chorus singing the first Christmas hymn. I kept my eyes on the light. I knew there was no heaven and thought there was no God, but there was loveliness and safety and a secret excitement contained in that time and place.

An hour later when I got ready for the second performance the red marks from my costume were still on my flesh as proof of my bondage. There is a photograph of the three angels in the alcove. A slender blond girl of sixteen standing between an exquisite child of five with long, almost white-blond hair kneeling on one side of her and me kneeling on the other. It was beautiful to be there, to feel the

As an angel in the Christmas Pageant at the Dalton School, 1935.

bright light on my face and hands, to press my palms together in adoration. I remember perfect happiness. The photograph shows a thin, dark, frowning child as the third angel.

Two years later I was on the stage, in a gold costume with a tight halo, gazing at an infant sitting on a pedestal holding a cross. In my last year at school I was the Annunciation angel and twice I was chosen to read the passages from the Bible that introduced the scenes. My religious training took place in a theatre. It became the church of my 3 life; existence there was as magical as what I dreamed of in the room with the mirror.

It was the dream made real.

Soon after I knelt as the angel in the alcove I learned how pleasant it was to have more to do. I began by writing a scene in our fourth-grade play which we adapted from a book called *The Princess Runs Away*. The book began, "The sky hung like a bright blue bowl over Egypt . . ." Those are the only words I remember. I look for the small book in secondhand bookstores without success. We painted the scenery on huge rolls of brown wrapping paper. I thought the boy who played a lute in one scene was beautiful but that it was wrong that one of the princesses wore pigtails, and that one was blond. There were four of us, one in each act. The scenes went too quickly and there was only one performance.

The fair princess in our fourth-grade play was Pamela Stillman. Her family lived in two adjoining town houses on Sutton Square. On Saturday afternoons Pam and I would roam through both houses and the garden by the East River. An elevator connected the houses, servants brought us cocoa, a trunk held complicated old-fashioned clothes that we used for costumes.

Sitting on the living room floor we plotted scenarios. Of course there were princesses, and often I would base my part on Frances Hodgson Burnett's Sara Crewe, a character I adored and wanted to resemble.

No one disturbed us. Time was ours. We acted our plays until I had to go home.

I look back on those hours now with loving disbelief. How could our trust in each other and in the reality of the situations we chose have been so strong? Why did it take the rest of my professional life to learn ways to refind that perfect trust and put it into my work? And why when that trust is threatened does it destroy my happiness in a way that is — hopelessly childish?

I was able to "be" anyone I wanted to be those afternoons on Sutton Square. But like most children when the person to "be" was chosen for me, without my own desire to be that person added to it, the results were painful. I know that if I had asked or suggested to my daughter at any time during her childhood that she act the part of another person she would have refused. The few times she was in a play at school we made her costume together and enjoyed it, but it has never been what she wanted to do. I told her about the two vacation trips my parents took us on, to the West Indies. My father edited the S.S. *Kungsholm*'s newspaper and had a lot to do with the day's activities planned to keep the passengers happy. The cruise director had the fine name of Burson B. Winecoop. He was handsome and vain and officious. There was a pretty blond girl on board who was constantly being photographed, and she had a nice name too, Candy Jones. There were races, movies and ship's pools, lectures and parties. The important event was the costume party. On the first cruise, when I was eight, my mother chose to have Tim and me be little native divers. She painted our bodies with black shoe polish and we both wore bathing trunks. Nothing else. I was horrified but silent. There is a smiling photograph of us in our costumes when we won the first prize. The following trip we were dressed up as newsboys carrying prop papers with *Kungsholm* headlines superimposed on the masthead. Fully clothed in neat rags, even hats. I look just as happy in the second picture when we won the prize again as I did in the first. Acting?

I lived two lives. A student and daughter for the world to see, an actress for myself. Life was getting complicated. I had difficulty sorting out my feelings. There was an enormous weight of love inside me in a place I thought of as my heart and it hurt to carry it back and forth from school. No place to rest it, to ease the pain, to rid myself of it. I was twelve years old and the pain was getting worse. I planned to turn over a new leaf to a clean white page. I would be a person with a goal rather than a dream. A pretty, not-quite-as-tall-as-I person, with kind eyes. That would be me on the next page of the book and all the other pages could be thrown away.

I saved everything about my life that I could find and I saved my thoughts, too. I wrote them down. By the time I was twelve I knew there was no clean page.

My teachers did not want me to be an actress. My Latin teacher, Lauralee Tuttle, who was married to a stage director, said, "I can't bear to think of you wasting your life waiting for the phone to ring." My history teacher, who was a fine writer — Elizabeth Seeger — wanted me to write history books. Helen Parkhurst, Dalton's creator and headmistress, felt I would be a disappointment not only to the school but to my parents, whom she seemed to love and admire almost as much as I did, if acting was to be my life's work.

But the theatre teacher, Mildred Geiger, had faith in a future for me as an actress from the beginning. While we rehearsed plays in the auditorium at Dalton I felt that future coming toward me.

At Dalton every holiday was celebrated with some kind of
performance in the theatre — Thanksgiving, the winter sol-

stice, Christmas, Lincoln's Birthday, the first day of spring and, at the end of the year, Arch Day, when every member of the school walked through a flowered arch to signify a going forth and growing up. Most of these festivals were staged by Mrs. Geiger.

Until I met Guthrie McClintic I thought of Mildred as the person I was acting for. Her standards were high and the productions of plays at Dalton in the 1940s were given time and care and were an important part of the curriculum. Theatre — acting in plays — seemed a natural part of our lives.

What I remember about learning to tell time is much like what I feel now when I learn a part. It is a kind of loss of innocence. As painful and unprepared for as the other loss that is whispered about and hinted at when girls begin to grow up. It is an expected thing. It happens to all of us. It will happen to each in a separate special way. The awareness of time passing. The awareness of one's own capacity to give and receive physical love and make love and make life. The feeling of exultation mixed with loss that follows the first few experiences. Then the confidence growing slowly within. The knowledge, secret and hidden within. I can tell time. I can make love. I can act a part.

Why are they joined in my mind? Because these things represent for me my only maturity. Without the ability to do these things I still seem to be the little girl in the blue angel costume.

Life goes by. There does not seem to be enough time to accomplish in daily living, much less in a career, all that you want to. Your use of time defines the kind of person you are off the stage — and on. When you are in charge of that time — the time of your life — you are happy, and as Thornton Wilder tells us, "He who has once been happy is forever out of time's grasp."

I have been wanting to think through more carefully my obsession with time. My habit when I find a subject that interests me is to find the dictionary definition. The dictionary is full of poems. If an actor had to choose one book out of all the books in the world, I think a wise choice would be an enormous overflowing dictionary, too heavy to lift. A piece of furniture for his life. For "time" there is a poem:

"The system of those sequential relations that any event has to any other, as past, present or future; indefinite and continuous duration regarded as that in which events succeed one another." It sounds like the prescription for a play. The second listing: "— duration regarded as belonging to the present life as distinct from the life to come or from eternity; finite duration." Time that has form. Like a play. The third: "A system or method of measuring or reckoning the passage of time." Three acts? Fourth: "— a limited period or interval." A scene? A moment in a scene? When I started to read Henry James's *Sense of the Past,* I was entranced with the idea that our lives could exist in more than one period of history, and that all time is *one* time. There are 67 listings in the *Random House Dictionary* and there is not one that cannot be related to stage time. The words are magical. The only painful entry is 42: "kill time."

By definition 53 we find this usage: "— time and time again, again and again, repeatedly," and I think of Gertrude Stein's love of her characters in the passage from *The Making of Americans:* "Always more and more I love repeating, it may be irritating to hear from them but always more and more I love it of them. More and more I love it of them, the

8

being in them, the mixing in them, the repeating in them, the deciding the kind of them every one is who has human being." In Stein's *Lectures in America* there is a section called "Plays," which contains some of the most original writing about the theatre I have read. She says she has found out something "fundamental" about plays:

that the scene as depicted on the stage is more often than not one might say it is almost always in syncopated time in relation to the emotion of anybody in the audience. What this says is this. Your sensation as one in the audience in relation to the play played before you your sensation I say your emotion concerning that play is always either behind or ahead of the play at which you are looking and to which you are listening. So your emotion as a member of the audience is never going on at the same time as the action of the play.

The actor reads this and having been in an audience responds to this feeling that makes him both uneasy and fascinated at the theatre. He knows too that his job is to live in the moment, the present moment that the author has given him. Stein must have known that, too, for she ends her essay: "It is in short the inevitable problem of anybody, living in the composition of the present time, that is living as we are now living as we have it and now do live in it."

The playwright is the master of time. The poet, too. The painter, the sculptor, the musician. All artists. And it is when we are most ecstatic that we, too, master time by forgetting it, changing it, shaping it, making it our own. Our act of love, repeating and repeating.

My father was obsessed with communication. He wrote books, plays, novels, criticism. He worked in the theatre, in   9 films, in television, in radio and at the end of his life he was the dean of the College of Communications at the University of Pennsylvania. He kept experimenting and changing in his work. From the time he was the music critic on the Philadelphia *Evening Ledger* until all he had strength for was to write to the editor of the *New York Times,* he was always asking questions and sharing his answers with an audience. He called the American audience the Great Audience, and wrote a book about them and what they looked at and listened to. He said that radio serials exist outside of time, "their people do not grow older and the listener is expected to know them forever." He said that we got to know these people the way we know our own friends and family and

becoming more familiar each time we see them, with the intonations of their voices, the way they laugh, what they are interested in; and we are supposed to care for them in the same way. We do not expect old friends to be dramatic or amusing every time we see them; the longer we know them the more content we are merely to be in their company; they populate our world, they are landmarks on our journey through life; and if we don't see them for several days, we want to know what happened to them and quite expect them to be a little repetitious when they tell us.

More and more he, too, loved the "repeating in them."

He celebrated the real, the natural, the good. He begged me not to become stage-struck and I promised him not to. I thought what we both felt about working in the theatre was too important to be approached frivolously.

When I was two and Tim was four his version of Aristophanes' *Lysistrata* was a success on Broadway. We grew
up among tangible reminders of that flush time that in-

cluded trips to Europe and lovely clothes and the Henderson Place house.

I saved the *Playbills* my parents brought home and cut out the reviews from the *Times* and the *Tribune*. As my allowance increased I began to collect theatre books. The collecting, the saving of words, became an obsession. I wanted a record not only of what I had seen but of what I was not able to see. I chose a profession in which memory plays an important part. A performance of a play can fade without a trace. It is difficult for the best critic or reporter to make you "see" a play with his words, but when it happens it can illuminate the experience.

Like most children I meant to keep a diary, but my life did not seem interesting enough to *me*. I was sure that when I became an actress it would change and every day would be worth recording.

It turned out to be true. As soon as I knew that I could be an actress and have a place in the theatre I was less afraid of life being meaningless. I was not planning or dreaming of fame; the dream was the work.

My grandfather's name in Russia was Sergius Seldes, but the man at the immigration office told him that was too difficult and wrote "George." He became an American citizen on October 11, 1886. He named his first son George, not after the name that appeared on his blue and red certificate, but after Henry George, the radical economist, whom he admired. His second son, Gilbert, born in 1893, was my father.

The brothers went to Harvard, were war correspondents in the First World War, and kept writing. George married Helen Larkin, who would become his partner in producing *In Fact,* a weekly newspaper that was the first publication in   11 the United States devoted solely to criticism of the press.

A Brearley School classmate of my mother's married the poet John Peale Bishop. At the ceremony my father met and fell in love with her but not her name. "I'll call you Amanda," he said, and in 1923 Alice Wadhams Hall became Amanda Seldes.

A longing to move from my own time to my father's, to share in lives before my life, to say aloud the words and thoughts I read in my childhood, pulled me toward the theatre as a life work and has kept me there. The experience of looking at the photograph of my grandfather, who died when I was two, and wondering what kind of man he was, asking my father about him, creating a vivid, imagined life for him, is much the same approach as I have now when I work on a part. Discoveries that make other lives real dizzy me.

I grew up thinking that my grandfather was an anarchist, but my Uncle George has told me that he was a freethinker, "not an atheist nor even an agnostic. He was a freethinker who accepted no religion but the moral teachings of such men as Buddha, Confucius and Jesus of Nazareth."

My father's manners were instinctive, springing from a childhood spent in a utopian colony that his father had created in Alliance, New Jersey, where he grew up with his brother and where their mother was midwife and postmistress until her early death. When the Alliance colony failed, my grandfather attempted to start another in New York at Croton-on-Hudson. It was to be called Belle Terre and in 1925 he sent out a pamphlet that included his credo:

That all forms of power, or ruling of man by man, is destructive of freedom and culminates in the subjugation of the weak by the strong and unscrupulous.

That mankind will not be happy until capital, as expressed in rent, interest and wages, is abolished.

That the mere abolition of such exploitation is in itself not sufficient to redeem mankind. True emancipation comes from enlightenment.

Conscious of his past, my father embodied the best of it. I grew up in a home without quarrels or cruelty, where time and thoughts and friends were shared.

The first play I saw on Broadway wasn't like a play at all. It was *Jumbo* at the Hippodrome, the last attraction to play there before it was torn down. The title part was an elephant and the most memorable performer was Jimmy Durante. He was a good friend to my father, but I did not know that until many years later when I saw in my father's will that Durante had loaned him a large sum of money. What I knew then was that he was lovable in a new way. Not like a parent or friend or character in a book. He was the first living actor I had seen — Tim and I adored him. We stepped into the sawdust ring after the performance and met him. I went home with my head full of dreams.

It is said that no one would become a playwright without having seen a play. But someone had to write the first play, compelled to set down one voice, then another, to record a conversation or a significant event. Seeing actors is not what made me want to be an actress. Seeing them simply heightened my desire to be one of them.

I was seven when I saw *Jumbo*, eight when we saw the musical *The White Horse Inn* at the new Center Theatre in Rockefeller Center, nine when I saw the comedy *What a Life*. The first serious play I saw was Robert E. Sherwood's *Abe Lincoln in Illinois*. I was ten years old and did not

13

know that you could ask to see a play a second time or I would have begged to be taken again. From the moment I saw Sherwood's Lincoln, he was a living being to me. When we studied him in school, I *knew* him.

Twice a week, after school, I would take the bus downtown to my class at the School of American Ballet. When my Aunt Marian realized how much ballet dancing meant to me, she gave me an extra lesson a week as my Christmas present. No one in the family thought I could be a dancer — they hoped I would not be one — but they did not discourage me.

At Dalton I had fine teachers who remained my friends long after I graduated. The best directors in the theatre are certainly teachers, too. At the School of American Ballet I had the happy fortune to be in one of Muriel Stuart's classes.

Film and television stars, descriptions of heroines in books, great paintings, the faces of our loves, influence our taste for the variousness of beauty. Muriel Stuart was a combination of what was wonderful to watch in another human being. There was not a moment when her body was not in perfect relaxed control and her face — a mask of life — was animated by concern for everything around her. She had been a teacher for many years when I met her. Her career had begun in England and included being a member of Anna Pavlova's company. Ballet teachers don't have time to talk or reminisce with their students, and Muriel did not refer to Pavlova once in the years I studied with her, but I could recognize the influence of that great dancer in her teaching. I had read many books, seen the brief films of Pavlova, and asked questions of all my father's friends who

had seen her. Exquisite. Ephemeral. Unique. They all

agreed. Theatrical. Seductive. Mercurial. When Muriel Stuart danced across the ballet studio to illustrate a combination of steps, I felt I, too, had seen Pavlova.

The discipline and difficulty of studying ballet exhilarated me. The concentration on a given set of problems, the repetition of the routine, released and freed my mind.

I was never promoted and did not deserve to be. Once in the elevator, Lincoln Kirstein, that marvel of inspiration and force for the ballet in America — and the power in the school — looked at me for some time (it was a slow elevator that threatened to make us late for class) and just as the door was about to open he whispered, "Watch your arms."

My energy never failed me but my strength did. My back

At the School of American Ballet, 1943–1944.

15

and my feet were not strong enough. After each lesson I would go home and bathe and wash out my leotard and tights and write down every combination of steps from class in a leatherbound book. After my parents had gone to bed I opened the door to the roof — my room was a single unit on the top floor of an eight-story building — and rehearsed the ballet class and improvised my own dances under the city sky. It did not occur to me that the residents of the Allerton House hotel across the street might be an amused audience to a girl with long arms wearing a white nylon nightgown in her nocturnal reveries.

There was an unbroken family rule that Tim and I could not go out on school nights. We would do our homework and read and go to bed. As I moved into the higher grades at Dalton and Tim went away to Exeter the rule remained. I did not question it.

One afternoon after Miss Stuart's class a young woman hurried into the dressing room at the ballet school carrying a list with names crossed out and added and rewritten down both sides of the page. "It's *Petrouchka* tonight," she bleated, "and I don't have enough supers for the crowd scene."

Nancy Norman and I were dressing to go home. She looked at me. We had been friends since the third grade — there was no need to say anything. I answered her unspoken question: "I can't, Nan. I can't go out on school nights."

"Oh, but for this! Just once! Call her, ask her."

"I can't. That's not fair, she'll think . . ."

"No, she won't. She'll understand." Nancy sensed that I did not want to put my mother in the position of having to say no. She also knew that if we were going to give the girl our names we had better hurry. It was five-thirty. She wanted us to be at "the Met," as she called it, by seven o'clock.

If I didn't make the call and at least ask, Nan would probably be deprived of the chance as well. *Petrouchka* had been part of the first ballet program I had seen, Stravinsky's music haunted my life, the Ballet Theater was one of my favorite companies. The woman interrupted our frantic whisperings.

"It's Fokine Night, don't you see? A tribute to him! All the stars will be in the crowd scene! Come *on*." Michel Fokine had died on August 23, 1942. This was the twelfth of October. The date of my first steps on a real stage.

My surprised, gentle-voiced mother said yes at once. She asked no questions, made no demands. It was perfectly fine with her.

Nan and I ran to a drugstore where they thought we were sisters, had melted cheese sandwiches and chocolate frosted floats. We arrived at the Metropolitan Opera House on Broadway and Thirty-ninth Street at six-thirty. Nan had taken me there many times as her guest and we had shared our hopes of becoming dancers. Perhaps she thought I would not become one; perhaps I thought she wouldn't either. But that night nothing mattered except finding the woman, who turned out to be "Alma." She arranged for supers with the ballet on a regular basis. She greeted us gratefully and directed us to a busy wardrobe woman, who gave me a dress and hat of blue taffeta. We were both tall; we played rich Russian women. Nan looked glamorous in dusty rose.

For about three minutes Jerome Robbins showed us how to get to the stage, what to do when our cue came, and 17 when to get off. Sol Hurok was trying on the costume of the bear. Nora Kaye was going to lead him on. Massine was in his sad, clownish Petrouchka make-up, nodding his head from side to side, moving about nimbly and carefully, acting the part before it was time to dance it.

We did exactly as we were told and were asked to come back and be in all the rest of the *Petrouchka* performances that season. I started to protest and Nan gave me that look again. "All right," I said and wondered what my mother would say.

My mother thought it was exciting. She loved hearing about it, and I described it all in a Russian accent, things I had never known before: the hush the moment before the curtain rises when a large company of dancers waits for the musical cue, the hurried roar of the curtain going up, suddenly understanding why the Met was called the Golden Horseshoe. From the stage I saw the shape outlined: a perfect half-circle of dimming lovely lights.

Alma gave us each a dollar. I decided to save mine, put it in a frame, keep it as a reminder of my debut. I broke the bill a week later to buy a Mounds candy bar. But I kept some of the snowflakes that came down on us from a canvas folded and shaken six stories above the stage. Little gray-white circles of paper in an envelope marked "Fokine Tribute."

Nancy and I practiced ballet in her room at home. Her mother had provided her with a barre and mirror. We listened to music. The Norman house was ornamented with exquisite photographs by Stieglitz and Steichen, paintings by John Marin, plants, flowers, shelves of books. Dorothy Norman was the editor and publisher of *Twice a Year* magazine. While Nancy and I were dancing and listening to music she was writing, planning, meeting with writers, painters, photographers, and presiding over home and family with calm beauty. She called me daughter.

I woke one morning when I was fifteen feeling light-headed. Had I dreamed something extraordinary? No, it was not a dream, it was a solution, a certainty that I was not going to be a dancer. I told no one. I kept going to the classes; I loved them even more being free of the necessity to excel in a field where I did not belong. I gave up that ambition and kept the love.

Allegra Fuller had inspired me to want to be a dancer and a skater because she was skilled at both. She was a close, dear friend from the moment of our meeting in the third grade at Dalton and it did not seem to surprise or embarrass her that many of the other girls wanted to be like her. Allegra's blue eyes and long light brown hair made her angelically pretty when she was a small child. She looked like a princess in a romantic novel. But she behaved like an unaffected, utterly honest human being.

I took skating lessons at the Iceland Rink on top of Madison Square Garden, where I had followed Allegra. I disapproved of Ned Wayburn's tap-dancing classes after seeing her lessons there. Paul Draper's artistry had made conventional tapping ridiculous, but watching Allegra skate made that kind of self-expression enviable. We went to see Sonja Henie together and it inspired Allegra to form a Skating Club at Dalton. We glided over the linoleum floors in white cotton socks and wrote down combinations of steps for homework, which Allegra would correct. I have that book. I was no good at skating on ice or linoleum. I had to give it up. I thanked my Aunt Marian for my expensive blue skating dress and the lessons. She had guessed my decision long 19 before I mentioned it. She was skilled in her own work; lack of skill made her impatient and brusque. Her nature was demanding, generous, pragmatic.

I was her namesake. Marian Hall was my mother's sister. The eldest of four children, she was the only one who had a profession. When she graduated from the Brearley School she apprenticed herself to an interior decorator and became one of the best-known decorators in New York in a career that lasted over forty years. It was to Auntie — as her nieces and nephews and godchildren called her — that all questions of taste were presented. Her dicta were my mother's laws. My long hair was cut short because "all the little girls in Paris have feather cuts." My "good" black patent leather shoes were exchanged for bright red leather ones — French and not precisely my size, but they looked pretty with a blue-and-white-striped cotton dress that Auntie brought back from one of her many trips to Europe. The couches and chairs wherever we lived were covered with lush, flowery chintz. My mother had a housecoat that matched a couch. A tasteful joke.

Auntie took us to the best restaurants, gave her relatives and friends lavish and appropriate presents, drank lots of champagne, and martinis with just a whiff of vermouth, and was interested in all that we did and saw and thought.

Tim and I loved her. We may have disagreed with much of what she said in her definite, warm voice, but even when we were adults we never quarreled with her. Her opinions were unshakable.

She wanted Wendell Willkie to be President of the United States. My parents were staunch Democrats. She asked them to leave her house after a bitter political argument. How 20 happy she was when Eisenhower was elected! Her life was among the rich. They needed their homes decorated and it was with them that she spent her most productive hours. We had dinner one night with a woman she described as "the richest in America." I could not help noticing that Ailsa Mellon Bruce's dress was on backward. When she noticed it she giggled helplessly and blamed her maid.

Auntie was the head of the family. In social matters even my father deferred to her. When my grandmother died the family as a unit of strength ceased to exist, but Auntie kept us together with her compassion and care. That I did not have a coming-out party or go to college or powder my nose were disappointments to her, but I told her what was in my heart more often than I meant to and read her my short stories because I knew she would keep my secrets.

Auntie never married. She had a lover who lived in Paris and she saw him twice a year there and whenever he could come to New York. He arranged for her apartment to be filled with flowers all year long and loved her from the day they met until he died. So did his wife and children. It was impossible not to.

My mother taught us by example, the example set in her life by her father, Benjamin West Hall. She was sixteen when he died, her sister Marian was twenty. They revered their father and could never love their mother fully when she remarried. He had been the beautiful figure of authority in their lives. The manners they were taught, we were taught.

My mother's mother had a photograph of my father on her dresser. She showed me the inscription, "To my lovely Mater, Gillie." She smiled. "You know, Lamb Pie," she said, "if the *Reader's Digest* ever asked me to describe the Most Unforgettable Character I Have Ever Met I would say your father, Gilbert Seldes — a Jew certainly . . ." I do not remember the rest. That was how I found out that the Halls and the Seldeses were different.

Her children called my grandmother Mater, so Tim and I did, too. She called me her Lamb Pie. She knew I could be an actress. We would go to movies together — double features in those days. Just as the second feature was ending she would squeeze my hand and say, "Let's see this one around twice." She bought me pretty dresses because I was too shy to ask my mother for them. And without meaning to, she taught me to lie.

Because I loved her I couldn't bear to disappoint her. She would ask me what my favorite color was — hers was red — and I'd say red. Blue was the answer, but I'd say red. And I'd get red dresses and red hair ribbons and we'd play an endless game in which the the house and furniture and flowers were all red. We'd go for drives in the car when she came to stay with us in the country, and I'd sit in the back with her and my brother would sit in the front with my mother and occasionally she would let him steer.

"You wouldn't rather sit in front, would you, Lamb Pie?"

"Oh, no, Mater."

Yes. I would have, but it was too late to change. The color red, the back seat . . . It went on for years. There was a lesson to be learned there, but I did not learn it. I recognized what I had done but I did not have the strength to change it. The best thing about being an adult is being able to say blue if you mean blue.

I played Elizabeth Barrett Browning before I had a chance to see Katharine Cornell play her in the revival of 22 *The Barretts of Wimpole Street* she had mounted for the armed services. When you are young there is no part you cannot play, and the longer and more difficult it is the more pleasure there is in playing it.

As the curtain opened on the Dalton School production of the play in May of 1945, before the first line was spoken I heard Mater's voice from the auditorium: "That's my granddaughter. Isn't she wonderful?"

Muriel Stuart came to Dalton to see *The Barretts,* too. It was not at my invitation; another girl in my class studied with her and asked her. I did not find out until after a class, when Muriel sent for me:

"I can see how much you love to act. If you are a dancer your voice will never be heard." Perhaps she said a great deal more; certainly the impact of those few words and the concern with which she said them guided me toward a choice I felt it was time for me to make.

It must have been during this period, too, that my mother told me, "It is foolish to expect to be happy. No one can promise you that. The important word in the Declaration is 'pursuit,' the *'pursuit* of happiness.' " I asked her if she was happy.

"I feel happy when I feel well." She had been frail since a childhood filled with illness. Her memories of scarlet fever haunted me. When Tim had it I imagined that he would die, but by 1940 wonder drugs made it a brief, unpleasant time that he minded most because of his isolation.

"But you feel well now, don't you?"

"Oh yes. But the time I remember best was just after Tim was born. Sitting on the beach in Bermuda. I felt well then." She said no more. I tried to imagine what it would be like to wake up and not feel strong and able to pursue the thing that might bring happiness. I had taken health for granted

23

and had not understood my mother's need for the constant quiet and care my father provided for her.

Before the war, sometime in 1937, my parents decided that they wanted a house in the country. For years they had rented places in the summer. One fall day we drove up to a gray stone Gothic house in Croton Falls, New York, and Auntie rolled down the window of the station wagon, waved toward the huge trees and barns and then the house itself, crying, "This is the place . . . And you must call it Strawberry Hill!"

It did look like Horace Walpole's castle, and she gave us a lithograph of the original Strawberry Hill for the living room. My aunt was enchanted by the prospect of her sister's family ensconced in this serious edifice. I can not imagine what my father thought. It did not seem like a house for him to write in or live in at the time, and as I look back it touches me to think of him fighting the weeds, pouring his earnings into a pit for a septic tank, paying the tree doctors who came summer after summer to try to save the elms, rushing to catch the 5:17 train from Grand Central that we would meet at Golden's Bridge.

Meeting that train was the high point of every day for me. It must have been for my mother and Tim, too. Strawberry Hill was remote from other houses and except when my father was home we scarcely left it other than to shop for food.

I used that house as a library. The wallpaper was dark blue and shone like damask. The furniture was prickly black horsehair and marble-topped tables. The rugs were dark and patterned, the mirrors ornate, the vases fluted. My Aunt Marian's generous contributions. I examined every book in my father's study and looked at the copies of *Esquire* magazine that were piled on a shelf in one of the dark corners. After reading his monthly piece, "The Lively Arts," I studied the drawings and photographs of naked women and nattily dressed men, which intrigued me. Fantasies began. New secrets.

It was the perfect setting for reading novels and imagining myself living in the novelist's world as I would learn to do later on when I began to read plays.

Why did the women in novels have such unhappy endings to their lives? Why did lovers part so sadly? Why were most marriages so unsatisfying? My reading troubled me. On the weekends during the summer we would all drive to Brewster and go to the movies. The same worries waited for me there on the screen.

How was I going to find a life that was strong and safe and good?

Could I find it in the theatre?

2

Robert Edmond Jones's costume sketch for Nijinsky's ballet of *Till Eulenspiegel* hung on our living room wall in New York. My father called him "Bobby." He lived in our building in a third-floor apartment with huge ceilings and dark walls.

I had read my father's *New Yorker* "Profile" of him and I knew and loved his book *The Dramatic Imagination*, in which I had marked my favorite passage:

An artist must bring into the immediate life of the theater . . . images of a larger life . . . Here is the secret of the flame that burns in the work of the great artists of the theater. They seem so much more aware than we are, and so much more awake, and so much more alive that they make us feel that what we call living is not living at all, but a kind of sleep. Their knowledge, their wealth of emotion, their wonder, their elation, their swift clear seeing surrounds every occasion with a crowd of values that enriches it beyond anything which we, in our happy satisfaction, had ever imagined. In their hands it becomes not only a thing of beauty, but a thing of power. And we see it all — beauty and power alike — as a part of the life of the theater.

This visionary artist filled the theatre with beauty from 1920 until 1946. His lights and costumes and sets were memorable for the color and craft of the designs and because, like James Joyce's epiphanies, they revealed "the whatness of a thing . . ." Even in his realistic sets he made the commonest objects seem radiant.

It was time for me to begin work in the theatre. I had wanted to study ballet and acting in the summers before I graduated from high school, but because of the war my parents felt I should do something useful. For two summers I had worked harvesting crops of fruits, vegetables and tobacco in New England. I won the prize as "the champion potato picker of the Deerfield Valley." All the time I was thinking of being on the stage. I learned soliloquies from Shakespeare on the way to the farms in the early mornings and rehearsed them during the lunch breaks. At night I read plays. All of O'Neill. Shakespeare's histories. Now there was a summer ahead of me that could begin my career. My father thought his friend Robert Edmond Jones could advise me.

Early in the evening of the second of January, 1945, I put on my best dress, navy blue with accordion pleats and a white organdy collar, nylon stockings, and patent leather shoes. I walked down the stairs and knocked on the oak double doors. A tall, gentle man with a birdlike body — a gentle eagle — asked me to come into the dining room, where he worked and ate at an enormous table.

"Sit here. We'll have B and B and cake. Will that be all right?"

Fascinated by his bright staring eyes, not knowing what B and B was, I nodded and obeyed. I loved the warmth and sting of it and tried to drink it slowly so that the time with him would last.

He told me stories about the theatre. He acted for me in a   27 bizarre, funny way. I felt I was *seeing* Sarah Bernhardt rip the bracelets off her arms in *Phèdre*. I wanted to shout "Bravo!" and laugh at the wildness of his performance. He used his voice and his face freely like a great storyteller. Suddenly he changed his mood and made me weep.

I don't know how long I was there. I came back to the eighth floor and kissed my parents good-night and wrote him a letter.

Two weeks later he sent for me.

He opened the heavy doors. "I've been away, shoveling snow in New Hampshire. Chopping wood. Writing. Drawing. Come in."

He stared at me. I stood still. Like all brilliant actors, he had transformed himself. "I've sent for you," he said coldly, "because I think I gave you the wrong impression of the theatre the last time we talked." I started to protest. "Come in and sit down and listen to me."

"The theatre is a place of ugliness and greed and corruption. You will be corrupted by it, too. Don't interrupt me, my darling girl. You are dreaming a dream about some kind of happiness and it will be destroyed in just the place you have chosen to make it come true."

"But if I work hard, if I want what is good —"

"Be still. Sit there. Listen. It is a business, too, you know. There are people in it only for what they can get out of it. You will be used, *used* —"

"But to be useful. To be like Ellen Terry!"

"You will have to find a Henry Irving to take care of you, to guide you. You cannot do it alone. The men you meet will not be the heroes you have imagined. Don't cry, don't be silly. You might as well hear this now while there is still time for you to be sensible about it. And what about your height?"

28

"What?" My height had hurt me as a dancer; it had not occurred to me it would cause me trouble as an actress.

"Where are we going to find actors tall enough for you to play opposite?"

"Some actresses are tall . . ." I thought of Katharine Cornell. I said no more. There was to be no cake or brandy and Benedictine and not much more talk. I still loved him, but I could not adjust to the onslaught.

He put his hands on my shoulders tenderly. "You'll be all right, won't you?" Did he mean would I find my way upstairs? Or more than that?

My parents were not at home. I went up to my room on the roof and got ready for bed. I did not dance that night. I had been chastened.

I fought against the truths of that second meeting for years. But I am grateful to him. He was, of course, the kind of artist he described in his book and I could not dismiss anything he told me.

His face looks down on me from a photograph as I write. I keep it on the wall to remind me of what he meant to me, not how he looked. It isn't the face I remember. My apartment is filled with photographs of my parents and their parents. I am looking for them. I am looking for myself. Enid Bagnold says, "Oneself is so unknown. Myself has no outline . . . I have become a woman I can't describe. I can see what I was but I have no idea what I am."

Most actors say they do not like to audition. I do. Unless someone knows my work I do not see any other way to find new, interesting parts to play. I much prefer reading for a part to sitting across a desk and discussing it. The ideal situation is for theatre people to see each other's work on some kind of regular basis. Too many people in the theatre say   29

My father, Gilbert Seldes, and my mother, Alice Hall Seldes, as photographed by Carl Van Vechten, 1932.

they cannot be bothered going to plays. They blame the public for seeing only the hit plays and then behave the same way. There is hardly a play without one or two good performances, some interesting writing, some inventive direction. And if there is nothing of any value in a production, something can be learned from the combination of talents that brought that into being, too.

The most difficult audition I had to pass was when I was sixteen. It was on a Sunday afternoon in the spring, months after my meetings with Robert Edmond Jones. My parents were reading the papers in the room where I am writing now. Through the years they had seen me in all the plays at school, but this day I was going to act two scenes for them. Why didn't we move into the living room? My mother was resting comfortably against the pillows, turning the pages of the magazine section. My father was smoking a cigarette. It was time to begin. The room was not really wide enough for both beds and the bureau and my mother's little dressing table with its chintz skirt. When the door was open it touched the end of one bed. There was no stage space at all. I asked if I could move some of the perfume bottles. I made the dressing table into the bar in Johnny-the-Priest's Saloon and began the long scene from O'Neill's *Anna Christie* where she tells her lover about her past. At first I was afraid to put my weight on the little table but soon forgot about it and everything except Anna. Then I put a sweater over my blouse, replaced the perfume bottles and stood as far from the beds as possible, preparing them — and myself — for the speech from the last act of Shaw's *Saint Joan*. My father smiled. He had heard me say it four years before at Strawberry Hill.

My father and I had been standing on the porch. I walked away from him, turned around and began. "Where would you all have been now if I had listened to that kind of truth . . ." I came to the end of the scene and waited for his approval.

"You don't really have the voice of an actress."

I panicked. What could I do? How could I learn? My teacher-father explained to me the value of criticism and that if I couldn't learn how to take it and *use* it, I could never be an actress. What I had thought would be a triumphant afternoon had been a sobering and valuable one.

The Strawberry Hill speech. I loved and believed every word. To act without doubt, with complete trust, gave me joy. The room became a huge hall in a castle. Ladvenu and

31

the Inquisitor and the Executioner were there, the dressing table was a prisoner's stool, my ankles were chained as I defended my faith. It was May, in 1431.

But it was May 1945. There were no more of Shaw's words to say. I looked directly at my mother and father for the first time since coming into the room. Their expressions were unfamiliar. Had we been mysteriously separated, or brought together? They embraced me. There was no more talk about my going to college. I took all the tests, wrote the letters and was accepted, but there was no question of my spending the next four years outside the theatre. I straightened the room, and we all pretended to look at the Sunday papers while my heart pounded and I felt faint with pleasure. They believed in what I wanted to do.

Near Dalton, on the corner of Eighty-ninth Street and Lexington Avenue, there had been a small bookshop. I loved to look at the books displayed behind the glass; it was a habit of mine to study them whenever the window was rearranged. One afternoon in 1939 a photograph on a book jacket looked at me. It was the haunting face of Katharine Cornell on the cover of her autobiography, *I Wanted to Be an Actress*. I had heard my parents talk about her. I knew she *was* an actress. I craved the book, but it was before I had an allowance that would permit me to buy it. I didn't say how much I wanted it, enjoying the secret longing. I listened to my parents talk about her and read her interviews and reviews. My father had written a profile of her for the *New Yorker*. He called her Kit, which was what both my mother and father called me when I was a little girl.

The night in 1943 that my parents took us with them to see *The Three Sisters* was the first time I had seen a play 32 directed by Guthrie McClintic and it was my first glimpse of

Katharine Cornell on the stage. We were spellbound by her stillness as she lay reading and whistling on the chaise longue while her sisters were reminiscing. Although she said little in the first act of the play, it was she we commented on in the interval. Shaken by the final scene, my father led me to her dressing room. It was the first and last time we ever went through this ritual together and it was quite different from shaking Jimmy Durante's hand and the elephant's trunk in the sawdust circle at the Hippodrome.

We passed some of the other actors' dressing rooms on our way to see Cornell and somehow got disconnected from my mother and brother. We were met by McClintic, who took us into a long room where Miss Cornell was sitting surrounded by her beloved dachshunds and vases of flowers. They talked with my father and smiled at me. Her performance of Masha was still in my mind, the excruciating moment of parting from the man she loved. Suddenly that special voice was talking to me: "Come and see me again, Marian. Without your father."

When she was playing in Anouilh's *Antigone* in 1946 I went to the opening night. A dear friend of ours, Lewis Galantière, had translated the play into English and this was its American première after a long and successful run in Paris. It was, like all McClintic productions, impeccably cast and directed. After the performance, there were so many people waiting to see Cornell that she stood in the center of the empty stage, still wearing her green robe with its golden-tipped sash, and we each spoke a few words to her.

I lived with my friend Nancy Norman for part of that year and I walked home from the theatre to Seventieth Street and Lexington Avenue without stopping to think what time it was or where I was going.

I saw *Antigone* three times during its run, and when a revival of Shaw's *Candida* was put in repertory with it, I kept going back to the theatre to see Cornell and her company. In *Candida* Marlon Brando played Marchbanks. I had seen Burgess Meredith play the part with Cornell in the brilliant production of 1943 that was mounted for the Army-Navy Relief Fund. Now another marvelous, unpredictable talent was existing in that lovely play. He took outrageous chances. The first thing I noticed were his American sneakers as he jumped over the furniture in Candida Morrell's conservative drawing room. His clothes, his *look,* were alien. This Marchbanks did not belong there. It made the end of the play, when he goes off into the night, infinitely touching.

I had seen Brando as Nils in *I Remember Mama* and in an extraordinary performance in Maxwell Anderson's *Truckline Cafe.* His Stanley Kowalski was still to come. Already the actors in New York loved his work and watched his career with fascination. He went from strength to strength, his work always daring, surprising, strong. It never crossed my mind that he would leave the theatre for films.

Brando was criticized for his diction and speech patterns, but I never had any trouble hearing or understanding him. He convinced me that he was the character he was playing in the specific situation of the play at every moment. The way he spoke was the way the character would sound. To have this remarkable talent is rare. The closest an actress has ever come to such perfection for me was Laurette Taylor in her creation of Amanda in *The Glass Menagerie.* The lilt and rhythms of her southern speech were so true to that play that it seemed all southerners must talk as she did. The essence of that musical regional speech made Tennessee Williams's words stay in the audience's memory from a single
hearing.

Brando also played the part of a messenger in *Antigone*. Clearly enunciated, passionate, desperate words rushed from him. When I saw him as Marc Antony on film the beauty of his speech did not surprise me.

I knew an actor in the cast of *Antigone* who was to become a dear friend when we played a scene together in a play with Katharine Cornell four years in the future. His name was David J. Stewart and he was developing into a strong and important character actor when he died of a heart attack in 1966. He had a special relationship with Miss Cornell in the three plays he did with her. She respected his opinions, and when they were on tour and Guthrie could not be there to watch the performance, she used to encourage David to give her criticism. I thought he would become a director, too, one day.

When David's friends gave parties he would ask me to them. The favorite place to go was Maureen Stapleton's apartment on West Fifty-second Street. There would be some beer and wine and a few potato chips and continual laughter and theatre talk. It was thrilling to be treated like a professional actor when I was still a student and to laugh with the others at Wally Cox's hilarious stories or wonder what Marlon Brando was doing behind the closed doors of one of the several bedrooms.

After a rehearsal of *Antony and Cleopatra* in which Maureen played Charmian — the part I'd hoped McClintic would give me — she sat on the floor in the center of the room and described the day's rehearsal with Katharine Cornell. They were doing the scene in the monument. As Maureen talked she began to act it out, part imitation, part inspiration. She had been so stimulated by watching Cornell that she lost all self-consciousness and enthralled us with that powerful scene. I remember particularly how rich and 35 clear her voice was that night. I always hoped Maureen would do more classical parts. Perhaps she will. Perhaps she does not want to. But I feel I have seen her Cleopatra.

In October in 1946 Eithne Dunne, who was playing Pegeen Mike in McClintic's production of *The Playboy of the Western World,* became ill and her understudy went on. It was Maureen and we all went to see her. It was a fine opportunity and Maureen was ready for it. Cornell was there to delight in her work and praise it afterward. When she came back to the apartment Maureen was carrying a signed photograph of the Playboy — Burgess Meredith — on which he'd written: "To Maureen — I seen ya when ya started." How we love to be there and recognize talent early in a career. Now that I am a teacher, I have that sweet proprietary sense of early recognition and it gives me joy.

Picasso has written that his early success was his rampart: "The Blue and Rose periods were screens behind which I was safe. Protected by my success I was able to do what I wanted." I feel that in the theatre the actor discovers his own talent and other people recognize it. It is self-serving for anyone in the theatre to say he "discovered" an artist. The best thing that one can do is to give that artist the chance to use his talent. Certainly McClintic was instrumental in many careers in this regard. When he was still a young actor, Burgess Meredith was asked what his ambitions were in the theatre. He said, "To play Hamlet — and to make Guthrie McClintic proud of me." I did not read this until after Guthrie's death in 1961 but I knew that everyone who loved him felt the same way.

A vagrant thought: Most of the other people on the bus were going to the McClintic office for interviews, too. No, only the girl in the dark blue pleated dress and white cotton gloves. Taking the gloves off would be something to do as I met "Apple," the receptionist, and Bill Worthington, the play-reader who suggested to Katharine Cornell that she do *The Barretts of Wimpole Street*. Theirs was the twenty-seventh management to receive the manuscript, which went on to become one of the great successes of its day. Cornell played Elizabeth Barrett over one thousand times.

Guthrie was sitting behind a large desk. Bright light from the window behind him shadowed his features, but I was aware of his searching, merry eyes that appraised me in an instant.

Sitting opposite him I began to know his face. It was a blending of the comic and tragic masks juxtaposed. I never got tired of looking at him. The questions came quickly, as did the suggestions. "The way to learn about acting is to be directed by many different people. Go to the Neighborhood Playhouse. That's the place for you now."

"There is some feeling at Dalton that I should go to college and . . ."

"Nonsense. A waste of your time. You are going to be an actress. Go to the Playhouse."

"I will."

He rose with me and I walked to the door.

"How tall are you, Marian?"

The dream was over. "*Very* tall."

"So is Miss Cornell."

"Yes . . . but she's beautiful."

"So are you, dear."

I fell in love with Guthrie McClintic.

I was to be directed by him many times, to spend hours — days and nights — talking to him, watching him, becoming a part of his life and later of Katharine Cornell's. 37

They gave me love and courage and strength and happiness in unending measure.

He let me watch him direct from a seat next to his in the front of the house, he used me as a stand-in for all the other actors when he lit a play, he let me come in and read with actors for new plays he was casting. But above all it was the talk and the stories that made my time with him so special. He was as in love with the theatre when I knew him toward the end of his life as he had been as a boy, when he had struggled to escape from Seattle and reach New York to begin a career. His book *Me and Kit* was titled *East of the Mountains* when he was writing it. He read it aloud to me, chapter by chapter, late in the evening, and I grew to know much of his life that was not in the stories he told over old fashioneds and the endless canasta games he played to win.

I had no tolerance for the drinks. But I was so enchanted with my hours with Guthrie that I would eat what he ate, drink what he drank. No wonder I lost at cards.

The canasta games began when they still lived in the house at 23 Beekman Place and in the "Log Cabin" at Sneden's Landing, but we played on trains on tour, at the splendid house Eric Gugler designed for them on Martha's Vineyard (Guthrie once called that island "my Bali Hai") and at the huge house made from a barn they built in Sneden's.

Guthrie taught me how to rehearse and act and create a part, and years later when I started to direct students at Juilliard a great deal of what I taught was what I had learned from being with him.

He introduced me to a world of theatre and to its most beautiful inhabitants. And he believed in me.

Robert Edmond Jones had suggested that my father call 38 John Huntington and arrange for me to see him. He ran a summer theatre in Cambridge, Massachusetts. I had endured one other such meeting. When Theron Bamberger interviewed me as an apprentice for his theatre in Bucks County, Pennsylvania, he took in my white gloves and my height. "How tall *are* you?" I was not afraid to answer because the part I thought he might cast me for was Essie, the would-be ballerina in Kaufman and Hart's *You Can't Take It with You,* and I felt that my height would make the character even funnier.

I got mixed up, as I always do with numbers, and I said quickly, "I'm ten six."

"What?"

"I mean, *six* ten."

"I couldn't give you a part if you were my grandmother."

I should have thanked him and left, but to fill the silence I said, "I'm five eight . . . and I'm glad I'm not your grandmother," and somehow vanished from his sight.

My interview with Huntington was more successful. He was busy, friendly, and strongly influenced by Jones's recommendation. He told me to show up at the Brattle Theatre on June 7, 1945, the day after I was to graduate from Dalton.

V-E Day. Incredible reports on the radio. The end of the war in Europe. Our beloved French teacher, Madame Frederick Ernst — exquisitely dressed and groomed — running through the halls, her make-up smeared with joyous tears, crying out the news. Four weeks later, twenty-four girls in white dresses getting ready to march down the aisle to *Pomp and Circumstance.* A ritual. From the balcony I had watched other classes graduate. Now it was my turn to hold a bouquet of dark blue flowers and to speak the invocation.

Lauralee Tuttle was our faculty speaker. The senior class   39 sat in the first two rows and listened to her counsel. I interpreted every word she said to mean: "Go on, be an actress. It will be all right."

The theatre was hot and had it grown smaller through the years? I was to come back and see pageants and plays and watch it diminish in size as I grew away from it but I never ceased to love it.

I wore my school ring. It was black and gold and ugly but it had the school motto on it: "Go forth unafraid."

3

I began to think of my first summer in Cambridge because a soft English voice asked for me on the telephone one day in 1976 when I was answering some *Equus* mail. It was Pamela Gordon: "You won't remember me." Before I let her tell me how she was or why she was in America I assured her that I remembered her perfectly, all our times together in Cambridge, and that even though we had not seen each other for twenty years — more — I felt close to her.

She had been in America many times before, but this time she called me. Mildred Natwick, one of Guthrie's favorite actresses and a dear friend, had told her I was in the play. It made a kind of link for Pam and the call was easy. We chatted and made plans to see each other.

When I arrived in Cambridge in 1945 I wore what I thought was the nicest outfit I owned, my new black wool suit. The June day was steaming hot but I wore it anyway. I got off the train in Boston, took a cab to Cambridge and presented myself at the Brattle Theatre box office, where Mrs. Huntington eyed me: "Hello, death warmed over." She told me that the men's room hadn't been cleaned out since last season and provided me with a can of Old Dutch Cleanser, sponges and rags. I went into the cellar and started to read and then erase the graffiti. Kilroy was everywhere. And words I had not read before. The room was damp and smelly. I didn't see how this could be part of my wonderful life in the theatre until I realized the comic possibilities. I read and erased: "Please don't throw cigarette butts in the urinal, you wouldn't pee in an ashtray." On my first day on the job, I lost my school ring down the drain.

In my rented room I hung my black suit at the back of the closet, and the next day I did filing in another dank section of the cellar. I longed to look at the old playbills in dust-covered stacks all over the disorganized room. On the third day I began my search for props. I went all over Cambridge and Boston looking for objects that could be borrowed for the theatre. It was difficult because there were shortages of most luxuries, but I felt it was a useful job. I knew that the right object for the actor on the stage is as important as the right objective. The only bad day I remember was during the matinee of *Alice in Wonderland,* in which I played the Tiger Lily, a playing card and a wicket in the croquet scene. I forgot the teapot in the Mad Hatter's scene. I pushed it down the long table with a broom handle, unseen, I still assure myself, by the audience.

Pamela didn't arrive until we did Agatha Christie's *Ten Little Indians.* She had to scream offstage and they didn't like her scream. I did it for her. I loved that. I was a pair of legs seen through the grille in *My Sister Eileen,* with Libby Holman, who treated us all like family. In *Her Cardboard Lover,* with Diana Barrymore, I wore an evening gown in a party scene. I felt thrilled to meet the daughter of an actor I revered, the wonderful John Barrymore. There she sat in the rehearsal hall, smiling at everyone, completely at ease. But it wasn't Diana. It was another slim, dark actress. Diana was late. Diana was on the front page of the Boston *Herald* because of some sort of mix-up with her husband. It was a bad time for her. The real Diana arrived looking tired and heavy and her hair wouldn't stay combed. Rehearsals bored her; unhappiness defeated her.

Pam, whose mother was Gertrude Lawrence, cheered me. She was funny, kind and hard-working. I did not think she wanted to be an actress, not the way I did, and as it turned out she did not stay in the theatre. When her mother came to see her one afternoon it made the shabby old auditorium seem grand and bright. We were engulfed by Miss Lawrence's easy charm.

In Pam's dressing room there was a piece of paper with "Dressing room. St. James Theatre." embossed on it. A loving opening-night message from her mother. I had not imagined being in a theatre long enough to have stationery printed. Gertrude Lawrence had been a star for as long as I could remember, but that particular piece of blue notepaper in Pam's mirror was what made her incredible career special to me.

Even in a career where you have not played all the parts you have dreamed of playing, there are parts you have played that you remember with disbelief. How could I have done that? After the life force of your acting is taken away and all that is left is the memory or perhaps a stilted production photograph, you wonder how your career *could* have progressed.

In my first year in summer theatre Bert Lahr came to Cambridge to star in a production of *Burlesque*. There was a little part of an actress I hoped to play. A pretty girl with a memorable figure played it and I was chosen to be   43 one of the girls in the burlesque line. I wanted to get out of it and just do props. But it was my job, and one day I found myself dancing for Mr. Lahr and he was laughing. Later he told me what struck him was that all the other girls were smiling and tapping away and I looked utterly miserable.

"Keep looking like that. It's *funny*."

I learned the routines from Ann Corio and taught them to other apprentices in Westport and Beverly, where *Burlesque* toured. Bert kept me with him, took me out to dinner, taught me some wonderful vaudeville routines and got me my Equity card. That meant that I would be paid more and would be considered for better parts by John Huntington. He cast me as Agnes in *The Late George Apley*. Mildred Geiger came to see me and we read my first review in the Boston *Herald*. I was a professional.

One night after a marvelous dinner in Boston at Ruby Foo's, Bert took me to the Old Howard burlesque theatre on Scollay Square. When my brother went to boarding school at Exeter one of the first adventures he reported to me was going to the Old Howard. It sounded degraded and daring. As I sat with Bert "studying" the girls, researching my part in *Burlesque*, I realized my brother had not described the audience. I was as fascinated looking at the various men in the seats near us as I was by the funny, unfunny spectacle on the stage.

Bert was driven to rehearsals in a black limousine. Sitting beside him and singing a song he loved, "Come Rain or Come Shine," whenever he asked me, I was aware of his moods and knew when to be silent. There were many questions I wanted to ask him: Why did he spend almost all his free time in the box office? When did he rest? Was he ever happy? His face was so heavy, his voice subdued, and only on stage did his eyes come to life. In Westport he told the driver to "put on the gas." I dared a question: "Why?" "I don't like this road." We sped toward a group of low buildings and stopped. Bert said, "Not here." But the car stopped. Bert told me that we were about to rehearse the skits and dances on the grounds of the sanatorium where his first wife had been confined.

A few years later at the Bermudiana Theatre I did two plays with Edward Everett Horton, whose sense of timing was impeccable and who was also willing and happy to talk to Christopher Plummer and me about comedy. He would take us to lunch when we were doing *Nina* or *Springtime for Henry* and delight us with stories that had no cruelty or jealousy or anger in them. He simply reported things the way he saw them and made us love him and laugh.

Edward Everett Horton had played Henry Jelliwell thousands of times. But he approached each performance as if it were the first. And in *Nina,* which he did with us for the first time, his patience and generosity were boundless. The sound of his perfectly modulated voice and the accuracy of his diction were as fine as a classic actor's. He loved the words. He played them to the accompaniment of laughter. Chris and I would stay up after the play every night and read Shakespeare and talk about his life in Canada. He was in his early twenties, but he had an enormous range of parts. When he met me at the plane he was in his make-up for the opening night of *The Playboy of the Western World,* in which he was playing Burgess Meredith's father. It wasn't until rehearsal the next day that I realized he was still a boy.

Except on the stage, where he was utterly at home, Chris seemed alienated. He drank too much. He told me that he had never known his father. One night when he was eighteen a man came backstage at the theatre and asked the 45 stage doorman if he could see Mr. Plummer. "Who shall I say it is, sir?" "His father."

"What was it like?" I asked.

Chris told me, "I felt nothing."

They did not see each other again. I ached for him, with no real father to love or remember.

Before I could choose to go to the theatre whenever I pleased I took the greatest pleasure in reading about the theatre of the past. I stopped spending my allowance on ballet books and bought theatre collections, criticisms, plays and biographies. It was my good fortune to know some of the writers I read. Auntie was a close friend of Stark Young, whose *Immortal Shadows* was one of my favorite books of essays about the New York theatre in the thirties. One of my father's oldest friends was Edmund Wilson. And in our living room E. E. Cummings described the performance of his play-poem *Him,* for which my father had written the program notes, with sweet excitement.

I began to "know" theatre people by reading about them and I got in the habit of going to the library — the theatre collection was still in the main library on Fifth Avenue, and there was a good collection of books and pictures on East Fifty-eighth Street, too — where I'd research the plays and players I was going to see on the stage. I continued to do this when I auditioned. It made it easier to establish some relationship with a producer or a director if I knew what kind of work he was interested in and was known for.

Actors are like detectives when they are working on a part, and in everyday life, too. We are insatiably curious and rarely satisfied. We can never know enough about a play, a part, other people or ourselves. I did hours of homework on the directors and teachers at the Neighborhood Playhouse as soon as I got home from Cambridge.

On the afternoon of my interview with Rita Wallach Morganthau, the director of the school, I walked west on Forty-sixth Street looking for a small theatre, but number 16 turned out to be one of many office buildings. The school that Guthrie McClintic had suggested was not in a playhouse as I had imagined it. In 1949 it would move to a new building with large dance studios and a small theatre of its own, but in 1946 we rented outside space for our final performances and during the school year worked in hallways, dressing rooms and ill-equipped studios. It did not matter what the setting was, the work was continual, obsessive.

The training at the Neighborhood Playhouse School of the Theatre included speech and voice and dance classes as well as acting classes and rehearsals for plays. For two years we trained with brilliant teachers — our major acting teacher was Sanford Meisner; Jean Rosenthal and Paul Morrison taught us stagecraft; our dance teachers included Martha Graham, Erick Hawkins and Nina Fonaroff. Louis Horst taught us to create dances to sarabands, gavottes and waltzes. I loved to sit in the curve of his grand piano and listen to him correct, suggest, evoke choreography from young actors who had never danced before.

We arrived early in the morning and stayed after classes to rehearse scenes for the following day. At night we went to the theatre. I saw almost every play that opened in New York, some two or three times. Much of the time at the Playhouse was joyous, but in the course of those two years we all had dark periods. A few of the young men had been part of World War II. Those who were more experienced 47

At the Neighborhood Playhouse, 1947.

felt the younger ones to be ineffectual. Some of the girls had been to college. The graduates of other drama schools must have thought the beginners inept. The class was shaped by dismissals or voluntary quitting, and eventually we emerged as a strong group of young actors. We did not take our good fortune for granted.

Our teacher was a product of the Group Theatre, which had helped to shape the course of American playwriting and acting in the 1930s. The names that Meisner mentioned were wonderful to us — Clifford Odets, Harold Clurman, Stella Adler, Irwin Shaw, Morris Carnovsky — and the actors who had gone to Hollywood — Franchot Tone, John Garfield, Frances Farmer. His reminiscences became part of our learning process. We loved to hear about them, and Meisner, who had eloquence and style when he spoke of theatre practice, turned our class into a small "Group." Like many other students, we hoped to stay together and form our own theatre, but we lacked a leader. The closest we ever came to being organized and productive is when we would meet at Richard Boone's apartment and rehearse improvised scenes for a television program he hoped to produce.

When I lived in Hollywood, from 1954 to 1958, I acted in many filmed and live television shows and in three plays. One was *Witness for the Prosecution,* in the round at the Players Ring; one was in La Jolla, Graham Greene's *Potting Shed;* and one was Clifford Odets's *Flowering Peach.* I was asked to read for Odets at the Carthay Circle Theatre, where the play was to open the following month. I had met him in New York at Dorothy Norman's when I was going to the Playhouse. Did he remember? I did not remind him. I came prepared to read for the part I had seen my beautiful friend Janice Rule play on Broadway. This production was to have   49

Jacob Ben-Ami as Noah and I wanted to work with him.

It is hard to remember words when you remember feelings. Odets was such a sweet and gracious partner in the conversation that I simply relaxed and answered his questions. Presently, when I thought I had taken enough of his time, I said, "Shall I read for you now?"

"Why? You have the part."

He had remembered our meeting. Dorothy was a good friend and it pleased him to have news of her. She had become through the years a close, dear friend of mine, too.

The production was a poor one — no one was proud of it — but I had that happy memory of a little time with a brilliant writer.

I told Sanford Meisner about it. He was teaching in Hollywood at the time and I saw him at a party. "Do you remember when I played Cleo in *Rocket to the Moon* at the Playhouse and you told me, 'All your acting is cliché acting'?" We laughed. "But now I feel shy about seeing you. That was ten years ago, and you told us, 'It takes ten years to be an actor.' I feel I haven't come anywhere near what I thought I'd accomplish." He took my hand. "I said — *twenty.*"

I did not see Meisner again for nearly ten years more. By then I was a teacher. Anne Sexton's *Mercy Street* had its first rehearsals in Wynn Handman's studio. Handman had been a student of Meisner's in the class after mine at the Playhouse. He, too, had become a teacher as well as the producer of the American Place Theatre. At a break in rehearsal Wynn told me that Sandy was using one of the other rooms for a class and that I should go in and see him. I waited until the door opened, saw that there was no scene being
50 acted, and went in.

Two decades now since my first meeting with him, a quiet talk about the possibility of coming to the Playhouse to study with him. I wondered if he knew that I had joined the faculty of the Drama Division at Juilliard. The same shyness came back, the same ridiculous need to please.

"Yes, I heard about it." His voice was soft and caressing. "How do you like it?"

"I love it! I adore it! I want to teach for the rest of my life. I had no idea what it would mean — I am so grateful to you — it's, it's . . ."

"Tell me about it, Marian. Tell me about it when you've taught for thirty years."

But he must still love to teach, I thought. He is so good at it. His work is seen on stage and film every day through his students. They are directors and dancers and technical people and teachers as well as actors. The names fill up columns in the school catalogue; some of them are famous and all of them are respected.

In February of 1946 it was announced that Michael Meyerberg was going to produce a play, based on a Chinese legend, called *Lute Song,* to be directed by John Houseman and designed by Robert Edmond Jones. I did not have the nerve to make telephone calls and had never gone to a theatrical office in an attempt to get an appointment. I wrote letters. My letter to Myerberg was answered and I had an appointment to meet John Houseman in his office at the Plymouth Theatre. The room was long and cluttered and the walls and rugs a grayish green. A restful room with a charming, urbane occupant who gave me his full attention even though it was obvious that there was nothing in the play that I could do even if I were a professional actress 51 and not a first-year drama student. I thanked him for seeing me.

"Not at all, not at all. It is I who should thank you. How else will I get to know actors whose work I haven't seen?"

I walked up Broadway, which seemed undressed and shabby in the afternoon sun, and looked forward to the time when I could see Houseman as a real actress.

Four years later I read in Sam Zolotow's column in the *New York Times* that he would direct *King Lear*. Another letter, an answer and an appointment. This time it was in a producer's office in the West Forties. I arrived early and was made to wait five and a half hours, part of the time in the crowded outer office and the rest in the lobby of the Dixie Hotel, with other derelicts who had no place to go.

It was not John Houseman who had kept me waiting but his producer, a young man named Robert L. Joseph. When he did see me he set up a reading at the National Theatre for the following week.

At precisely the appointed time I was called on the stage and acted three scenes for Houseman and Joseph. First Cordelia, then Goneril, then Regan.

"Where have you done this play, dear girl?" asked John in his gentle cosmopolitan speech.

"I've never done it — "

"Ah." We chatted for a moment, laughed about our previous encounter that seemed so long ago, and the audition was over. I did not get a part in *King Lear*. That season I played Electra with Judith Anderson in *The Tower Beyond Tragedy*, but it had a limited run and I was able to see Houseman's *Lear* with Louis Calhern three times.

Many years passed before I saw Bob Joseph again. He 52 was a friendly, gregarious man. I asked him why he had kept me waiting all those hours. "Why didn't you send your secretary out with a message?"

"Why didn't you leave? Lots of other actors did."

"I kept thinking you'd send for me."

"I was testing you."

"Testing?"

"I wondered if you were serious about being an actress."

4

As soon as the decision to be an actress happens — I was six when I knelt in the lights of that alcove in the blue angel's dress — it is impossible to imagine that you will not have a place to live in the world you have chosen.

I have watched actors strive for such a place, fight ruthlessly to keep it, and I marvel at them. My fighting is passive.

Is it because I expect to be chosen and that my career will happen simply because I *will* it to?

I wanted to be a serious actress, to play the classics and to contribute something important to the theatre. As the time came for me to graduate from the Neighborhood Playhouse, I confided my hopes to one of the voice teachers. "I'd love to get a part in *Medea* with Judith Anderson. I've read the Jeffers version. Or perhaps I could be in the Katharine Cornell production of *Antony and Cleopatra*." As soon as I had said what I wanted I regretted it. I saw her contemplate my chances, and she broke the silence with: "My dear Marian, you do not have the vocal technique to say 'Hello' to Judith Anderson."

Since that time I have kept my ambitions quiet. I wish I

were more ambitious and had tried harder to get certain parts; perhaps I could have accomplished more of what I planned at the start of my career. When I feel the emotion of ambition rising in me, instead of feeling powerful I feel weak. The only time that it sustains me, that foolish, glorious feeling, is just before I begin to work. It is possible to share it with the other actors even if nothing is spoken. When we meet to rehearse a new play, when we prepare for the first run-through, the first dress rehearsal, that energizing impulse that started us all in the threatre begins to work for us and renews our faith in what we are doing.

Long before those moments the individual preparations are started. For each actor there are a thousand private rituals. Before any important engagement an actor wants to feel well, look well and be free of other duties. We take care of our obligations and ourselves and approach a new part as if it were the best, the most important of our careers. It would not be possible to continue in the theatre if we were not able to achieve this state of innocence again and again.

Before I met John Gielgud in 1947 I had read his autobiography, *Early Stages,* had studied Rosamund Gilder's *John Gielgud's Hamlet.* I had seen him in *Love for Love* and *The Importance of Being Earnest.* I saw the Wilde play twice because I was laughing continuously the first time and I missed some of the words.

My letter of introduction remained in its envelope. He never asked to see it. I went into his dressing room. I did not tell him that this was the second time I had prepared for the interview. When Mrs. Morgenthau told me to "drop in and talk to John after his matinee" I had gone to the Royale Theatre on a Wednesday afternoon. *Love for Love* had its matinee on Thursday.

He talked about my father's books. He said that *The Seven Lively Arts* had introduced him to much of American "show business" in the 1920s. He asked me what parts I had played at school, asked about Mrs. Morgenthau's health. He had great respect for this tiny, formidable woman who kept the Playhouse running through the Depression and the war and whose love of the profession was evident in all she did.

Gielgud is a shy man. Michel St. Denis said of him as a young man: "He is restless, anxious, nervous, impressionable — he is not overconfident in himself . . . he is not distant, but he keeps people at a distance. He is not a person you get to know easily . . ." As he looked at my reflection in the mirror while he took off his make-up I felt at ease with him. He used the time with me to find things out, he thanked me and I felt that I would have the chance I wanted so much. I was luckier than I could have hoped, for after the year that included *Medea* and *Crime and Punishment* I worked with him again when I played for Irene Worth in *Tiny Alice*. Through the years we kept in touch. At Christmas, by my coming backstage to see him whenever he played in New York, chance meetings. Each time I see him I want to thank him again for the opportunity he gave me. My first job on Broadway. He is to me a prince of the theatre.

The letter from Robert Whitehead and Oliver Rea, the young producers who were making their Broadway debut with Jeffers's *Medea* in 1947, came while I was playing in a stock company in Vermont. It said that John Gielgud would like to see me for a reading on June 30 in New York City. After the final performance of one week's play and before 56 the rehearsal of the next, I got into an upper berth in a train that had no air conditioning and went to New York. There was too much time to spare after my arrival and before my appointment. The city was blanketed in damp heat. I walked; I went into Kresge's and looked at every counter. I read the *New York Times* standing in a doorway. My feet ached. I felt sick.

Arriving early, I was ushered to a seat outside a living room in a second-story hall of a handsome town house at 39 East Thirty-ninth Street. There were other actresses there, an older woman who would eventually play the leader of the Chorus and a young one who would play the part that I had come to read for. She was engaged to Oliver Rea and I suppose she had the part from the inception of the production. I was given the role of Medea's servant and the understudy of Oliver's wife-to-be.

Nothing in Gielgud's attitude would have made me feel I was not being seriously considered for the part. The reading was like an acting class. He coached and helped me.

Over the course of my career I was to play each of the three women of the Chorus, and the part of Medea in a summer theatre in Vermont. The play became part of my life.

Medea, directed by John Gielgud, ran for a full season in New York, was redirected by Guthrie McClintic for a season on the road, and his production later went to Germany, France and Hawaii. I was with it for the two seasons in America and the week in Germany at the Berlin Arts Festival in 1951. Twenty years later I played it again with Dame Judith, this time as the Nurse.

The Nurse's lines were the first words I read at any Broadway rehearsal. Aline MacMahon, who was cast to play the part, was delayed in Europe filming *The Search*. On the day the cast met at the National Theatre, Gielgud asked who would like to read for her. My hand shot up the way it used to at school and I was chosen to read before I could think of my presumption. Aline arrived a few days later, rehearsed brilliantly for a few days, and was fired and replaced with Florence Reed, who was the first choice for the part all along. There had been a tiff about money and billing; I presume she got what she asked for. She gave a vivid performance in the marvelous role. On opening night in New York, Aline's telegram was posted on the callboard: "CONFIDENT YOU WILL MAKE HISTORY TONIGHT. MACMAHON."

The night the play opened in Princeton to waves of applause Florence looked at Judith and said, "It's the greatest

The opening of Act Two in John Gielgud's production of *Medea,* starring Judith Anderson (*center*), National Theatre, 1947.

thing since *The Gesture!*" Judith said nothing. *The Shanghai Gesture* had been one of Florence's most successful roles, but somehow that night it was an insane compliment and was received without a reply.

Gielgud had said before the curtain rose, "We must try to make a frame around Judith's wonderful performance." He was utterly selfless about his acting in the play. He hadn't wanted to play Jason but they couldn't cast the part correctly, and Gielgud felt that since Judith had played Gertrude to his Hamlet he could return the favor by being with her in *Medea* for the first part of the run. When he left to play Raskolnikov in *Crime and Punishment,* Dennis King played Jason.

Judith had no understudy, so I played the part for Dennis at rehearsals. It was a chance to work with a fine actor and a witty man. I had such respect for him that when he suggested we might have an even more intimate friendship I was astonished. It didn't bother Dennis. I think it was his second nature to proposition everyone.

Ben Edwards's massive set for *Medea* was constructed in Fort Lee, New Jersey, in a building where they had made silent films. One morning the company got into a chartered bus and went out to rehearse on the set. It was drafty and uncomfortable but exciting to be on the steps that had until then been lines of tape on the stage floor. Later the cast sat in a circle and Gielgud talked about the problems of the set and how we should adjust to them. At one moment he paused and stared at me. His eyes stayed on mine for only a few seconds but I felt I knew what he was thinking: He was deciding that I could play his sister, Dounia, in *Crime and Punishment.*

For three weeks I said nothing but I kept remembering his look. On the train coming home from Philadelphia after 59 the tryout of *Medea,* I asked Robert Whitehead if I might be considered for Dounia. He was most polite but the answer was no. I tried to stop thinking about it.

Medea began its exciting run in New York. One evening there was an unfamiliar knock on the dressing room door.

"John would like to see you in his dressing room," said his dresser.

"Now?" I was still wearing my Negro make-up for the serving woman. Away from the warm stage lights it looked smudgy and strange, but I did not want to take the time to remove it.

Gielgud said that he had been thinking about me as Dounia, that there was even a resemblance. He turned his profile to me — smiling: "The noses! And you look like a daguerreotype." He chose me, took me with him into that greatly peopled play.

"I think I know the moment you decided," I said.

"I think you do."

Do the people who save love letters reread them through the years? If they do, is it painful or lovely? Is it better to leave them folded in their envelopes? The notes I have kept about my theatre life amaze me because they are not always what I remember. I think back to the time in *Crime and Punishment* with its extraordinary director, Theodore Komisarjevsky, its players — Gielgud, Lillian Gish, Dolly Haas, my teacher Sanford Meisner and a delicate, sweet woman, Alice Johns, who played my mother, the huge complicated set by Paul Sherriff, the play itself drawn from a masterpiece that defies dramatization — all these elements remembered make a mosaic of wonderful, happy times. But in the notebook there is a tone of despair. I was to disappoint Gielgud and receive the same criticisms from him

60

again and again during the run; Komisarjevsky was asked not to come to the theatre during the final days of rehearsals, and when he left many of the cast left with him. He had chosen a group of his students to be the occupants of the slum where the play took place. He spent much of the rehearsal time drilling them. "Crowd, crowd!" he would call, and the horde would appear babbling and laughing, improvising dialogue. Actors' Equity discovered this tribe in the midst of the professional company, found out that they were not union members, and they disappeared.

Lillian Gish, who worked diligently to please Komisarjevsky, was ignored in one of the note sessions before he left. She asked him if there was anything missing from her performance. He stared at her and said softly, "Yes." Long pause. "More rouge."

When the work began he was a dominating patriarch to the company. My first note reads: "Komisarjevsky thinks, coughs, broods, makes notes, follows script, watches, listens." Gielgud told me that Peggy Ashcroft had adored him. I thought of that marvelous actress as a young girl working on the plays of Chekhov with the man whose wife had been one of the most successful interpreters of Chekhov's women. The group seated around the table at our first rehearsal did not resemble the famous picture of Chekhov reading his play to the Moscow Art Theatre company, but the excitement of embarking on a new project was there. The actor who commanded attention that day was Alexis Minotis, who read Profiri Petrovich, the inspector who pursues Raskolnikov. He was demonic, fascinating.

During the first week of rehearsals I was still playing in *Medea*. Judith sent for me and told me that her friend, Minotis, was being let go from the cast of *Crime and Punishment*. I was stunned. I thought he was marvelous. I had 61 no information to give her about the change. The next day Vladimir Sokoloff began to work on the part. He was superb. Was he better than Minotis? Would Minotis have given the performance that was expected of him if he had been allowed to rehearse? It puzzled me to see a fine actor treated in such a way. I knew that young actors were always nervous about the first five days of rehearsal because, according to most contracts, the management could fire the actor until the fifth day without paying him anything more than the rehearsal salary. On the sixth day the tension lifted.

Sokoloff had known Stanislavsky. He was interested in the application of Stanislavsky's theories at the Playhouse. The need to act the separate "beats" of the scene, to find the "spine" of the character in the play — these were the phrases that made him smile. "Do you know that when Stanislavsky heard about the 'beats' in the scene he did not understand what the English word meant. He told us that when he talked to Americans and English about his way of working on a script he meant each little *bit* of the scene must be dealt with specifically." Bit by bit. Or beat by beat. That is the way an actor works on a part.

Komisarjevsky asked me not to move like Isadora Duncan. Gielgud said, "Be careful not to sway like a willow." Robert Whitehead asked me if I always hunched my shoulders. My tensions remained long after the sixth day.

There was no reason that I could not play the part of Dounia. It was not a complicated role. Perhaps I did play it simply and well once or twice. More often? I hope so. I let my passion for the theatre, for its occupants — the director, writer, producer, the other actors and particularly Gielgud himself — turn me into a lovesick girl instead of a professional actress. Gielgud once asked an assistant to tell me not to watch him constantly. "She never takes her eyes off me,

The curtain call of *Crime and Punishment,* National Theatre, 1948. Left to right: Richard Purdy, Sanford Meisner, Alice John, Vladimir Sokoloff, Lillian Gish, John Gielgud, Dolly Haas, E. A. Krumschmidt, Elizabeth Neumann, Alexander Scourby, M.S.

does she?" I never did. I found a place to sit in rehearsals where I could continue to study him without his seeing me. I had promised my father I would not be stage-struck but I was breaking my word.

On New Year's Eve the performance of the scene where Dounia sees her brother faint and rushes to his side was playing well. As he fell I went to him. Not like Isadora? Not like a waving willow? No, with strong, purposeful strides I went to him and knelt. A sound of bones breaking? Not mine. His. My knee, my weight, pressing into the beautiful hand of my beloved brother. My beloved actor. I lifted myself away, continuing the scene. Gielgud moved his hand swiftly and for the rest of the performance I thought he held

63

it as if it were a dead thing, useless and heavy. I knew that his hand was in a different place when I rushed toward him, that it was not my fault. It could not have been as we had rehearsed it and played it before. Surely he would acknowledge the truth of that when I went to apologize.

Because it was New Year's Eve his room was crowded with visitors. I could not see him. The next day was a holiday. The following night at the theatre I kept looking at his hand. It was whole and beautiful. He kept it by his side as I ran to comfort him in the fainting scene.

The play did not succeed. After its twelve-week run Gielgud arranged for me to return to the cast of *Medea*, where I remained happily until it closed in the spring and I took a train to another summer theatre to practice my craft in modern plays that had succeeded on Broadway and made audiences happy.

The bright lights in the alcove, the light described by Robert Edmond Jones in *The Dramatic Imagination*, the light Jean Rosenthal spread on the stage in her marvelous rehearsals that created an atmosphere for actors to work in at the Playhouse and most notably for dancers like Martha Graham to dance in, the light makes the space beautiful and memorable. It focuses the eye and the heart on the stage while the words are being propelled from the actors toward the audience. The light masks the flaws, enhances the perfections: It makes belief possible. It makes the theatre magical.

Technical rehearsals are particularly valuable for the actor. The director's attention is taken off them for many hours, and they are free to experiment and move in the stage surroundings that will become as familiar as their homes. If the comradeship between the cast and the crew is not born at these rehearsals the chance is lost and both groups suffer from that loss.

Respect and feeling for the technicians in the theatre were attitudes the McClintics were able to instill in all their companies because they could employ the same people in play after play.

Martha Graham has this encompassing magic to an extraordinary degree. Her use of all the talents, all the imaginations that surround her is remarkable. When you read her notebooks it is clear that she has been searching for ideas that will stimulate her from all fields, in all times.

Long after I was her student I appeared with her in *Mendicants of Evening* at the Alvin Theatre in 1975. At the Playhouse she had made me a costume for *The Eumenides*. At the dress rehearsal she had looked at what I was wearing and without a word disappeared, found two kinds of white material, tore them, twisted them and pinned them on me, shaping my body into Athena's in less than a quarter of an hour. Now she designed a dress for me as the Witness in her dance about youth and great age. When it was brought to the theatre I found it in her dressing room. She told me to put my things on her table. She shared not only that room with me but the wings of the theatre, where we would watch her other dances in the half-light spilling from the stage.

Jones said, "The secret lies in our perception of light in the theatre as something alive. Does this mean that we are to carry images of poetry and vision and high passion in our minds while we are shouting out orders to electricians on ladders in light rehearsals? Yes. This is what it means."

The space. The shape of the space in the mind of the writer. In front of the audience. How will it be filled? How will it be transformed through the imagination of the playwright into words that will inspire the director, designer and actors to make a living world?

Why is it that I would rather exist in that space — a stage in a theatre — than in nature's paradise, or in a city street, or in a library, or even in my own quiet room? What makes what happens there — in a theatre — more real, more beautiful, more lasting?

5

At the first reading of *Medea*, Judith Anderson was as simple and concentrated in her approach to the text as if she were starting a career. She developed her performance from day to day with enormous care. Certainly she had worked on the play for months before rehearsal, had worked with Robinson Jeffers on the text, but the day of confronting the material with the other actors and the director was a beginning for her.

Two years later, as the cast of *That Lady* sat around the McClintics' dining room table at 23 Beekman Place, I was startled and touched to have Katharine Cornell whisper to me, "I am so nervous. I don't read well. I'll never get used to it, feeling that I will be a disappointment to the others."

The theatre is thought of as a place of enormous egos and temperaments, but more often it is a place of vulnerability and innocence.

Rittenhouse Square in Philadelphia is shaded with greenery and shadowed by tall buildings, and in the Septembers that I have been in that city I have sat in the little park and dreamed of being an actress, talked about theatre with fellow actors, made plans, come to decisions. It is far enough away from the Locust, the Walnut, the Forrest theatres in distance of city blocks and atmosphere to seem a different world. There is peace there.

My memories of the city are bound up with the life in the square. When I came there in 1947 with the tryout of *Medea* I stayed in an apartment. Nancy Norman's grandmother lived in a comfortable, perfectly run building on the south side of the square, and Dorothy, like a guardian angel, had arranged for me to live with her during the two-week run. I envied the others their unattractive hotel rooms and felt awkward coming in late at night with traces of the black make-up still exuding from my pores. Even after a hot bath the sheets would be marked with the dusky smudges.

But I was happy. My life in the theatre had begun. For the hundredth time. I counted every pageant, school play, summer theatre job, Neighborhood Playhouse performance as a beginning. This was the best of all.

Why does the note "I feel ugly, unimportant, depressed" mar the page of the Spiral diary? Because it was taking too long. No matter how thrilling the experience was, I was not an integral part of its workings and I knew it. It surprises me that I could write it down. Such notes are rare in my many theatre diaries, but the feelings have not been uncommon. Suddenly, just before the appointed time for the curtain to rise or the red light of the television camera to flash on, an actor thinks, I don't belong here. How can I escape? Then the cue comes and we play our parts.

There was not enough acting for me to do in *Medea* until the following year, when I was given the part of the Second Woman of the Chorus. Because of my seeing the play through a character's eyes, the play itself began to live in an important way. What the other actors did belonged in 430 B.C. and had that reality for me. My notes about the tour were concerned with that life, and since I rarely took my eyes off Medea herself, what she did and felt and created out of words and passions on the stone steps of her palace became the fascination of my stage and real lives. They became one. Judith/Medea was the focus of that time for me.

Medea/Judith was not easy to serve. Her standards for behavior in and out of the theatre were high and she tended to distrust the members of the company. She loved us all at the beginning of the tour, but as the weeks went by and the strain of playing her complex, desperate character sapped her energy, she began to give notes to the other actors that hurt their feelings. They were taking her tone or moving on her lines or not watching her. It became a matter of pride to me that I could escape those notes, but of course a performance would come and I would be sent for and reprimanded. Even while it was happening I thought Judith was right. But it was difficult to deal with because in the following performance Medea seemed not to be there, only Judith — judging. Florence Reed once said that Judith's distrustfulness of other actors was "an illness of the mind." If so, it is an illness most actors share. We are trying to protect the reality we have created on the stage from moment to moment and whoever threatens that reality becomes an enemy. More often than not nothing is said, but when saying something is the habit or prerogative of a fellow actor it can be painful. I felt that somewhere during the tour Judith began to trust me and that she continued to do so in the other plays I did with her. She must have known, as I did in my actor's heart, that however differently I might go about it, I wanted the same thing to happen on the stage that she did. As the years went by and I acted with more confidence 69 and pleasure I knew that Judith's Medea had helped me, chastened and inspired me.

My father adored Judith. He called her his "serpent of old Nile." She was constantly giving me joking messages to send to him, and when he had to have a gallstone removed she wanted to be kept posted with medical bulletins. There was not always time to meet and chat backstage, so occasionally she would discuss things with me between the lines she spoke before her entrance.

"Death!" Medea would cry. As the Chorus reacted on-stage, a whisper:

("How's your father?")

"Death!" again. Deeper, more agonized.

("Did he pass his stone?")

Judith's directions to actors were mainly by indirection. What to avoid, not what to add. She hated extraneous movements, sounds or words added to lines, using the same tone of voice as the character who had just spoken. Martha Downes, who was in the Chorus during the long tour and became a dear friend to all of us, once asked Judith how to use a fan in a scene from *Tartuffe* she was preparing for an acting class. Judith took the folded piece of paper from her, put it up to her face, became Elmire and said, "It's not the fan . . . it's the *eyes.*" A lesson in comedy.

At the Biltmore Theatre in Los Angeles the opening of *Medea* had been a gala event. Many stars and celebrities were there. Lana Turner, dressed completely in white, gleaming with glamour, sat in the first row. How did she like it? she was asked on her way out of the theatre. "It was breathtaking," she murmured, "but I would have played it differently."

70   One summer I played Medea in a theatre in Vermont.

McClintic's stage manager, James Neilson, had urged me to do so, "somewhere, anywhere. You should have the experience of *playing* a part you know so well." The next time I saw Judith I reported — rather guiltily, I suspect — that I had played the part. Her eyes widened. "What did you wear?"

The old Theatre Guild on West Fifty-second Street was refurbished and opened as the American National Theatre and Academy in the fall of 1950. Robinson Jeffers's version of the Agamemnon story, *The Tower Beyond Tragedy,* was chosen as the opening play. Judith had played Clytemnestra in it at Carmel, California, and had wanted to bring it to New York for many years. While we were on tour with *Medea* I had studied the play and longed to be Electra in it. When the time came to read for the part in New York I ruined my chances by putting all my longing to be a great actress into the audition and dismaying Judith and the direc-

Clytemnestra (Judith Anderson) and Electra (M.S.) in *The Tower Beyond Tragedy,* ANTA Playhouse, 1950.

tor, Robert Ross, and the stage manager I read with, who must have thought I was wild, passionate, and insane. I was asked to understudy the part and once again to play a servant. I was ashamed and unhappy. I had prepared so carefully for an Electra I was not to play.

The rehearsals were a blur. I walked back and forth to my apartment on East Fifty-fourth Street trying to re-create my feelings of love for the play and the part I had to watch being created by another actress. She was the first person of my own age whom I heard use four-letter words in the theatre. Awed and repelled by her confident manner, I wondered if there were areas of rehearsal behavior I should investigate. I wondered what Judith thought. In the apartment I kept studying the part I now understudied. It was a good place to work. The former occupant had painted the entire place black. Walls, ceilings, the inside of the tub, the toilet and the sink. Black. The floors slanted toward Second Avenue and sighed when I paced up and down, working and reworking the part of Electra. The day before the first preview the director and Judith came to me and told me that I would play the part.

All afternoon I rehearsed with Alfred Ryder, who played Orestes. That evening there was a dress rehearsal. My walks to and from the theatre were ecstatic journeys. Judith helped me. Bob Ross's wife, Margalo Gilmore, helped me. They seemed as happy about the turn of events as I did.

I learned how to audition from my terrible audition. I learned how to act with greater discipline.

My joy in the play was tinged with guilt. It was not a good time for Judith. Her mother died the night we opened. The play was not a success. Was it wrong for me to feel such happiness? She denied me none of it, continued to care 72 about Alfred's and my work in the long second half of the play in which Clytemnestra did not appear, and made me feel like a colleague — a serious actress — and her friend.

I was in five plays with Judith; *Medea, Tower Beyond Tragedy,* the revival of Clemence Dane's *Come of Age* that McClintic directed and two later productions of *Medea.* Judith did not like to talk about acting or to hear other people talk about it. She'd mutter, "Stuff, stuff, stuff," and think her own thoughts. But watching her, night after night — *Medea* was the play I had seen most often until *Equus* — it was impossible *not* to learn from her grace and skill and discipline. She had learned acting by being an actress through years of rehearsals and performances with many different directors and players. But she had a special slant on characterization and a strong will of her own. Watching John Gielgud, and later Guthrie McClintic, direct her was exciting. McClintic went up to her and whispered an idea and I saw her leap off the ground like an animal in an ecstasy of discovery. She had played *Medea* for over a year when I saw that moment. I wish I could have heard what he said. Whatever it was transformed the entire final scene of the play and made her an even more pitiable and vengeful creature than I had seen before.

The long tour with Katharine Cornell in *That Lady* two years after *Medea* had similarities that were cloaked in dissimilar circumstances. Once again we actors found ourselves touring with a major star in what is called a vehicle. Not a classic this time but again the story of a woman's loves and fears and how they destroyed her life. But *That Lady* was romantic, lush. It belonged to Cornell because it was she who had read Kate O'Brien's novel and asked her to dramatize it. Judith had gone to Robinson Jeffers and asked him to write *Medea* for her. *Medea* was a success wherever we toured. *That Lady* was not. The critics did not approve of it, but the audiences came to see Cornell. She had played in all the cities we visited many times and they loved her. On paper, in account books, the play did not work. On the stage, in the theatre with Katharine Cornell, it did. Again and again she would tell me how much she loved the play and ask if I still did. It turned out that by the end of the tour she thought we were the only ones who were still faithful to it. She would say, "I wanted it. I've got it. I love it."

One snowy day walking to the theatre where a small audience was expected she said, "I think they were sweet to come. They'll find us at our very best." In less than an hour that audience would see the creature who was bundled in woolen scarves and fur-lined boots and a shapeless beaver coat transformed into a radiant Spanish noblewoman, resplendent in elegant costumes, moving quickly and sensuously across the sparsely furnished rooms of her castle. There she would fascinate and dazzle the people of the play, the players as well as the audience, for she had what is now lost in the theatre, an allure, a glamour, a personal charm that worked a magic on us all.

Part of it was her beauty. Florence Vandamm, who photographed the Broadway theatre throughout the twenties, thirties and forties, said of Cornell, "She has the most beautifully *interesting* face I've ever photographed." It was a mask that lived and changed and promised wonderful things. From the mask her eyes looked huge and her voice sounded rich and deep. When she was not on stage her glamour was of an entirely different kind. It was far more delicate, vulnerable, but no less spellbinding. Her ability to fascinate seemed effortless; her attention was thrown toward whatever she was doing at the time: cooking, playing 74 cards, reading, swimming, shopping, getting the mail. At

Martha's Vineyard, where she and Guthrie had a house that combined beauty and comfort, we would drive to Vineyard Haven or Edgartown to shop, stopping on the way at special fish or vegetable stalls where she knew the owners, their families and their problems. At the post office she would take a magnifying glass out of her bag and dial the number to open her mailbox. She had glasses but seldom wore them. It was not vanity. She had little of that. I think she wanted to be free of anything that constricted her. She wore no jewelry; her clothes were loose and flowing or, long before blue jeans were the fashion, she would exist in faded light blue denims throughout the summer months at the Vineyard. She loved the sun and took no particular care of her skin. Talk of food did not include dieting or the number of calories. She took good care of herself and of her company. A doctor's daughter, she loved to prescribe for others and she called herself a hypochondriac. The only time she mentioned her mother, she told me that she was extremely shy, that "she drank herself to death. It put fear in my heart when I was very young. But everyone loved my father; he was more of a hypochondriac than I am!" I asked her if her father had wanted to be an actor.

"My grandfather had a small theatre on the top floor of his house in Buffalo, and once every two weeks he would present an amateur play. John Drew, who was a close friend of his, thought my father could have been a great comedian. I remember two sets in that theatre, a white drawing room and an outside scene with lace trees. Oh, my grandfather would have been shocked to know that I became an actress! I'd rather cook than act." *I* must have looked shocked, because she added, "I'm not ambitious, Marianna, other people have been ambitious for me, but . . . something *forces* you to continue."

At a canasta session that lasted until four-thirty one morning we were talking about Ethel Barrymore. Guthrie said, "She's abreast of everything, a wonderful companion, an amusing conversationalist. She knows everything about everything — except the part she's working on!"

Cornell laughed. "She has more glamour than anyone else in the world. She's never *old*. You'll understand — some people — Ethel — I — feel *younger* now that we're older. People think of her wonderful voice, and of all her successes — but look behind that in any artist — there is hardship. I want to wire Ethel: LOVING MY WORK. HATING THE CRITICS!"

That was the closest she came to complaining about the disappointment of the New York run of *That Lady*. Guthrie made her laugh: "Remember what Mrs. Fiske said, Kitty, as she peered out at a small house: 'We're still in the minority.'" That reminded her of the time Mrs. Fiske came to dinner with her husband. Mr. Fiske was describing a play and his wife interrupted him: "Oh, you mustn't bore Miss Cornell with that play, it has nine acts."

"Nine *scenes*, Minnie," said her husband and continued with his plot outline.

A great many of the actors and actresses they talked about I never saw, but by being in a Cornell-McClintic production I was able to meet an extraordinary group of people who were a part of their theatre life. Cornell would send for me when Helen Keller was at the play. She told me how to hold Miss Keller's hand to my mouth when I talked to her. I felt afraid and wanted to call to Cornell not to leave me in the dressing room with her, but in a moment my fear was forgotten. I was "talking" with Helen Keller. What did we talk about? Our mutual regard for 76 Katharine Cornell.

That year I met Gustav Eckstein, Ina Claire, Constance Collier, Billie Burke, Margot Fonteyn, S. N. Behrman, Mainbocher, Pauline Lord, the Lunts, Marlene Dietrich. These are the names that are recognizable. There were many others who came backstage, or visited at the Vineyard or in the house at Sneden's Landing where the McClintics spent their weekends. Friendships happened spontaneously around them. It was taken for granted that the people they felt comfortable with would be comfortable with each other.

Cornell said that the only thing that lasted in the theatre was the memory held in the audience's consciousness. For many, the strongest memory of her was the sound of her voice. In conversation it was light and she was easily moved to laughter. It was naturally lovely. On the stage she projected a deeper sound. Her heroines had a passion that was reflected, caught, projected, in a variousness that made the audience believe she was inventing what she said. I thought all actresses should sound like Katharine Cornell, but no one ever has or will.

"It worries me that I have no other interest but the theatre," I said to Kit as we walked down a street in Columbus, Ohio. We were going to have lunch, do some errands and walk and talk.

"You are interested in living, in being a good human being. That is the most important thing."

"Yes." But could I live a life that was useful, important? I needed to ask her and did not know how. The questions I wanted to ask my own mother now crowded my head and made me feel dizzy. We kept walking and I said, "I couldn't love you any more if I were your daughter. This is something marvelous in my life."

"I hope you'll always feel that way about me. I think you

will. I've known it since the first time I met you. What you say makes me feel humble. I hope I shall never disappoint you." I started to speak but she went on, "At least as a human being; about acting — I'm never sure."

For the rest of that day I kept hearing: "interested in living." Seeing the words as if they were a headline in a paper. From that moment I stopped feeling apologetic about choosing to be an actress rather than a doctor or a nun or a savior of mankind. I was eighteen and I felt the world widen.

My scenes with Katharine Cornell in *That Lady* came at the end of the play. After we read it around her dining room table at 23 Beekman Place I did not rehearse again until ten days later at the Martin Beck, when Guthrie was ready to stage the last scenes. Until then he had let me sit beside him in the front of the house and watch him direct. I watched every rehearsal and performance of the play thereafter.

I was not prepared for a comment from Cornell when we had run our scene several times. She said softly, "You have a fault as an actress, Marian." So the dream was over. I was prepared for anything but I did not know what to say to her. She went on, "I have it, too."

"What is it, what can I do . . . ?"

"You tend to look upstage so that most of your face can't be seen in profile. You have to learn to find a way to look at the other actor but protect your own face."

I tried to remember what she told me and she never gave me the note again. But once, during the first week of performances in New York, as we were sitting together on the couch confiding in each other — mother and daughter — she put her hand gently on my cheek and turned my face toward the audience. It was completely in character, of course, but so generous and loving that I have never forgotten it.

Mother and daughter in *That Lady*, with Katharine Cornell, Martin Beck Theatre, 1949.

Guthrie asked me, "Could you bear to be with us for another play? It's not definite yet, but we will know soon. You're the only actress I know who could play it. It's not a supporting part. It might be the part to make you" — I thought, Don't say it. I don't want to hear it. If you say it it might not come true — "a star. I've known it since the first time I saw you, when you came into my office." He told me that I would always work, not have to look for parts, and that would give me a chance to develop. I believed him. And that part of it came true. I have worked continuously, but I was not able to live out his dream for me as an actress.

That Lady was playing at the Martin Beck when I received an invitation to come to the Plymouth Theatre to meet Mae West, who was casting some replacements in *Dia-* 79 *mond Lil.* She was in costume and make-up, sitting at a dressing table that had been arranged in the wings. The mirror had bright naked bulbs around it (bulbs I always unscrew so my eyes won't be tired from the glare). Part of the time Mae West looked at me and part of the time she looked in the mirror. In 1949 she was dazzling. I remember satin and diamonds and white powdered skin and smart eyes watching me.

"I unnerstan' yer playin' a Spanish girl down there with Cornell?"

"Yes, I'm playing her daughter . . ."

"How'd you like to play a Spanish girl with me?"

"Oh, I'd . . ."

"Just ask the manager and he'll fix it for you to see the play. Lemme know what yah think . . ."

I wanted to tell her that I planned to go on tour with Miss Cornell but there was no chance. The interview was over. She smiled. I thanked her. I was able to see the play because we were on different schedules. The Spanish girl turned out to be a strong swarthy woman who met her death by being strangled with the long, uncombed black wig she wore.

I stayed with Katharine Cornell, but I had had the chance to meet Mae West.

My childhood with the McClintics ended with the closing of *That Lady.* Just as I ceased to be Kit's daughter in the play, I began to be her friend in the rest of her life that I shared.

We did not do another play together although it was planned. Guthrie wanted me to be in *The Dark Is Light Enough* by Christopher Fry. "I've found it for you! You'll be with Kit again and you'll be beautiful!" It was arranged, but while I was visiting them with my husband at the Vineyard I realized that I was going to have a child. With any other producers it might have been possible to start with the play and leave it after several months, but Kit and Guthrie built a company, and it was not in the nature of their plans to replace an actor in the middle of a run. I surprised myself by not being more disappointed. "We've loved this play. I hope we'll be together again," Kit said.

"Once in a lifetime is wonderful . . ."

"Oh, I can't let it go at that. Whenever I read a play I'll look for the part of a daughter or a friend."

6

Thirty years ago when Kit said to me, "You feel things, emotionally, as I do, but don't articulate them," I was a listener. Whatever feelings I had I wanted to use in my work. In my daily life I seldom asked personal questions. I waited for answers to puzzlings situations I did not understand. My impatience to find reasons for behavior in others was cloaked by interested observance.

When I knew I was going to be married I went to the studio where my father was writing and told him at once. "Come upstairs and tell your mother," he said. He pulled me back into the room. "Tell her *first*." We went together to find her and were crowded once more in that bedroom. She was leaning back on the pillows reading, and I realized I was acting for her again as I told them both "for the first time." She called herself undemonstrative, but that morning she wept.

"Why are you crying?"

"Oh, darling! I thought you never would get married. You'd just . . . go on . . . and be an actress . . . and have your scrapbooks."

My father laughed. But what else could she have thought? I had not confided in her. The loves I told her about were theatre dreams and fantasies. Plays and parts and things that get written in diaries and put in scrapbooks. My undemonstrative mother held me in her arms choking between tears and laughter.

I had not confided in Guthrie, either. We met for lunch at the Gloucester House.

"Guthrie, I have something to tell you."

"What is it, my dream girl? My nemesis?" He grinned. I started again and he interrupted. "I am thinking of when I first met you . . . and the letter . . . I was not a little enchanted . . ." I blushed with happiness, feeling exactly as I had that first day, remembering it.

We ordered lunch. We drank wine and suddenly I told him. "Listen, Guthrie. I am going to be married."

He looked at me for a long moment. Then he closed his eyes and put his head down on the table. I reached for his hand.

It was a parting. I had lived the real part of my life as a secret kept from my family and close friends. After my marriage, when that time in my life was over and it was necessary to articulate it, my friends and family accepted my announcement with the same shock, surprise and puzzlement.

In the theatre the protected, private, most intimate moments of living must be examined, opened up, displayed — whatever the consequences. Choices must be made. The actor must dare to choose unsparingly. There will still be a sanctuary for secrets. On a deeper level than we can reach, the real soul of the character he creates will live, inviolate.

In teaching and directing, how delicately the actor must be handled. The real person must be investigated as sedulously as the text. The responsibility of sharing another's   83 feeling and perceptions can be devastating. The work can bog down, falter; mistakes are repeated in play after play with actor after actor for no apparent reason. Theatre people get sick of the very life that feeds them and makes them strong.

The image of the overemotional, always "on" actor exists for us all. It can be funny to see such a character on the stage, in a film, in a living room. But in most theatre biographies this "on" actor is a sad figure. The pages may be full of wonderful reviews, reports of standing ovations and huge salaries, but when the story is told one is left with emptiness. The glamour is gone, the reputation fades, opportunities lessen, lovers — if there have been lovers in the story — disappear and we are left remembering an emotional wreck, an alcoholic, a suicide: the character so often used in the novels and films that frightened me in my childhood.

I feared vanity, exhibitionism and the foolishness of unrealistic egotism: the blights of theatrical lives. Most of the notebooks and annotated scripts from the beginning of my career are filled with optimism and appreciation. They read like diaries. The theatre became my life and my work. I was free there to be — anyone. Everyone. Or to be perfectly one.

To find a part, to search for the character in myself and to communicate that being to my fellow actors in a play became my secret and my public life. I knew I would be happy. I could not have known how unhappy. Nor could I have known then that neither could be avoided no matter what path I chose.

Actors talk and write about other actors. It seems a natural thing to do. But the most fascinating person connected with a play is usually the playwright. When an actor's career begins, he either writes his own plays or finds a play in the library or is assigned a part in a classic play at school. When you read, think about, rehearse, play and live with a part, you feel you know the author well even if the actual encounters with him have been casual. Some part of his thinking and feeling and experience becomes part of yours. It is even possible to love the absent author, to feel that you know him through his words.

Because of Judith Anderson's generosity I met Robinson Jeffers in New York, and because of my own audacity I saw him again in Big Sur in the 1950s. We were doing his *Cretan Woman* at Stanford University and wanted permission to insert a speech from *The Tower Beyond Tragedy*. I called his daughter-in-law and she suggested that I come to Carmel and talk to him. The house that he had built was like a fortress and a sanctuary. Jeffers was a quiet, gracious host. *Medea* had meant so much to him that he seemed pleased to talk about it, and Judith, and to know how much both had meant to me at the beginning of my career.

I never knew Kate O'Brien well. She did most of the writing on *That Lady* in Ireland or at the McClintics' house and was quiet at the few rehearsals she attended at the Martin Beck. My first meeting with her was in Boston toward the end of the cross-country *Medea* tour. She came backstage with Katharine Cornell, and in my dressing room Cornell told me I would play her daughter the following season as she introduced me to Kate O'Brien by my character's name: Anichu.

Cornell was in awe of Anderson's performance, which she was seeing for the first time. "I could never play a part like that. Never. I don't have the power. Or the courage. I'm 85 not a courageous person. That's why I loved Antigone."

Was it just that element of courage in her performance of Antigone that made me run home from the theatre after the opening without any sense of the path I was taking? Elated, full of faith in human nature, in the inevitability of the triumph of good over evil? I reminded her of how much that play had meant to me and thought, too, of the kind of courage she had shown in her career. To become an actress-manager, to produce the plays she believed in, to tour them across the country. And in particular the tour to the troops in 1944.

"Other people made it possible for me. I have had such support. I would never have done those things on my own. Guthrie was ambitious for me."

I hoped I could find someone who might feel the same way and work with me. I felt I lacked the driving ambition to become an important actress, yet when I recognized these qualities in others I was offended by them. How to strike a balance and build a career that had dignity and usefulness as well as success?

In *The Three Sisters* Chekhov writes about a kind of courage in the face of the adversities of ordinary existence. I talked with Cornell about the final scene in the play, remembering another evening that was part of my early falling in love with a life in the theatre.

"I never played it right. Coming back from Europe after the *Barretts* tour I stood on the shore and looked up to the deck of the troopship where the soldiers were crowding the rail — singing and laughing" — she caught her breath with a sobbing sound — "and I knew *that* was the way."

"*Against* the emotion in the scene?"

"Yes."

But that was how I remembered it. Kit as Masha, her brave head high, Judith Anderson the beautifully stoic Olga, who began the play with such resigned remembrances of her father now holding her sister's wild feelings in check, and Gertrude Musgrove the beautiful young Irina grown suddenly old — I could see them, hear the band again in the distance.

I thought of Kit's career. Almost all the women she played were courageous. How odd that she should choose that word to describe a lack in herself. She began to whistle — the aria from *Eugene Onegin* that Masha whistles — and caught me staring at her.

"Well, I *whistle* brilliantly!"

Frank Corsaro, the director, wrote a play about his family called *A Piece of Blue Sky*. It was tried out in Fort Lee, New Jersey, in 1958, produced by Robert Ludlum, who now produces best-selling novels. I played the Italian woman based on Frank's mother and Shelley Winters played the Irishwoman who lived upstairs and loved his father. Frank directed the play and the cast was a good one. It did not have much success in Fort Lee and was never brought to New York, but the production was repeated for public television. Frank described his mother as "an old-fashioned woman in a world of no fashion." She was a devout Catholic, a dreamer, a woman who "managed" to carve out a life for herself and her family during the Depression.

My father came out to Fort Lee and at the performance he saw, a chair was set incorrectly on the stage. As the devout Catholic wife turned to leave the room she hit her shin on the chair and an "Oi!" escaped her. It was my father's favorite moment in the play.

I was happy doing Frank's play for many reasons. It brought me back from Hollywood, where I never felt at home, it gave me a chance to play a part that had not been created by another actress, and it was exciting playing with Shelley. Volatile, opinionated, incapable of stillness, this actress was fully alive on the little stage in New Jersey, so alive that at times all discipline was lost when her emotions took over the performance. In one fit of passion she threw an older actress to the floor in what was meant to be a verbal argument. The audience was amazed and greeted this new "business" with a spatter of applause.

Frank was outraged and scolded Shelley in front of the company. "But it got a hand, didn't it, Marian?" she asked. Before I could answer Frank said, "For the *wrong* reason!" and the subject was closed.

Most of the cast of *A Piece of Blue Sky* had been or were being analyzed. Shelley's only argument with me was that I did not see a doctor. When the rehearsals broke for a few hours each afternoon she wanted me to go to someone and discuss the play as she did. She threw down her script in disgust one day and said she would not rehearse until she had talked over the scene with her doctor. She went away, we waited, she returned, and the scene was rehearsed as before.

Oddly enough, the only other time I witnessed such a scene I also played a small part in it.

When Guthrie was directing *That Lady* I took the following notes:

We did our scene [between Ana de Mendoza and her daughter, Anichu], McClintic suggested that he had never liked Anichu asking her mother, "Did you have other lovers?" Cornell said if that question was taken out the scene would have to be rewritten. Both began to talk at the same time and to misunderstand each other. Cornell said to me, "You understand what I mean?"

"Yes."

"Anyone with feeling would."

McClintic: "Then I have no feeling . . . I shouldn't direct this play," and flung the script to the floor. A long silence. Then we began the scene. "And I don't want it in a *mood,* Kit. Don't act as if this was so monumental." We played our scene and the final scene of the play.

"You can hold my hand whenever you want to, darling. I don't want to make young gestures in this scene." I took her hand because I was frightened. I had never heard them quarrel before. Later in the dressing room she said to me, "Don't worry about the fireworks. He's forgotten it already. I'd be sick over it for a week, but perhaps it purges Guthrie. He's been up all night working.

Guthrie McClintic directing Katharine Cornell, 1948.

We'll work on it, you and I, and get the rhythm of the scene. That's all I wanted to do." And it was never mentioned again.

My only experience with a Eugene O'Neill play was a brief but intense one, and because I had read his plays for years and seen every performance I could, I feel that I knew him. One of the reasons was my friendship with the fascinating woman who was the last Mrs. O'Neill.

Paul Shyre had directed Sada Thompson in O'Neill's *Diff'rent*. She was not free to play it in New York, where he planned to put it on again with *The Long Voyage Home*. He offered me the part.

"You won't have to read or anything like that. I just want to take you up to see Carlotta and she'll pass on you."

The chance to meet Carlotta Monterey O'Neill delighted me. But how was I going to convince her that I could play the complicated neurotic heroine of her husband's play over tea at the Ritz-Carlton?

It was merely a formality. We met and talked and became friends. She gave me books about O'Neill and translations of his plays into Arabic and many photographs for my collection. It pleased her to know that I had started to read his plays on my own when I was at Dalton and had saved my allowance to buy the beautifully bound Boni and Liveright editions. I had hoped that she would talk to me about O'Neill and soon realized that it was her passion: to talk about him endlessly and amusingly. Long after the run of *Diff'rent* was over Paul and I would meet her for delicious lunches at Quo Vadis and she would continue her stories. Her startlingly handsome face would change, like an actress's, from joyousness to pain as her griefs overcame her. O'Neill was very much alive for all of us at those meetings.
90   Her sentences, her paragraphs, began with "Gene . . ."

We gave a performance for an audience of Carlotta and Paul the day before we opened. They sat more than halfway back in the small theatre. Michael Higgins and Robert Drivas and I wanted to act the play perfectly for her. Afterward, she said that I should do *Mourning Becomes Electra*. I had always wanted to play Lavinia.

"I do not mean Lavinia, I mean Christine. You could be Gene's Christine." I had not realized that I was getting older and could play a different range of parts. When Michael Cacoyannis sent for me to read for *The Cherry Orchard* in 1966 I read for Varya. He looked surprised. He had meant Paulina. He "taught" me the part — the way he wanted it played — at the reading, and said I could have it. But the production was never done and I was sorry, because I wanted to watch Lila Kedrova as Ranevskaya no matter what part I played.

We do not see ourselves in the real mirror or in the imagined mirror that is the audience. All those staring hours that ballet dancers spend facing that brutal studio mirror are not egotistical. You watch for the mistakes you make so you can correct them. Your eyes are on the form of your entire body, not your face. Even actors putting on make-up are looking at what to fix and change, not simply how to enhance their looks. After years of working on your face and body this way it becomes oddly impersonal. Part of the job. It is strange to go to Hollywood and be made up by someone else and to fear the eye of the camera on all your imperfections. "Where did you get those *scars*? Shall we pluck your brows? Do you have any close-ups today?"

When I was six years old we spent a summer in Connecticut in a rented house on Bantam Lake. A friend of my mother's constructed an outboard motorboat and Tim and I   91 were to be among the passengers on its first voyage. Two other children were invited.

Again and again John, the builder and captain of this rowboat-shaped ship, pulled the starter rope through the round groove at the top of the engine, to no effect. Suddenly a purr, then a roar, and the boat leapt, surged forward and we raced across the water staying near enough to the shoreline to call out to our parents, who were waving and applauding. I shouted over the roar of the motor, crouched on the prow. The other children and Tim were crowded in the back. One by one, they dove off into the lake. I wanted to join them and dove off, too.

The boat hit my head three times. The third time it knocked me unconscious. Tim says that when my head appeared above the water again I looked like an Indian. The propeller blades had slashed my nose and cheek. John jumped in and pulled me out, got me to shore. My mother drove us to a doctor. He asked her to hold my feet, my father to press down on my shoulders, as he sewed eighteen stitches into my face. "Her eye is all right," he said. "I think I'm going to faint. I've never done this before." He was barely twenty years old. He did not faint nor did my brave mother.

The bandages came off. "Don't look in the mirror," warned Tim. When I was alone I touched my face. The scars were like little twigs on either side of my nose. I did look in the mirror. They were black stitches, badly sewn, like hurried basting. I thought what I saw was the face I would have for the rest of my life.

When I was eight my mother took me to a plastic surgeon. I imagined he would look like the painting of a doctor by Otto Dix in the Museum of Modern Art, a

92 jowled, impassive monster with a round mirror strapped to

his head. He looked exactly like the painting. In a liquid German accent he gave his verdict: "No use for surgery. When she is sixteen, perhaps, a little face powder will help . . ."

No one in my family ever mentioned my scars again. I was obsessed by them, sure that they were the distinguishing feature of my face and always would be. But never once in my theatre life have they troubled me. Invisible from the stage, scarcely reflected in the dressing room mirror, they seemed to disappear and were forgotten.

The theatre, Aristotle tells us, is a medicine.

The mirror that we know best is of course Shakespeare's, in Hamlet's great speech to the Players that is often acted and quoted too glibly for us fully to understand its scope. There is a kind of warning in his counsel. If the players do not follow his advice they will not only ruin the play, they will commit an offense that calls for whipping. And the mirror. Most people stop quoting when they have said, "To hold, as 'twere, a mirror up to nature." They forget that Shakespeare said *the* mirror: *To hold, as 'twere, the mirror up to nature; to show virtue her own feature, scorn her own image, and the very age and body of the time his form and pressure.*

The writer has already made use of that mirror — his imagination, his memories, his dreams — and fashioned the play. Now the director and the actors join to bring it to life. They are a part of him, of his play, and he becomes a part of them through the thrilling, exhausting, never-the-same-twice experience of repeating his play.

If people want to call actors children sometimes it doesn't matter. There are times when our childlikeness makes our work come to life. This could be a description of a creative rehearsal:

> In an external respect it is easy to perceive when the moment has arrived that one ought to let the child walk alone . . . the art is to be constantly present and yet not be present, to let the child be allowed to develop itself, while nevertheless one has constantly a survey clearly before one. The art is to leave the child to itself in the very highest measure and on the greatest possible scale, and to express this apparent abandonment in such a way that, unobserved, one at the same time knows everything . . .

Rousseau? Dewey? It is Sören Kierkegaard. It is advice, counsel — like Hamlet's — with a warning in it. Let the child explore and develop on his own and he will meet the dangers of experience and learn how to deal with them in his own way. He will learn the "age and body of the time" through experimentation. He will learn to live in the moment, grow to be what Kierkegaard calls "the immediate man." This actor/child we are dealing with will also learn how to fail. In every rehearsal there is the time of despair. The child — the part the actor is bringing to life — seems to split away from the actor, and the self, the creative mind, lacks a hold on reality. Kierkegaard again:

> What really is lacking is the power to submit to the necessary in oneself, to what may be called one's limit. Therefore the misfortune does not consist in the fact that such a self did not amount to anything in the world; no, the misfortune is that the man did not become aware of himself, aware that the self he is, is a perfectly definite something, and so is the necessary. On the contrary, he lost himself, owing to the fact that this self was seen fantastically reflected in the possible.

*

For an actor, the days are full of life-or-death decisions. Your part becomes your life and if it is — if you are — threatened, your behavior becomes extreme to anyone not connected with the play. It is what analysts might call schizophrenia, which we are told is "a psychosis marked by withdrawn sometimes delusional behavior and by intellectual and emotional deterioration." This delusion, this conception that resists reason and logic and matters of actual fact, is often the state the actor finds himself in not only at rehearsal but in performance. He is separated: He is himself. He is the part. He is the child who learned the part and he is the artist playing the part. He can do no wrong. He can fail miserably. He lives in this nightmare/daymare throughout his working life. It is how he controls his "schizophrenia" that sets him apart from the indulgent amateur or the inspired nut.

The more I acted the less I wrote. But I kept notes. It was important to me to remember what happened at rehearsal, and every script I have has the director's comments written in the margin. Not just for my part, for the whole play. I learned how to act and direct from men and women who taught me as well as directed me.

My first teacher, Mildred Geiger, made such an impression on me that I find in an essay I wrote in 1945 at Dalton, called "On Acting As an Art," that the most fulfilling future for an actor is "to be a teacher in the school of the theatre." And a month later in an essay, "The Creative Process," "All art — each moment in the transient arts . . . must be strong enough to be re-lived."

Not long before I wrote that I had heard for the first time the exquisite phrase of Goethe's: "Then to the moment might I say, linger a while, so fair thou art."

We had a ritual at school that every assembly opened

with a spoken invocation. A girl in the class below me had said the Goethe. Her name was Eloise Brown. That year she had acted in Sophocles' *Electra*. I sat enthralled watching that masterpiece and I asked Eloise how she was so sure of what she was doing on the stage. "I am two people," she answered. "One is acting and one is in front of the theatre watching."

Enid Bagnold's *Chalk Garden* was a magical play. I loved her writing, I loved the part I played; it had a cast of talented, interesting actors and a rehearsal period that was full of lessons.

The director was George Cukor. The leading roles were played by Gladys Cooper, whom he had known for years, and Siobhan McKenna, who was a new actress to him, making her American debut. The producer was his old friend from Hollywood, Irene Mayer Selznick. In 1939 her husband, David O. Selznick, had fired George as the director of *Gone with the Wind*. David's wife — sixteen years later — fired him as the director of *The Chalk Garden*. Why? I was there and I am not able to say. A new director came in and did not improve the production. There were endless changes, and we rehearsed until the last minute before we opened in New York, but the play was always there in the language. It needed to be *played* for the words to become the actors' own. It was on its way to being just that with Cukor, but it was not happening fast enough. He finished rehearsal one day, the company traveled to Philadelphia, and he went on location with a film.

He told me something valuable about the part I played. "I want you to do only what *you* would do. Don't try to find things that the character would do — mannerisms and so on. Let it be *you* and we will see the character. That's what I used to tell Kate Hepburn." I followed George Cukor's instructions and felt happy until I received a written criticism from the new director. He quoted a line I said in the play and added, "When I hear you say it, it makes me wince." He said my part was hard to play, it was "a dog." It was, in fact, a lovely part and I learned more from playing Olivia than simply to ignore an alien opinion of a character.

As I played her, she seemed to change. I didn't feel myself changing, but the part began to develop and vary with each performance. I felt guilty. I thought the stage manager would come and ask me to repeat exactly what I did at the rehearsals. I did not realize that I was repeating what was rehearsed but in the creative way of an actor at last. The heartbeat, the temperature, the guts of the character, were mine now and the newness of each performance was nothing more than what should have been demanded of me always. It took me years to learn this about my own acting and to protect it. To be able to live within the discipline of a part.

My difficult times in *The Chalk Garden* were nothing compared to Enid's. She was asked not to come to rehearsals. Her beautiful lines were changed and rearranged without her being there to protect them. We were told that she stayed in her hotel room, writing, and that when she had a new speech she would pin it up on a clothesline her husband had arranged in the living room of her suite. She called these lines her "plums." Once she asked Gladys Cooper, who was having a bit of trouble learning her part, "Don't you want some new plums?"

"No," said Gladys.

When they did the play in London, directed by John Gielgud, most of the original text was restored.　　97

George Cukor is bright and impatient. He said to an actor in the company, "Do it this way . . . Do it that way . . ." The actor waited for the direction and George blurted, "Do it *the way it is!* True to this play, this part, not to any other." Listening, I knew he meant for the actor to find the answers to his acting problems in the script. And we had the advantage of being able to talk with Enid Bagnold. I asked her if Olivia, the character I was working on, was herself. "I am all the women in the play." The Enid who could say, "I have no idea what I am," could fill in the life of a character with thrilling insights. She described Olivia to me:

"She's dark, shy, rebellious, rich-natured . . . twisted into an early knot by a worldly, successful, witty, impatient mother. A 'scholar girl' who would have been soothed by Oxford but is tortured by 'coming out' in Mayfair. A deep heart, loyal, hungry for love, unable to express it.

"A rich-natured fumbling girl. A girl who had to 'find herself' and knew that the 'finding' was so difficult that the very clothes her mother superimposed on her threw her wrong, threw her off the track of herself."

My clothes in the play were designed by Cecil Beaton. When I heard his name I had not read the play; it had been offered to me on the long-distance telephone while I was acting in my father's version of *Lysistrata* at Stanford University. Beaton's name made me think of exquisite, delicate dresses. I had just had my baby and the thought of wearing lovely clothes delighted me. My clothes as Olivia were perfect. And hideous. Olivia was pregnant by her second husband, happily so. I asked Enid about that part of her life.

"Her first marriage was to her a sin. But she was caught, pushed, shoved, drawn . . . and then, too . . . the longing to please her mother and have peace at last. She loaded too much aching love on her child by her first husband. She was the first thing she had owned. She wanted to make up to her for what she herself had missed from her mother."

"And her second marriage — ?"

"Now she is different. She is changed by love, she has confidence, she has become rightly proud."

"And her relationship to her mother — ?" I was asking now about the major character in the play, acted with energy and brilliance by Gladys Cooper. Gladys had wanted her own daughter to play my part, and there were some unnerving rehearsals in our scenes together because in many ways Gladys related her feeling toward Olivia and me to her feelings for her own child. In her anger she would call out to Enid, "I don't know what I'm talking about." She did know, exactly, and soon became used to the fascinating difficulties of the scenes we had together. They were a joy to play. Her part provided her with plenty to draw on. Mine, which was a small part, was beautifully written, and all of the things Enid described to me were to be found in the seemingly inarticulate Olivia.

"She is unused to small change in talk, unhandy, unworldly, but desperately aware of her deficiencies. Through all the mishandling by her mother she never wavered in her loyal love, though she fought her."

"How?"

"By silences, by mutism, by gentleness, by drawing back, by wincing. She knows what is right."

The weeks of playing Olivia were important to me beyond the pleasure of having a theatre to come to and a part to play.

The director was replaced as well as the girl who played my daughter, but Enid had "directed" me in the part.   99

7

Edward Albee has helped other young playwrights by giving them a place to work and a chance to have their work seen. I had been offered a part in a two-character play called *The Four Minute Mile* by Arthur Hadley; it was to be directed by Stephen Aaron. I read it and felt I could not play it. Arthur Hadley came to see me. We talked for a long time and I decided to try. We played it for two performances in January 1964. I was glad I had changed my mind because I got to know Stephen Aaron, who would become a colleague at Juilliard. I did not realize that Edward and Richard Barr were deciding to use me in Edward's next play.

The play was *Tiny Alice* and I was asked to stand by for Irene Worth. Just asked — no reading, no interview. I was given the script and the job at the same moment. And out of that engagement — for Irene's voice, that delicate instrument, failed her — I played the part of Miss Alice with John Gielgud for three performances and Edward came to see me.

Miss Alice was a complex and mysterious woman and I was absorbed in her. Being a standby means that you do not have to be at the theatre at every performance; you simply let the stage manager know where you can be reached if you are not near your own telephone.

The American Place Theatre was planning a workshop production of a play by Mary Lee Settle called *Juana La Loca*. I had met Mary Lee only once, at a birthday party. She said, "I am going to write a play for you."

The afternoon of the first rehearsal of *Juana* the large cast was gathered around several adjoining tables. We believed we were in fifteenth-century Spain when the director was interrupted and told I had an important telephone call. I was afraid something had happened to my daughter. The call was from Mark Wright, the stage manager. Irene Worth had lost her voice and I would play Miss Alice that night.

I went back to my place at the rehearsal table and we finished the play. The director gave us some suggestions and dismissed the company. It was nearly six o'clock. As we said good-night he inquired politely about my telephone call and I told him. "I *thought* that's what it was and wondered why you didn't ask to be excused." I wondered, too, then. It had not occurred to me.

The adrenal glands began to work, my blood pressure rose. I ran from the rehearsal, found a taxi, went home and washed my hair, set it, put on the make-up I had devised for Miss Alice and went to the Billy Rose Theatre. Mark Wright was waiting for me and so was John Gielgud. Sir John, now, but still John to his fellow actors.

"Would you like to rehearse anything, darling?" he asked casually.

"I don't think so," I heard my own voice answer. It was   101 nearly half-hour. It seemed better to be alone and still. He smiled approvingly and the next time I saw him we were onstage together.

In the course of the play I had to seduce John. He knelt before me, and wearing a black lace negligee over a nude body stocking, I opened my arms — and the negligee — and buried his head in my belly, crying out my own name "Alice — Alice—" as the curtain fell, winding his body in the folds of my robe.

I had rehearsed it many times. The seduction of the young priest by the fantastically wealthy and powerful woman. It went beautifully.

It was the unwinding, the freeing of John from Marian, that terrified me. What were *we* doing in these outrageous positions? We hurried away from each other to prepare for the next scene. Each time we played it my heart pounded.

After my third and last performance of Alice, my dressing room glowed with a white azalea plant from John and a charming note from Irene. I went back to Spain in the fifteenth century with joy. That chance to work with John in a play by Edward Albee — what more would I wish for?

A part of my own in an Albee play.

My wish was granted. A year later I was reading *A Delicate Balance*. Edward wrote Julia for me.

I talked to Edward about Julia. He told me that the years of attrition had taken their toll on her. I looked up "attrition" and applied it to her scenes with her parents. Edward told me more about this woman who had been married five times and was still in her thirties, who mourned the loss of her younger brother and who fought — literally, with a gun — to keep visitors from taking over her room in her family's house.

Edward Albee's *A Delicate Balance* as drawn by Al Hirschfeld, Martin Beck Theatre, 1966. As shown, Jessica Tandy, Hume Cronyn, Rosemary Murphy, Marian Seldes, and in the backround, Henderson Forsythe and Carmen Matthews.

"She's hard to describe because she isn't 'anybody' when the play begins, in the sense that her character hasn't formed. It is the threat to her 'room,' her identity — whatever that may be — which brings her to the point of explosion and sudden fulfillment of her own nature."

That complicated nature included deep envy of her aunt, unconsciously incestuous feeling toward her father and love and fear of her mother. These parts were played by Rosemary Murphy, Hume Cronyn and Jessica Tandy. It was a powerful family to come home to every night.

"If Julia isn't 'anybody' . . . ?"

"She is an accumulator of attitudes, and if she has a personality it is a 'referred' one. Around her husbands she takes on a parody of her mother's behavior and attitudes. She's a child who, by the end of the play, becomes a middle-aged woman, another cripple in the house of life."

He "gave" me the part in more ways than one. Julia was difficult to play. I remember standing in the wings before the first preview, thinking, "I am afraid to go into that room. They won't understand me." My parents in the room, or the audience?

Edward Albee is mysterious as an artist and as a man. When you work with Edward or deal with his words, part of what makes the experience fascinating is the quest to understand him. Actors are not noted for their ability to describe the experience of acting or indeed their "approach" to a role, one of the reasons being that what seems confusing to an audience is clear to the actor. He has become the person of the author's imagination and is quite prepared to answer anything about the character within the context of the play. Explaining a part to someone who has not seen or read a play is treacherous and many fine actors get caught in interviews sounding fatuous or foolish. To explain an Albee play would be difficult for an actor unless he were to tell the story of the play from his own character's point of view. Edward told me "All my plays have dark corners." When I played Julia in *A Delicate Balance* I knew what was happening inside her at every moment. Years later, when I directed a group of regional theatre actors in the play, I might have answered the questions about Julia quite differently. I could see the play as an entity at last.

Edward behaves like a gentleman in the theatre. He speaks thoughtfully and quietly. He lets the actors find their way. It pleases me that in the past few years he has been directing his own plays. He knows what he wants and the actors respond to him with respect and love.

J. P. Donleavy saw one run-through of *The Ginger Man* when we played it off-Broadway in 1963. I met him before I played my part and not again, and have only the memory of his being there to make that afternoon the most important of all the performances of his play.

But when *A Gift of Time* was in rehearsal we had its author with us at every moment because he was the director as well. Garson Kanin's production plan was the most complex of any play I had been in and the technical part of the performance was as smooth — no, much smoother — than *Before You Go,* the one-set, two-character play I was in two years after.

It is a question of preparation. If the script is not ready before the rehearsals start, the gamble is lunatic. In plays and novels and films about the theatre there are scenes of frantic rewriting and rerehearsing out of town until the last minute before the curtain rises on a miraculously successful opening. I have found that what is performed on an opening night is usually as good or as ineffectual as it was 105

when it was conceived. There may be individual successes —
a splendid performance, a brilliant set, one scene that is
memorable — but if the work of the theatre has not been
done, the play does not live. Everyone who gambles loses,
the audience most of all.

I have had some especially good times in acting for a
human kind of mirror. I understudied Olivia De Havilland
in *A Gift of Time,* the play that was based on Lael Wer-
tenbaker's memoir of her husband's struggle against cancer,
The Death of a Man. One day, shortly before we closed
after ninety-one performances, Lael and her friend Susan
Greaves came to watch an understudy run-through with
Garson Kanin. No one else except the stage managers was
there, but the auditorium was full for me. I knew Lael, had
lived in her house in Sneden's Landing at the exact time the
play took place, when her family was living in Ciboure, in
the Basque country. I loved and admired her and the play
written about her. With her eyes on me, the afternoon
seemed to pass in a moment.

A longer time, and as happy a one, was when I
acted in a production of Anne Sexton's play, *Mercy Street.*

It was warm the day we started work and stifling in
Saint Clement's Church. Anne was tired from walking
around New York the day before. I had brought some gold
ballet slippers with my rehearsal clothes. Anne looked at
them longingly. I gave them to her and she wore them every
day to walk to the Algonquin and back again to watch her
play develop.

Anne came to many rehearsals. She sat for hours on the
hard wooden seats drinking beer and making notes. Her
dresses were always of bright unpatterned materials. Her
gray-green eyes were clear and her gaze seriously beautiful.

Often she was joined by Lois Ames, her friend and biographer, who was taking notes on the procedure.

It surprised me how open Anne was in discussing her personal life. Her husband, her children. Not only her words on paper but her life-giving personality created a world for us all.

In my copy of *Live or Die* Anne wrote my name and "who has worn my life and entered my death." I did not look at the inscription again until after Anne's suicide. It does not seem possible to relate that act to the existence of the radiantly beautiful woman whose life I knew at the American Place Theatre. We shared a time of creative work and lots of laughter. When Wynn Handman came in to see how things were going, he always caught the company drinking coffee out of paper containers and roaring with laughter at Anne's jokes or deep in a discussion of psychoanalysis in relation to religious experience. The complicated character of Daisy — partly autobiographical — was bound up in family traditions and church dogma. She was a romantic woman in a world of modern cruelties.

I trusted Anne about the words and she trusted me as an actress. She gave me the courage to try anything and I was guided by Charles Maryan, with whom I had worked on several plays at the New Dramatists' Committee. That group, like the American Place, worked with actors *for* the playwright, to give him a chance to see his work. The plays I did there were by a schoolmate from the Neighborhood Playhouse, Harding LeMay, who until he had established himself as a writer would go to work in a publishing house two hours early every morning and write his plays before the office opened. He was a passionate theatregoer and when we were at school we became friends by comparing our theatre memories. Our relationship was shared by the 107

As Anne Sexton's Daisy in *Mercy Street,* American Place Theatre, 1969.

brilliant Anne Meacham, who was in my class. We found working together as graduates enormously valuable; trained in the same way yet respecting our differences, we shared all the problems of putting on a new play in a short amount of time for a limited but highly critical audience.

With Anne and Chuck it was similar: professional respect and real friendship. The work was terribly hard because the play took place on a high emotional level, but the exhaustion we felt after rehearsals was healthy and warming.

I hoped *Mercy Street* would succeed and be played all over the world. It is the major remaining piece of Anne's work that has not been published and as far as I know there have been no subsequent productions. Perhaps its theme of madness and sainthood is too painful to provide pleasure in the theatre. If Anne had lived she might have worked on it further and perhaps written another play.

Anne sent me a poster-size copy of one of Daisy's speeches, the poem "For the Year of the Insane." A pencil portrait of Anne by Barbara Swann covers the upper half of the space. She wrote that she had thought of sending a photograph of herself "smiling and smoking" but I have instead her powerful eyes staring down at me, and pasted on the back of the frame her words: "With hopes that you will like it. It is sort of a collector's item now plus the fact that it is your words and your song."

At a rehearsal of *Medea,* John Gielgud said to the women of the Chorus, "You must speak the lines as if you were trying to prevent a great cloud from coming down." To stave off the inevitable, to fight for life against death. Every time I heard, and later spoke, the lines about the beauties of the Greek cities I remembered what he said. I have come to believe that acting is a kind of battle against the inevitable. A crying out against what must come into each life: the beauty and the joy, yes, but also the horror and pain and the inevitable ending.

All of us in our separate secret ways do the same thing when we find someone we love. We create another world, another time, another absolutely unique pattern that can be lived out and can conquer the terrors of life. And like love-making, the act of acting begins with questions, tentative seekings, waiting for answers, giving and receiving with the utmost awareness of the other person, and gradually thrillingly slowly, quickly reaching the longed-for and inevitable climax.

Each performance is like that. In an outrageous comedy or a serious play, the journey must be taken with the same sensitivity to the needs of others: one's acting partner and one's audience. Many actors have expressed this feeling in interviews. Does it sound childish? It springs from the guts of the actor, this need to relate one's ephemeral art to the realest, dearest part of his life. It also explains much of the inarticulateness of the actor about the act of acting because it is just as difficult to describe to another person as love-making. The needs and joys of acting correspond to the secret mysterious moments and memories of our lives shared with one person, rather than hundreds.

Perhaps this is one reason it always surprises me when actors criticize the audience. They are there, as Alfred Lunt once said, "to be wooed." They want to love the play. It is our job to let them do so. If we are careless or self-indulgent they will return to their own thoughts and leave us alone on the stage, alone, as it were, without our lovers. What is important, as William Gillette wrote, "is to give the same illusion of freshness on the 100th or the 1000th night as at the première."

The illusion of the first time. We seek that in our loving, too. We *learn* how to find it. Actors learn to find it in every moment of their work. It is their skill, their craft, their art.

"If you could play any part in the world, which would you choose?"

I used to name specific parts. Then I became cautious. If I said a great classic part I would be afraid to read in the questioner's eyes another question: What makes her think she can play that? I began to answer: "I would like to create a part. To have a part written for me."

It happened. After *Father's Day,* in which Oliver Hailey had written "Marian" for me, he wrote another play with an even stronger part with me in mind. It was called *For the Use of the Hall.* Oliver lived in California and sent me a copy of the first draft and I loved it. I told him I would play it anywhere he wanted. I also told him I thought he might do better to cast a star in the part. I did not mean a star could act the part better; it is simply that you get used to being told you are right for a part in the theatre and then finding out that the producers have decided to get a "name." I formed the habit of suggesting that idea before it was suggested to me.

But Oliver chose me and we worked together to find a producer. It was the first time I had the experience of trying to get a play launched and it was an education. The people who have said they will read anything that interests you appear to have forgotten what they said or lost the ability to read. People you've never known suddenly come into your life and are of real help. Days and weeks go by without a word. Scripts are unreturned. Then one day you hear of a man who has a theatre in Providence, Rhode Island, and you ask him if he will read the script overnight and give you an opinion. Adrian Hall reads the script and says yes. Oliver rewrites. I finish my fourth year of teaching at Juilliard and start another one. In the fall of 1974 we are ready to plan the rehearsal schedule and begin to cast the Trinity Theatre production.

They had good actors in the resident company. The only part they could not fill was that of the mother and I suggested a dear friend, Nancy Cushman. She read the script in one day and came to join us. Oliver was still in California. He planned to come to Providence during the last week of rehearsals. He asked me to telephone him every evening.

I told him what I could, but he arrived just in time. An actor cannot honestly report on the progress of herself or of the other actors. I thought I was finding the part, as we say, but when Oliver saw a run-through he disabused me of that idea and the real work began. By the time we opened I felt happy and strong as Charlotte. I loved playing with the Trinity actors and made plans for New York producers to come and see the play. We sold out, the reviews were good, our hopes were high.

A blizzard made it impossible for our guests to come to Providence. We received frantic telephone calls from people stranded on highways having to turn back to New York, reports of canceled airplane flights. When Gordon Davidson was able to come, the performance he had planned to see was canceled because of the snow. Roger Stevens saw the play but at dinner afterward never mentioned it. Herman Shumlin took the train from New York. He was warm and comforting but decided on another project for the coming season. The play did not come to life again until it was taped for television the following fall during the same week I started rhearsing *Equus*.

I never lost faith in it. The work in Providence was valuable for Oliver and for me, and the company had the experience of working with the playwright, which is a vital part of rehearsal when the exchange of ideas and feelings can inspire the writer and the actor to do creative and original work.

Before doing Oliver Hailey's play in Providence I had done his funny, painful *Father's Day* at the Golden Theatre 112 in New York. Our previews were wonderful, too. This part might be the one to rescue me from "featured" or "supporting" parts. At least I would be considered now for plays with the other actresses of my own generation whom I admired.

I am not envious of other careers but of opportunities. I wish I could have played so many parts. It makes me treasure the ones I do have the chance to play and not take them for granted. I have been in plays where the actors tell me they wish they could get out of their contracts. If I have ever felt that unhappy in a play I have hidden the truth of the unhappiness from myself until the moment for flight has passed.

Father's Day ran one night. I thought it would run a thousand and went to a matinee of *School for Husbands* the day after the opening because I knew I wouldn't have much chance to see other plays. I'd be *in* one. I went backstage to see Brian Bedford and he said, "You've been nominated for a Tony as best actress in *Father's Day* and I have for best actor. We're supposed to go to Sardi's now and get our scrolls." I had a batch of newspapers in my hand. I'd gone to Hotaling's before the matinee and bought the Bergen *Record* and *Newsday* and the Long Island *Free Press*. I decided to take them back to the Golden and leave them in my dressing room before the party at Sardi's.

Brenda Vacarro met me on the street outside the stage door. All her possessions were around her feet. Not just her flowers, but her make-up kit and her radio-phonograph. There was to be no second performance of the play. I leaned against the building and began to cry. A mixture of rage and self-pity and exhaustion. She looked baffled. It did not matter that much to her. She was going back to work in films, which she loved. I had counted on this play for four years and before it had a chance to live it was dead.

I went to my dressing room. It was stifling. The heat had 113 been turned on and all the bright flowers from the night before were dead and sweetly rotten.

I wondered how they had planned to let me know. I called my answering service. "There's a message from your producers: 'Don't — repeat — don't come to the theatre tonight.' "

"Nothing more?"

"No."

Sardi's was crowded with smiling people. Harold Clurman said, "I'll see you in the play tonight."

"No. You won't. It's over, Harold."

He pulled his tickets out of his jacket pocket. "Look!"

"They're no good."

My prince of the theatre John Gielgud heard us. He asked me what had happened. "I don't understand. How can that happen in America?"

I was given a parchment in a green leather case. I put it in my theatre bag and went home to call Oliver.

At the Wyndham Hotel the Hailey family was packing up, preparing to catch the eleven o'clock plane to California. Frank Gilroy, the playwright, came over. He was helpful and dear. Oliver called the producers and asked them to let him know about Walter Kerr's Sunday piece. They never returned his call. I thought of showing him the out-of-town reviews. They were so good. Meaningless now. Betsy Hailey made a big package of canned food, cookies, paper plates, for me to take home. I ate every bit of that food, even the stuff I did not like. Anything connected with the Haileys was important to me. He'd had a terrible blow and was taking it with humor. That was the way Oliver managed to get through his complicated, desperately difficult life. He was in charge of a large and temperamental family and he took them wherever his work took him. His mother, his invalid brother, his wife and two daughters. He planned each day the way he planned his work and for the most part they stuck to his script. There was no room for sentiment, but that night it forced its way in. There was a lot of rough embracing and laughter that kept being choked with tears.

A few nights before, Oliver had turned down a huge movie deal, his agent knowing he could get even more after the reviews were in. When he got off the plane in California his agent told him the price had dropped $180,000 from the day before.

I had decided to take taxis that year and had opened a charge account at Sardi's. I didn't take the taxis and never used the account until *Equus* opened. *After* the reviews came in.

In 1968, when John Houseman suggested I be a teacher, I thanked him and refused his good offer.

"Why not, dear girl? You are eminently suited. Why not?"

I did not want to tell him that his invitation made me feel he did not consider me a successful actress and that therefore I would be available as a teacher. I underestimated John — and myself.

Three months after his school opened he called me and explained his plan to train young American actors for a repertory company that he would produce.

"You are needed here, Marian. We are going to do a reading of *The Trojan Women*. You are the one to do it."

"I can't, John. I'm doing a program, excerpts from James Agee's writings at the Theatre de Lys. I'm in the midst of rehearsals."

"When will it be over?"

"February twenty-second."

"Start teaching on the twenty-third."

115

I did and have never stopped and now I cannot conceive of a theatre life without teaching. John let me teach an acting class after we did *The Trojan Women* reading and the following year I began to direct plays at the school as well.

I was serious about becoming a fine teacher. For a long time I did not admit it. I held teaching in too high regard to think that I could do it, and many theatre people are of the opinion that acting cannot be taught. I felt that without my training I would have much less to offer, but I saw actors without training move ahead quickly in the Broadway theatre.

It is in the use of what you have learned that you prove its worth or worthlessness. A poor teacher or director is worse than none, but part of being in the theatre is learning how to adapt to the situation each play presents. The cast of characters offstage is full of stars, temperaments, talents, dolts, dears, bastards, teachers, artists, lovers and friends. Onstage they must be assembled into a amalgam of talent, the best of each person used with imagination and energy, resulting in an ensemble of artists.

While I was directing *The Trojan Women,* Michel St. Denis — with whom Houseman had created the Juilliard School — was directing Yeats's version of *Oedipus Rex.* His production of it for the Old Vic New York season in 1946 with Laurence Olivier was one of the greatest events I had ever seen on a stage. Now he was sharing his expertise with first-year students in a new theatre school. Where else could they have had such an experience? Such a teacher? When our rehearsals were over St. Denis and his wife, Suria, and I would share a taxi downtown and discuss the day's work. What colleagues!

The students from my first Juilliard class were the original members of Houseman's Acting Company. It had been his 116 dream to send a group of young actors touring the country in classical plays. Our actors were carefully prepared. The course is four years and includes every sort of training an actor needs to sensitize his mind and body as well as his talent. Most of the faculty work in the professional theatre in addition to teaching at Juilliard.

How is talent trained? By creating the proper atmosphere in which it can grow. If the technical skills of the actor are improving by being trained and tested, the natural gift for acting that led him to the theatre will grow stronger. The actor is given problems that are increasingly more difficult to solve. Parts to play, scenes to work on, that stretch his abilities. The important thing is that his talent is in use. The worst thing for an actor is through mischance or laziness to spend the hours and days and years of his life not doing what is important for him. Once the decision to be an actor has been made it is necessary to find a place to work, to study, to train. And after the training period has been fulfilled the situation becomes more serious. It is no good to wait for the right part, the great play, the most talented director. The actor has to ready himself to learn from experiences in all the media. If his goal is serious theatre, that is what he will do after a time of apprenticeship. For many the goals shift. Most of the actors I studied with did not stay in the theatre. But I am convinced that the two years they spent at the Neighborhood Playhouse made their *lives* more productive by sensitizing them and allowing their talents to develop.

How can the mystery of talent be described, expressed, explained? The closest answer I have found was written by Albert Einstein: "The fairest thing we can experience is the mysterious. It is the fundamental emotion which stands at the cradle of true art and true science. He who knows it not and can no longer wonder, no longer feel amazement, is as good as dead, a snuffed out candle."

8

Equus will be a living part of the theatre when my life is over. It will be put on the stage, all kinds of stages, through the years. It is the first new play I have been in that I know will have an important influence in the theatre long after it has closed on Broadway.

Because I had a part in it my life as an actress changed. I had worked consistently in the theatre all those thirty years, but I had never been asked my opinion by an interviewer, I had not been stopped by strangers on the street to talk about the play, I had not been forced to become a ticket agent (for *Equus* and every other successful play on Broadway), I hadn't had my caricature drawn for Sardi's and I had not walked into the theatre night after night without checking the callboard to see if the closing notice had been posted.

All those things that *Equus* brought me were fine things. What it could not bring me was the kind of part that demanded total commitment of my time and energy. I continued to teach acting at Juilliard, I worked on a dramatic radio program every week, did occasional other acting jobs and writing as well as the eight performances of the play. I wanted something more.

I dreamed of having parts that would absorb all my attention and love so that there would not be room for anything else in my life. In the dream, along with the part would come important relationships with the writer, the director, the producer, the stage manager and the other actors: a feeling of responsibility toward the play that would be integral to its success. I "act" that now. I have all the same feelings that were dreamed but have not been able to convert them into my real life in the theatre.

The function of a supporting player is a fascinating one. You work just as diligently on your part as the major actors, but when the time comes to play it, over and over, part of the skill is in knowing what *not* to do so that you become part of the structure of the play and remain there, strong — and supportive.

I know this from playing these parts in play after play, but also from the lovely times when I have had the major part and viewed the play from that other, happy angle.

I am not talking about stardom now. That is something quite different. For an actor to play a great part anywhere to anyone who will watch is a joy. It is the opportunity we all crave. And when you taste the glory of it, it is hard to be satisfied with less.

A friend of Peter Shaffer's told him of the event that propelled him into writing *Equus:* A stable boy had blinded twenty-six horses. The friend knew no further details of the alarming crime and Peter did not try to find them out. He wanted to find his own explanation for what had happened.

He invented everything in the play except the crime, which he modified, and he discussed his ideas with a distinguished child psychiatrist.

In the play there are eight characters who speak — the boy Alan, Dr. Martin Dysart, the boy's parents Frank and Dora Strang, the stable owner, the stable girl, a horseman, and the magistrate Hesther Salomon, who brings Alan to the hospital in the small town where Dysart practises and urges him to take him on as a patient.

The action takes place on a square of wood set on a circle of wood. Upstage from the playing area, forming a backdrop, are "tiers of benches in the fashion of a dissecting theatre" (Shaffer's words, even though he has also likened it to a railed boxing ring).

On either side of the stage stand two metal ladders on which are suspended the masks worn by the actors who play the horses.

When the play was in rehearsal in London both author and director felt that the illusion of horses was not succeeding. They wore their brilliantly executed masks, but the sound of boots on the wooden floor was unconvincing. During the run-through Peter passed John Dexter a word on a piece of paper: "Hooves." They had them created, six inches high, heavy metal bars attaching a horseshoe shape to the actor's soft shoe. A true strong sound rang with every equine step.

About John Dexter, the author has said, "He directs powerfully through suggestion. Into the theatrical spaces he contrives flows the communal imagination of an audience. He enables it to charge the action of a play with electric life. He is a master of gesture and of economy."

120   The *Equus* audience surrounds the play. On the stage

benches sixty people join the actors at every performance. They become part of the play.

I felt I would get the part of Hesther Salomon in *Equus*. I had saved the reviews of the play when it opened with the National Theatre in London in 1973. My father had subscribed to the *Manchester Guardian*, and for several years after his death those delicate, inky-smelling pages that were difficult to cut without tearing continued to arrive.

I had been introduced to Peter Shaffer by John Gielgud in May 1960. We had been at the same theatre on Fifty-fifth Street seeing a Russian film of *Othello*. Years later I saw him again at a big party at Roddy MacDowell's apartment. Peter's play *Five Finger Exercise* was playing on Broadway. We said hello, but I was too shy to talk to him and he was more shy. I doubt he remembers either meeting.

I had met John Dexter at Stratford, Connecticut, in 1969, when he was directing *Hamlet*. As part of my contract Michael Kahn had asked me to understudy Gertrude. The play was given to me in script form with all the moves written in. I learned it but never played it. My reason for being there that summer was to play Olga in Michael's production of *The Three Sisters* and that must have been where John first saw me act.

The bus from Providence got in at two in the morning. I went home, unpacked, bathed and washed my hair and went to bed. My appointment to read was at the Ambassador Theatre at 11:00 A.M. My class at Juilliard was at 2:30 P.M., a first rehearsal of *A Month in the Country* would begin at 5:00 P.M. I used to dream about days in the theatre like this one.

The stage manager greeted me with a hug; I said hello to Kermit Bloomgarden, the producer, who was sitting in the front of the house. John Dexter came up on the stage and put his arm around me.

"You may be too young . . ."

"How old is Hesther?"

"Oh — about forty-six."

"I'm forty-six."

He thought I was joking. In a way, so did I. I felt ageless that day. *For the Use of the Hall* had been a life-giving time for me. I felt strong and young and that I could act any part, any play.

We looked into each other's eyes for an important moment. Had he decided?

"Shall I read now?" I always ask to begin as soon as possible. The tension gets worse with every passing moment even when people are friendly at an audition.

"Are you ready?"

"Yes."

Bob Borod, the stage manager, read with me. Bob had had his first New York job with *All Women Are One* thirteen years before.

That was a three-character play with one woman in it who impersonated three other women. We were going to play in an off-Broadway theatre that seated 199 people and the salaries were to be minimal. I had to read for the part seven times. The author wanted Sophia Loren for the part of the lusty Italian widow. At one of the later readings I asked him if he had offered it to her. The director suggested I pad my breasts for reading number six.

We read Hesther's first scene. It went well. I asked Dexter if I should continue. "No, it isn't necessary."

Peter Shaffer came up on the stage and expressed surprise

that I would read for such a part. I was grateful for the chance and thanked him. Good-bye to Kermit, thank you to Bob, and I was on my way home to prepare for my acting class with the orange-covered English edition of the play in my hands. I was not asked to return it.

In March Kermit called me and asked if I would like to play Hesther.

Between February 4, 1974, when I read for Hesther, and the following September, when we began to rehearse, something happened that gave me more than the usual confidence in working on a part. I had heard from a friend of Peter Shaffer's that he was "writing up" the part of Hesther for the New York production. I tried not to think about it too often for fear that when I did see the script the changes would be few. As it turned out, the speeches Shaffer wrote for Hesther made the part stronger and more human. I was sorry that when *Equus* was reprinted for America the original text was published and her new words were not included.

The easy give-and-take between an actor and a writer either happens or it doesn't. When you learn a play from a published version, as I did *Equus,* it seems foolish to question so much as a word. The only line cut in the New York production of the play was one of Hesther's. In England the actors playing the parents were older so a reference to their ages in the first scene was dropped. Not a word was added — for over a year.

The added word was a beautiful one: Yes.

In the second act at the end of the scene between Dysart and Hesther, where she tries to make him deal with the boy's problems before his own, he ends the confrontation by saying simply, "I'll talk to you," and she leaves. When we were rehearsing to reopen at the Helen Hayes, John said, "Didn't Hesther say 'Yes' when we did it at the National?" Peter thought for a moment. "May I say it?" I asked.

"Yes." After two years.

When *Mercy Street* was produced, Anne Sexton wrote that she had found "a family for my art." *Equus* gave me the theatre family that all plays do, an unusually close one because of the length of time we stayed together. In addition to providing me with a platform to act on, it gave me the courage to write some of the things I had been wanting to express about acting. Fifteen years ago I started collecting my theatre notes to write a book and gave it up because I thought no one would read it. I feel now that it may be read in part because of the tremendous interest in the play. That I will not have been writing for myself alone.

The orange book has some signatures in it now. The author's and the actors' who have played Dr. Martin Dysart in New York — Anthony Hopkins, Anthony Perkins, Richard Burton — and the first Alan I played with, Peter Firth.

I admitted to Peter that I had never worn glasses in a play, that I saw clearly only what was happening directly in front of me on the stage. Everything Hesther does in the play is concerned with the Doctor and I never took my eyes off him when I was on the platform. When I was seated on the side and watched I could see everything, but nowhere as clearly as Peter could with his young eyes. He wrote in my book, "It doesn't matter that you never *saw* the play. Just being there was enough."

I kept my eyes on the Doctor, the actor, the character, the man. Whoever played the part, I loved.

I have loved a thousand times. I loved the light in the alcove and thought I understood the act of worship then, when I was six years old. I loved the plays, parts, actors, rehearsals, performances at school and wept at my graduation because I was afraid it would never be as wonderful again.

I loved the work and the dancers and the teachers at the School of American Ballet, where I tried too hard to become a dancer. And as I began to be an actress in the "real" theatre I found things to love in every actor I worked with. To act without love is cruel. To the other actor, to yourself and to the play.

The love I am describing is based on an understanding of the other actor's world as well as your own, a perception of his problems in the play not only in relation to your part but to the whole enterprise. A caring that is beyond what is written in the script or staged by the director. If this caring does not exist, the space we have come to fill remains empty. The play cannot live.

If it exists, this caring love, everything seems possible.

During the run of *For the Use of the Hall* in Providence, I came back to New York on Sunday evenings, taught my classes at Juilliard on Monday and returned Tuesday afternoons. The first time off coincided with the Juilliard Christmas vacation. On January 2 my production of James Saunders's play *Next Time I'll Sing to You* was to join the repertory of the Acting Company, composed of Juilliard graduates at the Billy Rose Theatre. I arranged to have a rehearsal on the last day of 1974. The theatre had been called the National when I saw Ethel Barrymore there in *The Corn Is Green,* when I read for John Houseman's production of *King Lear* and when *Medea* opened there in 1947. I enjoyed walking to work, passing the wonderful library, strolling   125 through Bryant Park. *Medea* was over by 10:15 P.M. If there was a good double feature on Forty-second Street we used to go to the movies after the play. We did not know enough to be afraid in those days and the films were of the best.

Twenty-seven years later the National had another name and its blue décor was now red. These changes had happened before I played there in 1951 in *The Wall*. I felt happy to be walking toward it, happy that my actors (as I thought of them with pride) would be making their New York debuts where I had made mine.

There was not much time to work. We had a runthrough. They were fine in the play. I went back to the dressing rooms elated and overheard another director telling my dear actors, "Just get out there and *sell* it!" My heart sank.

On the night of January second Houseman told me they played beautifully and were well reviewed. On the same night I was in Providence. We opened *For the Use of the Hall*. The most beautiful roses in the world were there. Sent by Patti Lupone, the only actress in the cast of the Saunders play. Why isn't there a way to make roses last? You must be a Shakespeare or a Gertrude Stein. But I can still see those roses.

The scrapbooks I kept about Judith Anderson and Katharine Cornell and John Gielgud still give me pleasure. The box with *Ondine* on the label is dear to me. In 1954, when I worked with Audrey Hepburn in *Ondine,* she behaved in such a way that my admiration for her was on a par with what I felt for my early idols. I expected so little, I got so much. She was generous with her talent and energy; her beauty and spirit transformed the Forty-sixth Street Theatre into a seascape. I loved watching her rehearse and act and

126   was sorry the play had to close in June after only five

months. Nearly twenty Junes later Audrey was in New York. We saw each other again. First at Sardi's, where we nearly missed each other because I had become nearsighted and did not see her sitting three tables away. When she was pointed out to me I sent her a note, and she could hardly read my tiny handwriting without glasses. It made us both laugh. What did we talk about? Our careers? No, our children.

The following Monday she came to see *Equus*. How beautiful Audrey makes other people feel! That is her magic on and off the screen. The dark and gentle eyes that I had first studied as she listened to Alfred Lunt's direction were now beguiling me again. I thought of how obediently she had followed Mr. Lunt's suggestions. The gossip in the company was that since she had fallen in love with Mel Ferrer, who played opposite her, he was giving her different directions after the rehearsals. I did not believe it to be true. He did not respond to direction as Audrey did, was ungracious to the older man in front of the company at times, but the production of *Ondine* had been largely Mel's idea and it would have been ridiculous for him to sabotage it by redirecting Audrey.

Lynn Fontanne came to many rehearsals to watch her husband direct. Occasionally he would look out into the auditorium and ask her a question with a look or a shrug and always received an immediate answer, either verbal or by some strange language of the heart. Once he called to her, "Lynnie, I want the King to acknowledge the court the way that woman did . . . you know . . . when we were watching from the balcony . . ." He raised his arm and cupped his hand and jiggled it at the wrist in an adorable way. "You know . . . Lynnie . . . ?"

"Queen Mary, dear."

I remember Miss Fontanne walking near me once and

saying softly, "I have something to say to you but I am afraid you won't understand. It's not really important." I asked her to tell me. "Well, my dear, I can hear you *breathe*." I had never thought of it before, but I realized at that instant that I was inhaling with such force that it made a sound. It would have become a bad habit. I was grateful to her for telling me. She also told me that if *I* thought I was beautiful the audience would too.

I came back the next day in my best clothes and Miss Fontanne stopped me after the rehearsal and said, "You look like a medieval beauty today. You can look as beautiful as you want to whenever you want to. Just *think* it. That's what I do."

Princess Bertha in Alfred Lunt's production of *Ondine,* 46th Street Theatre, 1954.

This intention, this need to look like, to *be* other than you are, exists in everyone. The actor heightens it. Makes use of it. Glories in it. As soon as you can believe you have become the character the writer has written, the craft of acting will allow you to convince an audience. Of one, or a thousand. When I had come to read for the part of Princess Bertha I had only an agent's description of the part: "It's the heavy in the play with Hepburn." I thought he meant Katharine Hepburn and if it was a "heavy" I decided to wear a plain suit and dark sweater. By the time I read the script at the theatre I knew I had made a mistake, but it was too late. I learned to stop people when they described a part to me. "Let *me* read it."

We called them Mr. Lunt and Miss Fontanne. They referred to Audrey as "the little girl." They delighted in her success as we all did. What was difficult to express to them was our delight at being in their presence. There are no knights and dames in the American theatre, but it has its royalty. The Lunts were ours. Their work, their discipline, their offstage behavior, were exemplary. They were universally admired and it was Lunt who Sanford Meisner praised most highly of all American actors to our class at the Playhouse.

He was friendly, accessible. He loved food and was a fine chef. He shared recipes with us. He was interested in our lives. When the news came by telephone one night during a performance in Boston that my mother had died in Florida it was Mr. Lunt who spoke to me first.

I remember the comfort but not the words.

Mr. Lunt no longer acted on the stage when he directed *Ondine,* but occasionally he would show Mel how to play part of a scene and step into his place. He would become Hans, the knight who loved the water nymph Ondine, and 129 for a few moments I would be acting with this marvel. Afterward he would mutter to Mel, "I am doing this badly, of course." By that time Mel's attention would have wandered, and if I were lucky Mr. Lunt would repeat the lesson, as perfectly and precisely as the first time, adding again the gentle disclaimer.

When Alfred Lunt died in 1977 his great career was noted in the papers and magazines, and three nights later many of the people who had worked with him stood under the marquee of the theatre named for him and his wife as the lights on the other Broadway marquees were darkened for several minutes. We shook hands, kissed, embraced and walked away in silence, remembering him.

A list of names. In the paper every day. When you are young you never look at the page they appear on. Then slowly, illogically, you begin. And one day, out of the unknown names swims, clears, stands a name you love. A man you knew. Your mother. Your father. A dear friend. Someone you had forgotten.

A woman who was in love with my father read the news of his death over someone's shoulder in a crowded subway. I had been calling her all that day to tell her. The shock of how she learned of his death was almost as unbearable to her as the realization that she could no longer share part of her life with a wonderful man.

We try to keep what we love alive. We do it by our daily living and by our work.

My need to learn about other people's lives through books and plays has been a need to make life more vivid as I am living it. Not to let the days go by unnumbered or without meaning. And the longer I have lived the more I have counted on the life force of work to keep me alive.

"The search for truth is in one way hard and in another easy. For it is evident that no one can master it fully nor miss it wholly. But each adds a little to our knowledge of nature, and from all the facts assembled there arises a certain grandeur," wrote Aristotle.

Children and actors look for teachers to be guides in their search.

9

On September 17, 1974, the *Equus* company met at the Lyceum at eleven in the morning. The lovely old theatre was uncared for, dusty, welcoming. We greeted each other affectionately — new friends and old. There was no need for Dexter to make a speech about the play. We had read and studied it. Most of us knew our parts that first day except for Anthony Hopkins, who had the longest role to learn in the shortest time and, as if realizing this, read it so quickly that the cascading words were nearly incomprehensible. The way he was going to play Dysart was his secret. When an actor gives a brilliant reading the first day some directors beg: "Do that again, play it that way," and all the love and care you give the part to make it grow and develop simply makes them impatient. They want what you showed them first. Dexter allowed Hopkins time to grow.

With *Equus* I decided to turn over a new leaf.
A new actress. A new part.
Hesther Salomon. Lovely name. Lovely woman. Warm

and understanding. A wise and good friend. Capable of sharpness if the Doctor — her friend — became too indulgent. Capable of love (hidden, discreet) to give him the courage to say what was in his heart in her presence.

In the beginning I could do no wrong. I was told all the encouraging things an actress wants to be told. The part became me, took over, acted me.

Day after day of disciplined rehearsal. The play was strong, the language powerful. The director and author worked as a team. Neither minded if you asked the other a question. It is not always so.

Claude Chagrin, the French mime who had created the movement for the horses in the National Theatre production, not only re-created it for the New York production but conducted an intense movement class each morning for half an hour at the start of rehearsal.

There were seventeen of us. We all took the class. And after it one actor read a poem while the others lay still on the floor, breathing deeply, listening.

Dexter's voice would break the silence: "Who wrote that? Does anyone recognize that?"

My hand would shoot up the way it had at Dalton.

"No, not *you,* Seldes." He called me by my last name for a long time. Often with affection, sometimes with a curious edge in the sound. (Meisner used to call me Miss Geddes at the Playhouse. Barbara Bel Geddes had made a lovely success on Broadway in 1946 and it amused him to confuse our names. It was not the first time. Norman Bel Geddes had designed the set for *Lysistrata* in 1932, so Geddes and Seldes had gotten misused from time to time. I live in the same building as Norman's widow and she and I get each other's mail.)

John teased me whether I gave the answer or I didn't. I did not mind. His love of language was our strongest bond when I began to know him.

We lost our shyness. John would be there, watching, encouraging, insulting us one by one. We strove to be good, as children do, longing for his praise and quick to praise each other and to laugh at what we could not help finding ridiculous.

Later in rehearsals he would refer to these lessons, demanding the kind of precision with words that we had achieved with our bodies. Literally begging us to do as Shakespeare suggests Hamlet's Players do.

I used to read to my mother from her treasured copy of *The Oxford Book of English Verse*. Before I took an English class in school I knew most of the shorter poems in it. At Juilliard I taught a class in poetry to actors. I had read often at the Poetry Society of America and since 1972 had been reading poetry on the "Today" television program. This was the first time I had experienced its use in a rehearsal. Dexter's use of poetry and movement in the development of the play helped mold us into an acting company.

When I started to work in the theatre actors and actresses dressed carefully for rehearsals. Particularly for the first reading. Gielgud mentioned at one of the early rehearsals of *Crime and Punishment* that Peggy Ashcroft wore a different frock to rehearsal every day and that pleased Komisarjevsky. I made a note and did my best. Today everything is casual and entire casts rehearse in blue jeans and T-shirts, even when the characters are supposed to be wearing long skirts or some kind of formal attire. Odd. At Juilliard you can suggest to the student that anything he does to make the circumstances close to performance level will help in the transition between rehearsal and performance. But directors do not always ask for these approximations in professional rehearsals.

At the Plymouth there were always remarks about the clothing we wore to work. In general the men in the company dressed more carefully and showily and talked more about clothes than the women. But the day that Richard Burton gave us a farewell party I wore what I thought was my prettiest dress. It was pale blue with bright anemones patterned on it. An actor looked up and asked, "Did somebody shoot a couch?" Well, one of my favorite scenes in *Gone with the Wind* is where Scarlett decides to make a dress from the velvet curtains.

When you have a job in a play you take more care of the way you look. Most actresses who have reputations for being difficult about their clothes are simply anxious for that part of the performance to be given as much care as it deserves. Little time is left for choice of costumes, changes in costumes if they are not right, and no provision at all is made for the chance that the clothes decided before rehearsals start may not be suitable by the time an actor has worked on a part for several weeks. There is usually an uneasy compromise.

At the first preview of *Equus* I wore a brown knit suit that had been purchased at Macy's. Its rich dark color contrasted subtly with the various browns of the horses' costumes and fit into the scheme of earth colors used throughout the costume plot.

The skirt clung to my body, the jacket did not. It rolled up in folds around my waist. I mentioned this to the woman who had bought the suit. "Oh, just smooth it out each time you get up," she suggested. I did not want to do that. I did not want to wear the suit. It was not my idea of what 135

Hesther would wear. I wore it and after the performance I walked home depressed, wondering how John could have accepted the way I looked.

At nine in the morning a clipped English voice was on the telephone, "We'll meet in front of Bergdorf's at ten."

"I can't. Rehearsal is at eleven. John will —"

"I've spoken to John. You cannot go on the stage in that tatty suit."

The voice belonged to Eric Harrison. I knew I should obey it. Eric and I went to several department stores and an hour and ten minutes later I walked into rehearsal wearing a splendid, expensive brown suit. I wore it until it fell apart.

The gentleman who solved my problem was the wardrobe master of *Equus*. There has to be some sort of a title for the *Playbill,* but those words do not describe what Eric did. He handled the entire wardrobe without any assistance; he chose all the replacement costumes. He bought the suits for the Dysarts and the jeans for the Alans. All of that was to be expected. But the rest of Eric's function in the company is harder to describe.

He took care of us. He provided a place for the actors to meet and have tea and coffee before and during the performance. There were always cookies or cake and fruit and candies. He cared about the play, listened to the performances and was critical of any falling off. He despised carelessness. Being a friend of Dexter's he was in constant touch with him. He knew all the gossip about our play and every other play in New York, on the road, and in England. He gave delicious parties in an apartment filled with paintings and the sound of the best stereo set imaginable. He had a remedy for everything. He could be cruel and biting and funny and soft. It depended on the day or his mood. He was, of course, a star.

When we had been running for about two months he asked me to come to his apartment for dinner. I said it was not possible, that I did not go out between shows, I had to rest. Nonsense. Rest at his place. Eat good food. Come on. I went often and he cared for me, fed me gourmet meals and let me rest. He was wildly entertaining on all subjects — politics, sex, the very rich, the very talented, the untalented — and most of all himself.

Anthony Hopkins, that generous, wondrously talented man, was the best Dysart I could imagine. Not better than any other actor; better than any dream I had of the character. Acting with him was what acting should be. The give-and-take of life on the stage.

He loved acting and gave his full attention to every detail

Equus curtain call, Plymouth Theatre, 1974. Left to right: Mary Doyle, Everett McGill, M.S., Peter Firth, Anthony Hopkins, Frances Sternhagen, Michael Higgins, Roberta Maxwell.

of his performance. Always prepared, *ready* to work, he energized the routine and made it exciting.

He had worked with John Dexter before. They strove in concert to find just the right move, pause, inflection, the strongest motivation for each moment of the play.

At a certain point after several weeks of rehearsal the temperature changed. Discontent. Looks. Avoidance of looks. Directions given with a cruel edge in Dexter's voice. Nervous laughter from the others. He was joking, wasn't he? They're old friends by now, aren't they?

Selfishly I took pride in the knowledge that although Dexter could go after Hopkins, it would not happen to me. I was secure. I knew he had the right actress in the right part.

How many days passed before *I* heard that edged voice? When did I change from a graceful confident magistrate to an incompetent amateur actress? What went wrong?

Just as it is fruitless to bring up old arguments when a quarrel is over, there is nothing to be gained by dwelling too long on the slights — real or imagined — that we feel in rehearsal. Because it is my nature to want to be directed and led during this time it is natural for me to give the people who are helping me — the writer and the director — all that is their due, and more. I think I have learned to take criticism sensibly, and yet when John Dexter called from the front of the house, "Watch those Jewish hands, Seldes!" I was as startled and hurt as when my grandmother had unintentionally wounded me about my father thirty-five years before.

Boris Aronson, the stage designer, is a lovable genius with a marvelous accent that makes stories he tells or stories about him delicious to the ear. Boris said, "Dere are only two rules in de theatre. Vun: Dere iz always a wictim. Two! *Don't* be da wictim."

In the dictionary I find two definitions for *victim:* "VIC-TIM: A living person or an animal offered as a sacrifice in a religious rite. 2. A person injured destroyed or sacrificed under any of various conditions. Synonyms; prey, quarry."

In 1923, when he was thirty-five years old, Uncle George was living in Vienna. He wanted to see Freud and interview him for the Chicago *Tribune*. When Freud refused he turned, "in desperation," to Alfred Adler. He asked him, "What *makes* a dictator?" George had been thrown out of Italy by Mussolini after spending four years there as a correspondent. Adler was interested in what George had to say about Mussolini and their conversations formed the basis for a piece he sent to the *Tribune* that was published on December 16, 1925, and that, Adler said later, "introduced him to America."

The important subject for George was Adler's theory that the behavior patterns of all human beings are set in the earliest years of their lives. George did not become Adler's patient, but he said, "I feel his views shaped me — my pattern — more than those of my libertarian, nonconformist, freethinking father in my childhood. Adler told me that every man and woman, living and dead, had experienced the feeling of inferiority, and that from childhood on everyone struggled to overcome it, and that all of us seek the equation of our individual inferiority, the tests of our behavior pattern, through relationship to society, to one's work, and to sex."

Adler had told him that when he was young he felt victimized or ignored by his peers. He was nearsighted and timid and was the victim of verbal and physical beatings. He 139 determined, he said, that he would become a famous man, a doctor, a humanitarian.

While George was in Germany he attended the rehearsals of the première of Shaw's *Saint Joan* at Max Reinhardt's theatre. The cast included the dazzling young Elizabeth Bergner and a group of eminent actors. They welcomed George because he had a copy of Shaw's preface, which they had not seen. At a rehearsal of the trial scene Reinhardt lost his temper and screamed at the talent gathered on the stage: "Remember, you are *not* actors!"

In seeking an explanation for the behavior of dictators George — the gentlest of men and one of the wisest — reexamined his own life and career and gave up newspaper writing and returned to America to write books.

He refused to be a victim. He chose to be a passionate muckraker, a truth-teller, a reformer.

I thought of trying to catch John Dexter in a piece of fiction. To allow myself the chance to write his thoughts about me, in answer to so many of my thoughts about him.

I would set the story in Sardi's, perhaps changing the name of the restaurant, and we would be having a late supper after the theatre just as we did when *Equus* was in preview. There would be a third person there, as always. A young actor. It would be his first time in the theatrical restaurant. John would be offering us the chance to play in *The Sea Gull,* just as he did. And then I would have him look across the table at me and think, I am offering her the chance to play Arkadina, but she is still so much Nina. Perhaps that is what both draws me to her and irritates me. Am I a kind of Trigorin to her? She is in love with the theatre, ardent, emotional. But she is more than twenty years older than Nina and it's a bit unseemly. That naïveté should have been burned away by now. How will I use it in Arkadina? Can I strip her down to what she, Marian, must really be? A talented but disappointed actress? A lonely creature who makes the best of everything because she fears that's all there is?

Then I would write a section from my point of view. The facts of my life that are strong and wonderful which I do not share with John. I will see his thoughts in his eyes and the rest of the evening I will *act* Arkadina for him. I will for the moment destroy all Nina's love of life and substitute for it the world-sickness that Arkadina exists in. John is more comfortable with that side of my character.

How would I end that story? It would be lovely to make the actress (me) have a great success and grow and forgive. Or would I have her clash with John at the last part of her career and make it a sad story like so many theatre fictions?

I had been warned by Tony Hopkins that the warmth and brilliance John Dexter was lavishing on the company might change without warning. He spoke from experience. After several plays with him at the National Theatre Tony had vowed never to work with him again. Actors' vows are not to be taken too seriously. A part like Martin Dysart and a chance to play in New York were too good to refuse and most directors and actors have the ability to forget hard times and ancient grudges.

I could not hear Tony's warning. I was in the midst of the most creative experience I had had for many years, certainly since becoming a teacher, and I could relate it all to my teaching.

After nine months of playing Dysart, Tony went to Hollywood to make several television specials. I sent him a post card: the Oskar Kokoschka poster of the tortured, twisted woman in the red dress that is at the Museum of Modern 141

Art. Beside the artist's credit I wrote that it was a portrait of me at a Dexter "brush-up" rehearsal. That card elicited a passionate treatise against Dexter's treatment of actors which Tony asked me to "pin on the notice board for all to see." More important, it was a cry to me to give up any kind of "negativism and cowardice." Full of four-letter words, because it amused him that I did not use them, it ended with the simple command: "Get straight."

I followed Tony's advice. It was time to evaluate John's treatment of me as methodically and dispassionately as I would a problem with a student or with another actor. I had been repeating a pattern of idealizing a person who was doing his job in his own way and letting comments and criticisms take on far more meaning than they were meant to have. I had to work on Hesther to prevent her from becoming sentimental and emotional. John was right in his demands. His manner — the language, the onslaught of words and feelings turned against me in front of others — were things I had to learn to deal with. The director could not be my father or Gielgud or Guthrie or Alfred Lunt or any of the other gentlemen who had guided me in the past. This was another time. Just as I had gotten used to the feeling that young boys were directing me when I first did television, I now must adapt to a kind of witty brutality and translate it into terms I could use in my work.

After the bad times were over I did not forget them. They were valuable. It was impossible to respond completely to some of the methods John used, but it was also impossible to ignore his value to me. I needed to go through that miserable passage to arrive at a place where I could be an actress he could count on to react to his direction without fear or cowardice. To welcome it. When I learned to smile at what John chose to do to me and to make John laugh, I knew that our relationship had developed professionally and socially too, and that we could give each other pleasure as well as work with each other.

Equus was still in previews when people began to ask the cast, "How long do you think it will run?" After a few months, "Are you going to stay with it?" Later, "Are you still in it?" and inevitably, "When is it going to close?" When we played our six hundredth performance I thought of James O'Neill, who played *The Count of Monte Cristo* over six thousand times in the course of twenty-five years! He was a last-minute replacement in the New York production and was not pleased with his first performance. He said, "The public saved the life of the play." In *O'Neill,* the Gelbs comment: "The play that was to bring him the popularity and wealth for which he had yearned, simultaneously put a strict limitation on his career. It became a trap from which he never escaped . . ."

Laurette Taylor's daughter, Marguerite Courtney, says that her mother decided to close *Peg O' My Heart,* in which she had made an enormous personal success, after a year and a half in New York because she had not worked all those years for success to have it imprison her forever in one role. She was a great admirer of Sarah Bernhardt and wanted to have a career with more variety in it.

"I could never be a Bernhardt," she said; "there just isn't enough of me."

But there was too much to accept the "trap." She quoted Peg: "Ye can't cage the Irish. They'll die on your hands." She played the part six hundred and four times in New York and over a thousand times in London, again deciding to close it when there was still a public waiting to see her in it. Why did she submit to what she referred to as "bondage" 143 for a second time, and for twice as long? Her daughter says that her stay in England from 1914 to 1915 had been the time of her greatest personal happiness.

The knowledge that life is good enhances the joy of working in the theatre. The discipline of acting makes the happiness of life outside the theatre doubly precious. We read in the papers about our more popular actors, we have all heard rumors about our colleagues and we think our own thoughts and nothing surprises or dismays us. There has been a sense of liberated private living in the theatre for a long time; what is happening now in the real world seems overdue to most creative people. We expect to be judged by our work. We accept the judgment each in our own way.

The aristocracy in the theatre is talent. A cast will forgive an actor almost anything if they think he is a good actor, and will withhold even the meagerest compassion from an actor who does not do his part well. That cruelty is based on discipline and it is one of the things that keeps a professional company alive and sensitive. Nothing the director or stage manager could say is as damning as the expression in the eyes of your coworker when you have done poor work.

How can it be always new in a long-run play?

That is our task. If an actor cannot fulfill that task he cannot be called a professional. We have seen extraordinary performances by amateurs and children and people who have had too much to drink at parties. But to be able to repeat something good is to have real power. The craft is in how you prepare each time for that repetition.

Each actor has his own way. Students ask how to prepare. It is useless to tell them. You have to find your own way and each part teaches you something new. A way to find security in the moment before you begin the life of the play. It begins when you wake in the morning for some. For others you can see it happen in that second before the door opens, before the lights go on, before the first word is spoken.

There is the ritual in the dressing room, private for some, gregarious for others. The look of the room, the temperature, where each article of clothing is set — yours and the character's — mementos from other plays, as far back as high school. Farther? I have a little china cat Mildred Geiger gave me. When I am not working in the theatre it goes back to its original box with cotton around it and stays in the dark until there is another dressing room for it to ornament. A different robe for the theatre. Special towels, soap, cologne. Brushes and combs. The actual tubes or sticks of make-up, the brushes. An occasional new cosmetic, produced that year, that will change everything and make your old face new for a new part.

There are rituals backstage in the wings. I watched Katharine Cornell hold her hands above her head and shake them gently for a few moments before she went onstage. Her large beautiful fingers fluttered in the air and then came to rest. She told me that she had done this since 1928 because she was self-conscious about the veins on the back of her hands. "Oh, yes. I keep doing it. I think it calms me. Of course I know it lasts for about ten seconds!"

I used to kneel down just before I went on in the final scene of *That Lady* so that the cracking sound in my knee joints would never be heard on stage. In another play a stagehand reminded me, "I used to see you praying just before your entrance every night."

One night there was a certain confusion in the wings. A new actor, Martin Brooks, was taking over for Douglas Watson as Cornell's son. Certain last-minute adjustments were being made. Kit said to me in a whisper, "He's awfully good, isn't he?" I missed Douglas terribly because I admired 145 him, but I nodded, knowing Marty was excellent. "I'd like to be one of those who help him." She already had. In the quiet of the wings I was thinking of so many actors she had helped when the moment was shattered by an electrician's voice growling, "Will you deck hands get your outdoor livery outta Her Majesty's room!" The costume and prop men cleared the stage, Cornell raised her arms above her head, the exquisite hands danced and the play began.

Constantly learning something new is what makes a life in the theatre so stimulating. Painful, too, but that is to be expected. But even in the long, long run of *Equus* what was routine became ritual and the rest was fresh every day. Before he goes on the stage the mature actor does not need to say to himself "I have never said this before or done this before." The very act of walking on the stage insures that condition of innocence. An actor's faith in the situation the playwright has given him is the core of his work. Without that faith acting is silly, humiliating, feckless. And acting without that faith is boring and full of lies. Finally, the actor and the public know this and a career comes to an end.

A drink or two can give an actor an illusion that his faith is still there. That is the temptation. It seems easier to have the drink or smoke the forbidden weed than to bend the will toward the work at hand. How odd it is that so often the condition of being drunk or hung over is forgiven or not mentioned or laughed about. Tragic, really. Because for an actor there is always so much more to learn.

Many of the students I teach plan to work in regional theatres, where they can continue playing the classics and work with talented companies. More and more of these theatres are building reputations with audiences and critics.

There were not as many opportunities when I was young and I was grateful for the summer stock companies that hired resident companies. For seven summers I worked in various theatres, and without those jobs I would not have had the opportunity to work with Dame May Whitty, Elissa Landi, Victor Jory, Libby Holman, Franchot Tone, Eileen Heckart, Neil Hamilton, Ruth Chatterton, Judy Holliday, Vincent Price, Lillian Harvey, Freddie Bartholomew, Buddy Ebsen or Orson Bean. It was in the various stock companies that I first played Oscar Wilde, Jean Giradoux, J. B. Priestley, Lennox Robinson, Emlyn Williams, Lindsay and Crouse, S. N. Behrman, Lillian Hellman, Tennessee Williams, Ruth Gordon, Moss Hart, and Aristophanes.

The work was done under pressure; there was never enough time to study and rehearse; and as soon as one play was running we were working on the next one that would open the following week. The pressure of live television shows reminded me of the panic that sometimes accompanied opening nights in stock. But much of the work done under that pressure was exciting and in some cases important. I thought that Ruth Chatterton's Regina Giddens was one of the finest performances I had seen. I played her daughter in *The Little Foxes* one summer in Vermont and the part of Birdie Hubbard years later when Ruth joined the company at the Bermudiana Theatre in 1952.

For two summers at Kennebunkport, Maine, I worked with James Noble and Archie Smith. We played Noel Coward and Robert E. Sherwood and we all acted and sang and danced in a production of *Lady in the Dark*. It was the second musical for me. The first was *Alice in Wonderland* at Cambridge. The first lines I spoke as a professional actress were written by Lewis Carroll. I played a Tiger Lily.

Showboat was a musical that appealed to me because of 147

the character of Julie that Helen Morgan created. My father had written about Helen Morgan in *Esquire* and she wrote him a sweet letter of thanks that she asked him not to show to anyone. In it she confided she wanted to study to become a better actress. When I was offered the chance to play Julie I worked on her songs ceaselessly to overcome my nervousness at not being a trained singer. G. Wood played the piano for "Bill" and helped me with the song and the character. He thought if I learned to drink I'd be a better Julie. The most difficult part of playing Julie was that the actor who played Captain Andy professed to have known and worked with Helen Morgan. I could not meet his standards. I did not tell him that I did not meet my own. I still walk down the street singing, and practice for that time when I will dare to play in another musical.

When acting is poor it is called "stock" acting or "ham" acting. There was a lot of very bad acting in the stock companies I played in. Many of the movie and television stars who came in the day before the opening and moved the resident actors around the stage to fit their needs were not talented theatre actors. I worked with drunkards and dullards and it amazed me that week after week they would go on to other theatres and "get away with" their second-rate work.

Cornell had written in *I Wanted to Be an Actress* that she had learned a great deal from working in stock companies. She said it was important to learn what *not* to do.

It makes me smile now, but it was terrible to see established actors stumble through performances. One summer a fine actor arrived to do his part beaming with good will and the vague grin of an alcoholic, which I had not learned to recognize. He held his script for the rehearsals and on the opening night seemed calm and a bit sleepy.

He started the play with energy that soon flagged and his eyes were seldom on his acting partner. He had written his part on bits of paper and hidden them in the hat he wore, in the newspaper he carried and on a coaster which he placed under his prop glass. Because his hands trembled the newspaper prop was the deadliest. He could not read what he had written. The hat failed him too. The page flew out of the hat as he made a flamboyant gesture. It was an actor's nightmare taking place before our eyes. What is extraordinary is that the reviews were good, the audience applauded the star they had come to see and the following nights the cast got used to his bizarre technique that kept us alert and fascinated.

I smile now because I remember the sweetness of the man, but he represents a part of the theatre that is depressing. He wanted to be a fine actor, he was richly talented, but his drinking killed his career. There are actors now who rely on the stimulation of drugs in the same way. For a time it is possible for them to function under the influence and the stimulation of any number of "highs" but the future looks empty. Survival in the theatre demands a discipline that not everyone has the patience to practice. There are times when every actor, writer and director would love to have some sort of easeful release from the tension. That is why during the half hour before the play we are always so careful to ask if an actor is preparing before we disturb him in his dressing room or in the wings. The gathering up of his strength and confidence is one of the essentials of a good performance. It is the substance of an actor's life.

10

Anthony Perkins played Dysart and Thomas Hulce played Alan when Tony and Peter left *Equus.* Tommy had been Peter's understudy and went on the first matinee of our previews. Perfectly prepared, he gave a fine performance.

I met Tony Perkins as a professional actor on the stage of the Plymouth Theatre when he began to rehearse Dysart in June 1975. The stagehands remembered Osgood Perkins. Here was his son: serious, charming, utterly committed to the part. My father had admired Tony's father and had often told me about his performance in *The Front Page, Uncle Vanya* and *Goodbye Again.*

Osgood Perkins appeared in twenty-five plays on Broadway between 1924 and 1937. He was popular with audiences and critics and had a distinguished career. Tony was six when he died and when I first met him he was fifteen. It was in Boston, where June Walker was appearing in a play. Her son, John Kerr, was a friend of Tony's. I met them both at a party in June's suite at the Ritz-Carlton. I was eighteen and felt older. Tony seemed like a serious, charming child. We had a long talk and when I arrived at Kennebunkport to begin the summer theatre season I found an inscribed copy of a play from Tony which I treasured.

After playing Hesther with Tony for a short time I had the chance to play the part of Dora Strang, the mother. Frances Sternhagen was going to take a five-week vacation. Dexter was in Europe, so Peter Shaffer directed me for three rehearsals. It surprised me how nervous I was at the beginning. I knew Peter quite well by that time and I certainly knew Dora, since long before rehearsals when the first actress who was cast for it changed her mind and decided not to be in the play ("I'm a star. I couldn't sit on the stage all night"). At that time I thought of asking to play her instead of Hesther. Dexter advised me: "Stay where you are, dear. Hesther's a marvelous part."

After the first rehearsal with Peter I couldn't wait to come back and show him what I had learned. I did the scene in the second act where Dora defends herself against the doctor's painful questioning. She is challenged and her guilt and rage pour out in a long, brilliantly written tirade. He came over and embraced me. "We don't need to rehearse anymore." And as I was leaving he said, "Are you going to play it that way at every performance? You'll kill yourself!" I did not have to answer. Yes, for the actor and for the character those moments onstage are times of life and death. Even in repose, in the subtlest, most restrained moments, the actor has that choice — life for his character or nothingness. In a long run it is essential to choose *life*. In the long run, too. Always.

Frances came back and played Dora again and I went back to Hesther. When the play had run for twenty months Frances decided to leave. She was respected and loved by the company. When the play opened it was inconceivable to me that any actor could be replaced. I knew Tony Hopkins and

151

Peter Firth had nine-month contracts, but I never accepted the reality that when June 30 came they would leave and we would go on without them.

At the first-anniversary party at the Oyster Bar in Grand Central Station, amid all the gaiety and consumption of seafood, I mentioned to Peter Shaffer — John Dexter was not there, he does not like large parties — that I was anxious to make a change.

"You want to play the Mum, do you?"

"Yes, I think if I'm going to stay with the play that it would be better for me and for the play."

"And will John put you in?"

"He said he would."

"Well, it's fine with me, dear."

I was not the only actor who wanted Peter's opinion that evening. Tony Perkins cornered him near the anniversary cake and asked, "What do you really think of my performance?"

An act of folly. Everything Peter told him was negative and Tony did not forget it. I wonder if Peter had forgotten it months later when Richard Burton joined the company and Tony offered to come back after Burton's engagement and was refused — or twelve weeks after that when Burton left the company and Tony Perkins *was* asked to return?

However much these events hurt him, Tony behaved like a gentleman and never did less than his best. I was outraged at his treatment. It did not occur to me that I was to be treated in much the same way.

For the moment I looked forward to working with John on a different part. When I reported my conversation with

Peter to the stage manager a rehearsal was set up for me two weeks hence.

Elated, I thought I had made a choice about my career instead of just letting things happen. I worried about Frances's going because I knew it would hurt the balance of the play. But her mother died, so she decided to leave sooner than planned. She needed to be with her family. Mary Doyle, who understudied both Hesther and Dora, was delighted that I wanted be the Mum, as she preferred playing Hesther. All was well.

Shocking then to be stopped by the stage manager on my way to the second act one evening and have him tell me that they were reading other actresses for Dora.

"Oh," I said, "that can't be."

I gave him a shortened version of my Dora diary. There wasn't time to talk about it. But as I sat on the stage after playing my last Hesther scene I began to feel something had gone very wrong. After the curtain call I asked where I could reach Peter Shaffer. In London at Claridge's. I called the next day. He'd gone to Greece — the place of the doctor's dreams in our play, the place of beauty and truth. Unreachable. John Dexter? Having oral surgery. Better not call him for a few days. Kermit? Ill and not to be troubled with a little thing like this. I called the coproducer, Doris Cole Abrahams. Her mother was in the hospital. Doris was spending the days and most of the nights there. I began to dislike my thoughts. Was I being greedy?

When we were rehearsing *A Gift of Time* during the first week I acted many parts that were later played by other actors. Ruth Gordon came to the rehearsals and at the last run-through before the "real" actors came she asked me if I'd miss playing all the parts. Thrilled to be talking with her 153

I said, "Oh, yes, I love them. I'd like to play all the women's parts in the play."

"So would I," she said, "and the men's too!"

In the week my problem was being discussed the company manager was never backstage at the theatre. For a long time I did not call my agent to tell him what was going on because I kept thinking there had been a misunderstanding and it would be settled by a message from Peter Shaffer. No message came. In fact, the original message from the stage manager was added to: "Peter doesn't think you are ideally suited for the part." Painful. Probably true. But if you are an actress it is not being ideally suited that concerns you about a part, it is how to act the part so that it seems to be ideally suited to you.

This took place during the final week of Juilliard's term. A week of seeing plays, teaching my final classes, counseling the graduating actors, comforting the ones who would not return. How could I tell these confident or frightened young actors that I was on the same seesaw of discontent?

One night there was a knock on my dressing room door. A loud, demanding knock.

"Who is it?"

"Doris."

"Just a minute. I'm not dressed."

"I don't mind," she said and pushed open the door.

"I do," I said and pushed it shut.

A few seconds later I opened the door. She came in, lit a cigarette, emptied a glass dish onto the dressing table and used it as an ashtray. "I understand there is a crisis," she said.

"Is there?" I asked.

Long silence.

"I mean, it seems that there is some confusion about your playing Dora."

I told her my story.

"Well," she said, "we'll have to wait until we can find Peter."

"When will that be?"

"I don't know. He's scouting locations for the film."

"I think it should be soon," I said as steadily as I could. "I have to make my plans."

She began to tell me about her mother's illness. I felt foolish. Her parent was dying and I wanted to find out about a part in a play.

"We all love you, Marian," she said.

"I don't want to be loved. I want to be treated like a professional. Please let me know as soon as you can."

She crushed out the cigarette and left.

The company was aware of my unhappiness. I stopped going down to the coffee room. Everyone was behaving as usual, but I read betrayal into every look.

Six days later the same pounding on the door.

"Just a minute."

"How long am I going to have to wait out here?" Doris called. I pulled on a robe, and in she came. She told me that she and John Dexter were going to make a decision without waiting for Peter.

"When?"

In two days.

Three days later over another cigarette she told me we would go ahead just as originally planned and I would play Dora after Frances left.

"Doris, what can I learn from this experience?"

"What?"

"What can I learn . . . ? I don't want to go through this again. It is silly and painful. I feel unhappy and humiliated . . ."

"But this has been a happy time for you, hasn't it?"

"My time in *Equus?*"

"Yes."

"Some of it, yes, very happy. And some of it has been extremely difficult and I want to learn something from it so that it doesn't happen again. Or if it does, I'll know how to handle it." She looked vague and anxious to leave the dressing room. "Well, what can I learn?"

"Nothing," said Doris.

I did learn something. To fight for what I had been promised. The worst that could have happened was to find out that someone (I am not sure it was Peter) did not want me to switch parts. The best thing was that I didn't simply give up and accept the situation, which I am often tempted to do.

As a matter of fact, when I knew the part was mine I asked for a raise. I named the amount I thought Dora, Hesther, and the father should have been paid from the beginning. I was given a message "from the management" that it was absolutely out of the question. It was 5:59 of the afternoon in which the contract was being typed. I told my agent I did not believe the message. He sounded a bit upset.

"Just wait," I said.

He waited. They called. I got the raise. And Michael Higgins did, too.

If only money did not get mixed up with pride. To have no pride as an actor is fatal. To have the right amount is almost impossible. It gets in the way of good work; the lack of it prevents your taking chances, daring to go further than you have before, risking whatever reputation you have —
156 not with the public, but with your director or playwright.

You need to know they will allow you to rehearse awkwardly, embarrassingly, in your search for certain elements in the play. Not carelessly, but with the kind of abandon that only comes with real love.

Our happiest theatre memories are those when that love exists in equal measure for the actors and the audience. When the play is received as love is received, with trust, unquestioningly. Because it is being given with confidence and truth and, yes, pride. Beautiful pride.

On the appointed day, John Dexter, perfumed with alcohol and exuding charm, strode into the rehearsal. I bought a housedress and wore it for the first time. I did not want to look (to Dexter or to myself) like the actress he associated with Hesther. He stared at me. *"Wrong* dress." Not "Hello." *"Wrong* dress." He looked at the shoes I had bought for Dora. They passed muster. In two hours we did three of Dora's scenes over and over. He suggested a heavy walk. I asked him if I should change my hair style and color (yes). Hands still. Head still. Find the center . . .

"This is a character part for you, Seldes."

Yes. We worked hard and the time passed quickly.

"Thank you."

"Don't thank me, it's my job. If I come back and see you 'acting' I'll have something to say about the Jews."

He quizzed me on a Bea Lillie song that I did not remember. It gave him pleasure. He was in complete control. He had told me that although he did not see me play the part (when I took over during the first summer) he *knew* what must have been wrong.

"Don't show us her feelings. An American woman would have handled this differently. An Englishwoman doesn't show her feelings."

157

Right. I can do that. He wants to be sure I do not confuse what Peter asked me to do with *this* rehearsal. This is *his* work. He did not waste a moment. He worked with intensity and pleasure.

All the work on a part is helpful in some way. All the pain and humiliation, the delight and fun, find their way into the human being you eventually play. I went to the dressing room and read the play again and put his notes into my script.

The day I rehearsed Dora with Dexter I began my final week as Hesther. I was saying good-bye to that part and thinking of the new one. I began to *see* Dora in myself. I started to move as I wanted her to as I went about the chores of the day. It made playing Hesther more interesting than ever because the contrast between the two women was so great. Yet I would find so much of Dora in myself that it shocked me. Her fury at what circumstances had done to her relationship with her child nearly drove her mad. But as John reminded me, she was English, so she tried to conceal what she was feeling.

She would not, as I did once, run with a long knife in her

John Dexter.

hand to scare away a man who was yelling about a child's crying, would she?

My daughter was three months old and I had put her out in the sun. It did not matter that it was lovely California Sunday sun beating down on her and Stanford University while I was learning my lines in *Lysistrata*. It was hot and uncomfortable. She began to cry. I decided to stay for another few moments and then give up the sun bath. Before I made my move a man who appeared to have the same proportions as King Kong strode down the street. His hulk blotted out the sun. I thought he was going to do something terrible. My husband woke up and stood in the doorway and saw me with the knife (I had not realized I had raced in and out of the house to find it and was holding it, much less brandishing it). He laughed with surprise and admiration as the man slunk away.

Those deep, maternal, protective feelings can make you smile after the fact, but all the feelings I had about my daughter's life were real feelings, not theatre feelings. I did not question them. I must play Dora like that. Hesther asks questions, listens to answers, receives. Dora fights for her life. For her child's life.

I took my script with me to the hairdresser's, where I planned to spend the day. I was going to have my dark hair stripped and dyed. I thought of my daughter's tawny brown hair. I would have asked her for a lock of it to take with me but she was scandalized by the *idea* of my changing my hair, so I arranged to have it done while she was away at college, and by the time she came home she would accept it as a part of my work. My note for the hairdresser about the new color: like a light brown deer or a lioness.

Dexter hates any kind of stage artifice. No wigs, make-up, few props. The most prominent objects on the stage were 159 the actors and the silver horse masks. The most important things were the words.

I played Hesther nearly seven hundred times. I always loved her words, and the words the Doctor said to her. Now there were three performances left. Because the changing of my hair color took a full day I played Hesther once with blond hair. The stage manager told me that until I spoke the ushers thought it was a different actress. No deer or lioness was conjured up by a glance at my mane. There was no animal as blond.

The new actress for Hesther had been chosen and rehearsed. Before the matinee she and I had our pictures taken in the top dressing room of the theatre. It was too expensive to have a picture call, so we had separate head shots. The room was sweltering. I was afraid to look at my brazen, blond self in the mirror.

I pulled my new hair back from my face and knotted it at my neck.

"Where shall I look?"

The photographer was a friend. He had come to Juilliard several years before and taken pictures of my acting class, and had done all the *Equus* pictures.

"Just beyond the lens. Chin up. That's it. That's it." He took about ten pictures skillfully and speedily. I ask him if I might loosen my hair and have a picture taken of me as a blonde.

"Look up, down. You're beautiful. You're about to say 'I love you.'"

I wondered how it would turn out. I never saw it. And the others? Would they be Dora, unbeautiful, unloved?

I went downstairs to my own room. I thought the new Hesther should have her own time with that camera before the audience's eyes were on her. She was nervous. There is never enough time for a replacement to rehearse and she was upset because Tony Perkins stood in the wings for a few moments when she was rehearsing before the matinee. What she did not know is that Tony is by nature abstracted and more nearsighted than I am. He probably did not see her. After my first performance with him he told me:

"It's as if there were an Indian blanket between us." I knew I must find more ways than just my eyes to reach him. Burton and Hopkins saw everything. Tony sensed things, but his way as an actor was a private, lonely way. It worked splendidly in the part. One night when I leaned forward to kiss him on the cheek his upstage arm reached out to me and he touched my arm. It was so unusual, so startling, that it moved and unsettled me. He did not mention it in the intermission nor did he repeat it at the next performance. Perhaps it was just an accident, perhaps he was simply trying to steady me. Such a little thing. It made the whole evening special for me — as Hesther.

On the final night I played Hesther he moved to a new position so that he could take both my hands in his and hold them for a moment before I left the center of the stage and returned to my place. Our private/public good-bye. He said everything by saying nothing.

I stayed in my own dressing room and followed the same routine when I played Dora, but a major change was the position where I sat on the stage. I sat by Hesther in the first act and alone on the small bench in the second act.

In my old place I had been almost too aware of the actor next to me. Shaffer had not given the character of the stable owner, Dalton, any words in the second act. I knew that it was torture for whoever played it to sit there with no task. If he were a student of mine I would suggest that the audience is still interested in his reactions. How do they know he will not suddenly get up and interrupt Alan and the girl or come into the Doctor's office with some new evidence? But all three actors I sat next to found it impossible to be still. Often the audience members sitting close to us were disturbing. One man took off his shoes and his feet were bare. He crossed his legs and one huge, too white, clean but odorous foot appeared next to Dalton's lap. It was funny and offensive. But we did not talk to anyone during the play so there it stayed for an act. Distracting.

One evening a young boy said "Munchtime" to his companion and took out a package of Pepperidge Farm cookies just as we were finding out Alan's relationship to his parents in the center of the stage.

As the run lengthened, some of the actors started to disappear from their places on the stage after their scenes. It was a matter of foolish pride to me that I did not do that. My pride is one of the things that keeps me disciplined and wears me out. No one else in the world cares that I cannot bear to miss a cue, or sign in late, or leave the stage. It was the same at school. I wanted a perfect attendance record. When I was in the fourth grade I missed a week of school and years later I missed four performances of *Equus*. Why is it that I still want to find the books where that information is recorded and erase it?

The experience of missing performances was an odd one. I fought the doctor to let me go back to the theatre. He wouldn't even let me talk to the stage manager. He made the call.

"You are not to talk, to whisper, to make a sound, until I tell you that it is safe. You may burst the blood vessel on your vocal cord. You must get a pad and write everything down."

162   He treated my throat, took wonderful care of me, and the

cord healed. The appointments became part of my professional life and I looked forward to them. I was grateful to Dr. Wilbur Gould for his severity. I had always let the theatre be my doctor, knowing I would feel well enough to go on when the time came. But this illness was a combination of the flu and teaching and rehearsing with Tony Hopkins's understudy all at the same time. Tony had contracted phlebitis and had to rest for several weeks. We missed him but the play survived his absence. His understudy, Alan Mixon, was prepared and skilled.

When people said that they had seen *Equus* three or four times, I wanted to say I have seen it over eight hundred times.

We did not praise each other night after night; some actors never mentioned the performance. When an understudy went on we all talked about it, but in general it was the Dysarts — particularly both Tonys — who liked to talk about the play. Tony Perkins was obsessive about his Dysart. He could never get enough notes from the stage manager or enough comments from the cast. Actors who were with him in *Look Homeward, Angel* said he was the same then, wanting to dissect his scenes each night.

In *Equus*, because its life was long, the temptation to give the other actors notes was great. I am a teacher and I make it a point never to do so, and if I am asked I try to say little. Not because I don't have ideas, but because I cannot see the play as part of the audience. Actors are not audience or critics. Their concentration must remain *inside* the play.

For both the parts I played I worked out a scenario so that I was in fact acting the part all through the play even though I was not in the scenes.

In much the same way that a novelist plots out the life of his characters, the actor fantasizes, ideates, dreams about 163 the character he plays. When that character is speaking, acting, moving on the stage, the playwright has given the actor his complete life. But in a play like *Medea,* as a member of the Chorus, or as a witness in *Equus,* there are long stretches of the play where the actor is still and silent. To fill these spaces with life is what we had to do in the long run of *Equus.* I based my life as Hesther, the witness watching the story of Dysart and the boy unfold, entirely on my feelings as Hesther for Dysart. I felt that the times I sat and watched from the side were part of the performance I gave on the stage and that there should be no beginning of one or ending of the other. From the time I left my dressing room to take my place on the bench Hesther's life began and it did not end until the lights dimmed for the last time.

It seems to come with stardom, this need to give notes, and it should be discouraged. When I started out in the theatre we were instructed not to criticize the other actors. If something seemed uncomfortable we were asked to speak to the stage manager. Both Cornell and Anderson did this. It is better for the morale of the company, too. If you feel you are being tested by the star as you are playing it makes it hard to act well. You find yourself trying to pass the test, to get the pat on the head at the end of the evening. That has very little to do with why we are there on the stage.

Sharing the problem with your fellow actor and the director or stage manager in a professional way is the answer. The best thing to do, the right thing to do, is to rehearse. But it is hard to arrange. We are not allowed to use the stage without paying a crew. When we do have brush-up rehearsals they are mainly note sessions from the director because it is difficult to get a complete cast together after a play has opened. All the unions have rules. When Richard Burton came into the play, we had to vote as a cast to give

164

up our day off to rehearse with him or he never would have had a day of work with the actors when they did not have to think about the play at night. The management was prepared for us to turn down their request. Kermit came and told us we were loved and respected. We said we would be quite happy to rehearse. He did not seem to hear us. He said how important the extra day would be. We agreed and told him we just wanted to be told in advance what the hours were. He reassured us. "You'll be told everything . . ." and began to explain his position again. "Kermit, the actors want what you want." He smiled, amazed. It was easy to arrange. Communication between management and actors is a tricky thing. The McClintics came closest to solving it, in my experience. The artistic people were the producers and there was no conflict. Like everything else about working with them, that relationship was special and enviable.

The success of *Equus* seemed to make everyone greedy. In three years the various companies had grossed over ten million dollars. The enormous difference between the stars' salaries and everyone else's was unfortunate. A fact of life. As the play continued to make money week after week certain actors would ask for raises. Each had to fight with the management for the smallest increase. But I am learning that if an actor doesn't ask there will only be bottles of liquor at Christmas and cast parties in restaurants to which the press is invited. We were not ungrateful for the holiday remembrances but we knew they were part of the production's write-off. A little like being taken to lunch and having your host jot down your name as a reminder to take the cost of the engagement as a deduction on his income tax.

Some business lunches are for the business of being interviewed. The first serious interview I had was with John

Corry of the *New York Times*. The "news" was that I was going to play a different part in a play that had been running for over a year. When I received the call from John Springer — the press agent for *Equus* — I was not sure how to accept the invitation. I liked Corry's pieces about actors that had appeared in the *Times,* I was flattered to be invited, but I was afraid that the interview would turn into a discussion of my opinion of the three actors who had played Dysart. Louis Sica, Springer's assistant, assured me that nothing of the kind would take place and we made the appointment for the following week.

Al Hirschfeld came to the Plymouth and made a witty sketch of me. It is the second one of his drawings of me in a play; the first was in *A Delicate Balance*. It was such an accurate "takeoff" of my performance that the first time I saw it I felt threatened, as if I had been caught in the act — of acting.

Louis's first idea was to have the interview in my apartment. It would have been nice because I am surrounded by the furniture and paintings and books that have been here for thirty years. But the walls that enclose them and the ceiling that covers them were in a state of such frightening disrepair that I did not think the *New York Times* would find them fit to report on. Like most apartment dwellers in New York in the 1970s, I was having a quiet battle with my landlord. I kept hoping that after thirteen years of polite pleading he would repair the leaking roof that spoils my ceiling and fill the cracks in the walls. It was a stalemate. The landlord was silent. I continued to write requests for attention as I sent in my rent check. I got to know the secretaries who answered his telephone. Once a man came to look at the damage. He said it was absolutely frightful and

166

that something would be done at once. The ownership of the building changed hands. I never saw that man again.

A French restaurant in the East Sixties was the setting for our rendezvous. The food was delicious. Louis and John Corry and I talked about the theatre and our lives in connection with the arts in New York with the ease of old friends.

I took it for granted that Corry would have seen *Equus*. He had not and this surprised and pleased me. It made the range of subjects we could talk about wider. We spoke of writing. I had brought a piece by Joseph Conrad that I was going to read to my students at Juilliard. The connection between art forms — all the arts — has always been part of my teaching. I read to Corry, ". . . to snatch, in a moment of courage, from the remorseless rush of time a passing phrase of life, is only the beginning of the task." He liked it and took the entire paragraph with him. He told me he was going to finish the book he was writing that afternoon.

We joked about my dyeing my hair, we spoke of the ballet and the years I had spent training to be a dancer, and Louis told him something of my acting career before *Equus*. We had been at the restaurant for over two hours. It was time to go.

John Corry said to me as Louis was paying the bill, "Of the three actors who have played Dysart . . . ?" I looked over at Louis and he smiled. I looked at John Corry and decided that I trusted him and that I would answer his question honestly and fully. I think I did. I told him my feeling about the long rehearsal period with Hopkins and his effect on all of us, of my knowing Tony Perkins when I was eighteen and my delight in the happenstance of our working together. I said that whereas Richard Burton was 167 exciting to act with because he was unpredictable, Tony was utterly professional and you could count on his performance. I used the word "quixotic" for Burton, meaning to say "quicksilver"; I used "predictable" for Tony and remember adding, "That's *not* the word I mean, but you understand, utterly . . . reliable."

There is a family joke about me, that when faced with a question of comparison I say, "I don't compare." Of course I do. Often. But I find that I am careful about verbalizing my preferences because I usually pay dearly for my opinion. When I was in *That Lady* with Cornell a friend of my mother's who had been an actress came for tea one afternoon. She asked me about touring with Judith Anderson in *Medea* and I tried to evoke the special feeling of that tour for her. The closeness of the company, the feeling we all had that this play was a rare chance to work in a classic in cities where a great actress had not been seen in a Greek play for decades, our parties after the play, our journeys on trains and buses. I told her something of the pre-Broadway tour with Cornell, too, and of what it meant to play in Buffalo, where she was born and was welcomed back with each première as a favorite of the whole community.

"Who is the greater actress? Cornell or Anderson?" The question came from nowhere. My answer was, "I don't compare them," but I did not say it. I leaned forward with my hands pressed on the glass-topped table, resenting the question and unprepared to answer, and the table split — suddenly and silently — into two huge pieces that crashed to the floor. In the confusion the question was lost.

The evening of the day the John Corry interview appeared I was stopped on the way to my dressing room by Tony.

"You didn't mean to say that, Marian. I'm sure you didn't mean to."

I had been teaching and thinking of other things.

"Oh, in the *Times* . . ."

"In the *Times*. You didn't use that word?"

"Predictable?"

"Yes."

"I did use the word. But in a longer sentence, Tony. It was not meant to be used against your work. I'm sorry . . ."

"It's no good being sorry. I have to go out there and play this part and everyone in the audience will be thinking 'He's predictable.' "

"That won't happen. They are seeing it for the first time. Most of them won't have read the piece. Tony . . . I'm so sorry."

"It's no good being sorry."

I went up to my room. I was sorry. Sorry I had hurt him, sorrier that the first New York interview in my career left me feeling a little sick. I vowed to be more careful if I had another chance.

When the news came that they would like to put my caricature in Sardi's, an appointment was made for the artist to come to the theatre to meet me. He trudged up the stairs, knocked on the door; I opened it. He looked at the bare, gray little room and asked, "Is this *it?*" I assured him it was not only it, but the best I had ever had.

I was prepared for this encounter. Hair freshly washed and curled. Lavender cashmere sweater. The same make-up I wore on the street and on the stage in *Equus*. None of the actors used make-up and only two of the actresses, and even they did not use much. I remember when the ritual of making up used to take most of the half hour before the performance, even when I was playing a straight part. Now it is 169 the opposite. I wash my face. It's like getting up in the morning. Teeth, clothes, hair.

I offered Richard Baratz the other chair and prepared to pose for him. No posing. He took my picture several times with a Polaroid.

"Have you seen the play? Would you like to see it as my guest?"

"Could I bring my girl?"

"Yes." He told me I was the only actor he had drawn who had asked him to a performance. He did not go to the theatre very often; he had never seen me work. He came and liked it. Ten days later he brought me the picture. There I was. Not in my lavender sweater, but wearing full make-up with bright red lipstick to match the bright red blouse I seemed to be wearing. I had a huge button at my neck with the *Equus* logo on it. I looked like an elderly showgirl. He had photographs to prove it. The eye of the beholder?

I should have used my dictionary. I would have been prepared for the "judiciously exaggerated peculiarities and defects" that Richard captured in his drawing.

He told me he made his living as an engraver. A week later he brought me a delicate print of a country scene. I kept it in my dressing room.

I played Dora, with my blond hair twisted back and pinned at the nape of the neck, for a week, and to celebrate I called Frances to thank her for the lovely flowers she sent me the night I started playing a part so closely associated with her. A bouquet with predominantly lavender and purple sweet Williams and chrysanthemums. And a card signed by the ever-helpful florist: "Francine."

I tried to make her laugh with stories of how we were all reacting to each other in our new roles and I confided that the actress who was playing Hesther did not like the part and was covering her disappointment with a kind of gallows humor offstage.

At the Sunday matinee I told everyone that Frances sent her love. Tony Perkins stopped me on the stairs.

"Do you think Frances is rich?"

"I don't know. Perhaps her mother left her some money . . ."

One of the reasons Frances left the play was to settle her mother's estate. But the major reason was to have more time with her family. Tony kept looking, eyes piercing mine, always waiting for me to say more when I had no more to contribute. I filled the pause.

"If I didn't know her and just met her I wouldn't think so . . ." Frances dresses and behaves with simplicity.

Tony smiled. "I would" — and he walked away.

He is fascinated by money and has the reputation in the company of being rather tight with it. Most companies expect stars to be more generous than the rest of us, but the truth is, they are not. In *Equus* Tony Hopkins, who was paid the least of the stars, was the only truly generous one we had. Ask the doormen, ask his dresser, ask all of us who had food and drink and wonderful talks with him during the rehearsals and for the nine months he was our Doctor. The members of the original New York company all carry the silver key rings he gave us on opening night — rider's crops with a horseshoe pendant with his initials and ours.

The days I teach I come to the theatre with the same sort of excitement I feel after a fulfilling rehearsal. The teaching blends into the professional world and adds to it. All my students had seen *Equus,* some two or three times. When

171

Tony Hopkins played the Doctor he came to my classes and was the best student in the room. He absorbed and shared everything.

Some of the Juilliard students (the school is only ten years old) have appeared on television, some on the Broadway stage, many in the Acting Company. They are all professional. The actress who played for me in *Next Time I'll Sing to You* with unique distinction and wit, Patti Lupone, flew to Los Angeles to play the title part in *The Baker's Wife*. Friends said she was lovely in the part. The "word" in New York was that it would close before it came to Broadway. She will get other offers. But if she doesn't? Should she have stayed with the Acting Company? How can I dare to advise these students I care for so much?

When I see Patti again will I tell her that her starting salary in *The Baker's Wife* was more than twice mine in *Equus*? No, I do not think so.

On the Monday after Tony told me *Equus* was going to close in New York, the telephone rang and Ken Marshall, a third-year student from Juilliard, called to ask me if I thought he should fly to the Coast the next day to test for the lead in a TV series based on the Irwin Shaw novel *Rich Man, Poor Man*. He had not seen the long TV film of it

Teaching at Juilliard.

shown earlier in the year but he had bought the novel, read it and liked it. They wanted to sign him for seven years.

"Who is *they?*" I asked.

"Universal. It's presold and if it doesn't catch on after the first thirteen they'll put me in something else. But I want to be an actor, you know the kind of actor I want to be . . ."

He wanted to be a serious actor in the theatre. He wanted a career that would have importance. He wanted to play the great roles. He was one of the few married students at Juilliard. He was twenty-six. Good-looking. Talented. A joy to teach. He was developing into a real actor. Should I have said, "Stay in New York? Don't even go to do the test?"

Instead I asked, "What does your wife think?"

"Oh, she wants me to be the kind of actor that *I* want to be . . ."

What can the theatre offer him in New York now? Will another year at Juilliard be more valuable than the exposure (as they call it) and the money from an important series? What if it fails and he is free in October and can rejoin his class?

"Are you prepared for it to fail? Are you prepared for them to take another actor at the last minute even after you have tested?"

"Yes."

I told him I thought he should go and do the test. I felt that his need to study and learn would remain strong. He would not be seduced by the TV world. Yes, go. He thanked me. We talked a little more. As always, as he did after class, he said, "Have a good show tonight." I was so touched by the refrain, I did not tell him we were now dark on Mondays.

11

Do actors plan their careers? When I read autobiographies there seem to be patterns, shapes of years, blueprints followed. But in living the life of an actor it seems I have made few decisions of real importance. I have been able to say no to what was not worth doing. But that has been comparatively easy because I have been lucky enough to be steadily employed.

We read of the choice between theatre and film for successful actors. Will Brando ever come back to the theatre? Will Robert Redford wait as long between plays as Richard Burton did when he became a major star?

I don't have many mementos of the few films I have been in, but I remember some times that make me smile. Being called on a Friday to come to California on Monday to begin work as Herodias in *The Greatest Story Ever Told*. I knew I could not be the first choice for the part. I went to Hollywood and stayed for a month. I had the chance to work with George Stevens for about three or four hours out of that month of work. The rest of the time was spent in make-up or waiting. In the theatre you do your own make-up and you know what will hurt and how to avoid the smudging and blotting that will make you have to start all over again. The make-up man, Del Armstrong, usually did Lana Turner and Rita Hayworth. He was as handsome as a movie actor and used to take them out on dates. I wondered if their eyes teared when he applied the black liner on their lids at seven in the morning. I kept spoiling his beautiful work.

One day, all made up, hair dressed — a process that took over two hours — I was not used until the afternoon and I sat in the background of a scene where my film daughter, Salome, and a troupe of Inbal dancers repeated the same dance for hours. There is a brief shot of the dance in the picture. Not of the background. That was to be expected. What I did not expect was that the dancers would be told "That's a wrap" without my hearing it. I sat in my position in my elaborate make-up and costume and crown and the huge sound stage got quiet. I had decided to read through the Bible during my time on *The Greatest Story* so I pulled it out from its hiding place under the embroidered cushion and began to read in the half-light. The quiet deepened. When I realized I was absolutely alone I felt ridiculous. I was locked in the sound stage. Queen Herodias took off her crown, groped through the other dark sets until she found a door that would open, went through the process of getting rid of her exquisite trappings, called a taxi and went home.

The next day was better. There was to be a close-up of my reaction to Herod as he watches Salome dance. I was dressed and robed and given two thin, nervous Saluki dogs who followed me and spoiled most of the takes that morning. In the afternoon the setup was the same but the camera position was changed and Mr. Stevens told me to hold the look with Herod a bit longer. Yes. "Ready?" Yes. The handsome make-up man checked me. The dog trainer brushed the dogs. I wanted to tell him, "They won't be in the shot," but you learn that the second assistant director will take care of things like that. "Action." I walked slowly through the room preceded by my daughter. She looked at Herod, then I did. But in place of José Ferrer, who had been sitting there all morning, was a short man who looked like an aging full-back. Hunched forward on the throne, staring forward. When his eyes focused on mine and the close-up was being taken he winked and stuck out his tongue. "All right for you?" George Stevens asked William Mellors, the cameraman. "Fine." There was no sound, no need to check. And they didn't ask me. That close-up is in the picture.

There was more freedom in the work provided by television. In the course of a dozen years I was able to act with Frances Starr (who had been a Broadway star for David Belasco), Fay Bainter (who had played the title role in *Lysistrata* and told me things about the production that my father loved to hear: When a member of the old man's chorus had to be fired in Philadelphia the management tried to find a gentle, careful way to dismiss him. After all the planning a stage manager simply blundered the news to him in front of the entire company. The actor looked out toward the auditorium and said in deep Shakespearean tones to the director and producer, "For this relief, much thanks").

In television programs I played with Walter Slezak, Burgess Meredith, Betty Field, Art Carney, Jackie Gleason (as we watched Gleason suffer through the long hours of rehearsal with drinks of straight liquor followed by chocolate ice cream "to put out the fire" Art commented, "Fat people are happy . . ."), Brandon DeWilde, Angie Dickinson, 176 Walter Matthau (we were husband and wife in *Othello* —

Iago and Emilia), Cloris Leachman, Patty Duke, Victor Jory, Shirley Knight, Joseph Schildkraut, Lee J. Cobb, Melvyn Douglas, Luther Adler (we played Mr. and Mrs. Molotov), Roddy MacDowall, Paul Douglas, Tom Tryon, Arthur Shields, Josephine Hutchinson, Eli Wallach, Oscar Homolka, Claude Dauphin, Edward Asner, Kim Hunter, Hurd Hatfield, Charlton Heston (as Macbeth), Judith Evelyn, Eddie Albert, Jean Stapleton, Alan Arkin, Telly Savalas — it would take ten theatre lives to find oneself in such company.

With some of these talented actors there were reunions on the radio and once or twice in films. Charlton Heston and I spoke of working together again and we almost did. When he played John the Baptist in *The Greatest Story Ever Told* two of the four lines I spoke were requests to have him decapitated.

In Hollywood in the 1950s there was a wide variety of programs being filmed for television. I was able to play some interesting parts, and some dull ones. An interesting one was a Mrs. Danvers-like woman in a half-hour filmed show with Joan Fontaine in a part not unlike her lovely·performance in *Rebecca*. A dull one was with one of the most fascinating actresses in the world, Bette Davis. As soon as the agent said she was the star of the hour-long mystery show I agreed to do it. The part of the police matron who escorted her to trial gave me the chance to work with her. As I stood by the camera waiting for my cue the cameraman said, "Will the tall girl move a few inches to the right?" She must have seen my involuntary wince because Bette Davis put up her hand and said, "Her name is Marian Seldes." Afterward she told me, "At Warner's when I was a star I introduced everyone on the set."

"Oh, I didn't mind his not knowing my name . . ."

"I *know* what you minded. We're all self-conscious about things. But you shouldn't be. You love it, don't you?"

"Acting?"

She nodded.

"Very much."

"So do I."

She loved her children, too, and told me about Margo, the adorable child she adopted who turned out to be hopelessly retarded. We talked of men and marriage intimately. When she gave Glenda Jackson her New York Film Critics' Award at Sardi's in 1971 I said *Father's Day* was about to open. "I'll be there for your first night," she said. She had a project in mind for us to do. On the opening night I received a dear telegram from her saying she would be at the second night. Another reason for my unhappiness at its precipitate closing.

I did not seem to have any control over my acting in Hollywood. In a scene in a Disney picture the director told the actor playing my husband to walk over and shove a cookie into my mouth. I was appalled. But we did the scene. It was not used. The first scene I ever did in Hollywood was not used either. It was for John Frankenheimer in *The Young Stranger.* He came to the house to see my husband and while he was there offered me the part of a mother who comes to a police station to see her son. I had to do it, no one could be better — all that. I remember saying, "It sounds like the kind of scene that ends on the cutting room floor!" John assured me it was integral to the plot. I did the scene. It is on the floor, but you do see a woman walk out of the frame and say "Good-bye." That was my Hollywood debut.

I was cast as a fictional Biblical princess in *The Big Fisherman*. There were some nice scenes in the part. A few were difficult to play because Frank Borzage's thoughtful way of cueing me into the scene was, instead of the word "Action," to gently grab my rear end and push. Nevertheless, I took the work seriously and, when the best scene in the part was going to be shot, arrived on the set ready and anxious to work. I had practiced how the strength would leave my head, then shoulders, then arms and hands; how my breathing would change as the energy failed in my body; and how finally I would sink to the floor, dead.

The scene was prepared by the technicians. They were all in a fine mood. We were shooting the picture in Palm Springs at a leisurely pace. The accommodations and the food were of the best. Borzage asked, "Are you ready?" I was seated so I was safe. "Whenever you say," I answered.

"We'll run through it once for sound and then we'll shoot it."

I began what I had prepared. The movements, the trembling, the gasping. All as I had hoped, seeming real, seeming like dying.

"Hold it," said the sound man. He explained to Borzage that the sounds I was making were impossible to record.

The cameraman went over and whispered something to him, making gestures that said "No good."

I thought I might have another chance. But no, a decision was made. Borzage came over to me and asked, "You couldn't just, well, fall out of the frame, could you?"

"Yes," I said meekly.

"And could you lie there? Still? Not panting or anything and we'll play the rest of the scene over you?"

And that is how I died in *The Big Fisherman*.

There were better experiences in film in the East. A 179

documentary for the Mental Health Film Board called *The Lonely Night,* and Nancy Hanks in *Mr. Lincoln,* written by James Agee. I would not mind looking at either of them again.

Irving Jacoby wrote and directed *The Lonely Night.* It was filmed on location around New York and much of the cast was nonprofessional. The adviser on the film was Dr. Thomas Rennie, who had been one of Zelda Fitzgerald's doctors. He wanted a film to be made about her and we talked about her book, *Save Me the Waltz.* It pleased him that my mother's memories of Zelda were all happy ones. They used to go shopping together and it amused Zelda to surprise the saleswomen. She once complained about the width of the skirt on an evening dress. She said it was not wide enough. The saleswoman and my mother looked at the yards of material. Zelda suddenly sat down and spread her knees as far apart as they would go. "I play the cello!" she exclaimed.

I showed Tom Rennie the letters my father had saved from Scott. Serious letters about writing and letters in doggerel about life. With them is the lovely Christmas card with the photograph of the Fitzgeralds dancing with their daughter and a water color of a blue flower by Zelda which epitomizes grace and calm.

Mr. Lincoln was produced for the "Omnibus" television program, but the company was as close as on the documentary, and Norman Lloyd, who directed most of the scenes I was in, tried to make the Lincoln story as simple and stark as a documentary. Norman had played the Fool in the Houseman production of *King Lear* and he directed an Alfred Hitchcock television show I did in Hollywood, but this was 180 the first time I had the chance to know him. When the series was completed he arranged for us to see a screening of it. He was renting Houseman's Henry Varnum Poor house in New City at the time. We travelled by bus. The actors, the crew and Jim Agee, who stood in the aisle, hanging on a strap, talking ceaselessly.

Jim appeared in the film, too, and was with the company during its sojourn in Kentucky, where most of it was shot. He was a friendly, loving man. His stories about Chaplin — whom he revered — held us spellbound as the bus careened around the icy curves of the highways. Long before the trip started he had fortified himself with drink and he did not stop drinking all day and night. It did not occur to me that he was poisoning himself, courting death, he was so vividly and sweetly alive.

The second unit scenes of *Mr. Lincoln* were directed by a young man named Stanley Kubrick. He worked with intensity, skill and humorlessness. He wanted to make his own films and went on to do so.

Audiences remember films in terms of images and plays in terms of moments. I have never taken part in a memorable film and I have never considered anything I have been a part of in television to have lasting importance. It has been done too quickly. I have seen programs with exciting performances in them and know some actors who can be fine on dramatic programs that continue day after day. (If I were on one I would not want to call it a "soap.") The best thing about television and film is that they can make you feel you are actually in the specific place the author intended. But simply putting a camera in that place will not make it happen. The atmosphere of a television studio or a movie sound stage is as sensitive as that of the living theatre. When the situation is false the work that is produced there is false. 181

When the program "You Are There" used the news correspondents of the network to interview Cleopatra at her
death or Queen Isabella as she decided to give Columbus
the riches he was seeking, I was there and they were there,
but *you* were not. You were probably wondering how in
heaven's name we got there.

As the technicians at the CBS studio on Vanderbilt Avenue raced against the ticking of the relentless electric studio
clock the floor manager's voice boomed into the dressing
rooms: "Five minutes to air, company onstage."

Kim Stanley — our Cleopatra — dashed back to her
dressing room, dissatisfied with her make-up. She pulled the
black wig away from her tawny mane of hair, grabbed a
pair of manicure scissors and with ferocity and hurried carelessness started to cut off her eyebrows and was drawing on
Cleopatra's as the urgent voice called, "Places, places, Miss
Stanley." Several seconds later, apparently in control of her
heartbeat and her talent, the marvelous actress slipped into
her place in Egypt and Walter Cronkite's voice set the scene.

In radio too we must be able to snatch Conrad's "moment in time" and make it real. The opportunities for marvelous writing to be heard on radio are boundless. It costs so
little and you can take the audience anywhere. Everywhere.

I played Hesther and Dora and hundreds of other women
as well during the run of *Equus*. Himan Brown produces an
hour-long radio show, "Mystery Theatre," on CBS and I became a part of a group of actors in his stock company. We
all doubled — which is fun to do — and played parts of
every age and nationality.

At nine in the morning the cast met at Studio 6 in the CBS
building on Fifty-second Street. One reading of a story none
of us had seen, ten minutes spent putting Hi's cuts into our
182   scripts, and then we were "on the air." Not live, as in the

old days of radio, but taped. Before noon we had completed the program.

The radio actors I have worked with are skilled professionals. There is no time for anything else. Hi does over a hundred programs a year and in the third year of his mystery series he began an adventure series. He hopes to do a great play series next. Radio acting used to flourish in New York; now there is little chance to practice the craft.

Hi hears the world. There is no play I have done in the theatre that he would not prefer to listen to on the radio. Produced and directed by Himan Brown. One day he will do *Equus*. Perhaps I can double as Hesther *and* Dora.

Ten days after the successful opening of the national company of *Equus* in Hollywood John Dexter was back at an *Equus* rehearsal in New York. No one was sure when he had seen the play with the new actors in it but everyone was apprehensive. What kind of a work-through would it be? The new actors had heard enough about Dexter to fear him. I assured them that whatever the pain, they would benefit from what he said to them, that the most difficult thing to cope with in a Dexter rehearsal was to have your work ignored.

He arrived, as always, exactly at the appointed time and was ready to work. He asked us to sit together at one side of the stage, "so I won't have to keep looking 'round and be blinded by Miss Seldes's new hair." We gathered on the benches at stage right, sitting close. We were united.

He was brutal about the horses, told them that he demanded only two hours of their time a day and that they appeared exhausted and diffident. He told the dance captain to put them to work. He gave Tony some approving, positive statements about his work on the role over the last six 183 months (an odd choice of time since for three of those months Burton had played Dysart), but it was meaningful to have the leading player praised so highly in the presence of the cast. He was hard on the new Alan, but helped him in the rehearsal. He gave me notes with no sting in them. Then he clapped his hands together, rubbed them, smiled a sweetly diabolical smile and we started a run-through.

When we came to a spot with a new actor he stopped and repeated the scene or the section of the scene as often as necessary to make his points clear. Most of the notes had to do with timing and intention.

Performances after a rehearsal are interesting. How much have we been able to absorb? What will work better, what still does not work? Since John had said everything in front of the company we were able to judge the results, and although nothing was said that night, what we noticed with surprise was that in several cases the actors chose *not* to do what John had asked. He would hear of this and it would not be as pleasant when they were told a second time.

John had asked Tony Perkins to wait for a moment after the rehearsal.

The next day Tony inquired, "Do you know why John asked me to stay?"

"No."

"Can't you imagine?"

"To make up for the way you were treated when they asked you to leave." A thin smile. "No." I couldn't imagine. "Why?"

"He came over to the side of the stage and sat near me and said, 'I bet your *father* toured.' "

So according to Tony the compliments were just to soften him up so that he would at least play Washington on the 184 first lap of the tour.

The strongest point of John's rehearsal was to say the words, to tell the story. To come in, give information and leave. It is an unsparing way to approach a play but in this situation it worked. He asked Tony not to work on his comedy points. In fact, to let them go. Tony nodded. But at the evening performance he said he was trying to find a *new* laugh to replace one of the ones John wanted him to cut! He asked several actors what they thought of the audience's response. What could he do to get a bigger laugh?

12

Who is the audience? What does it mean to the actor? Is it what it looks like: a group of people? Or is it one person the actor invents and puts there to watch: a part of himself that is neither the actor nor the character but what the great Italian actor Salvini called "a third self"? Is it like the dancer's mirror or a huge camera? A lover? An enemy? George C. Scott used to tell me that he faced the audience the way a matador faces the bull. It was a contest for him, life or death.

Has the modern audience been changed, possibly corrupted, by film and television viewing? In 1945 Max Beerbohm said that the great actors of the Victorian and Edwardian eras were even more ardently worshiped than ours. "Yours, after all, are but images of idols, mere shadows of glory. Those others were their own selves, creatures of flesh and blood, there, before our eyes. They were performing in our presence. And of our presence they were aware. Even we, in all our humility, acted as stimulants to them. The magnetism diffused by them across the footlights was in some degree our own doing."

Dexter feels that I am overly influenced by the audience. I wonder. It seems to me that it is an important part of the performance and that its reactions nourish the play. To hold rigidly to what you have rehearsed in spite of its reactions would be foolish; to *use* what it gives you within the discipline of the performance can strengthen the playing.

Every few years there is a feature article in the *Times* or *Playbill* making gentle fun of actors in long runs, usually quoting the famous George S. Kaufman remark that he is calling a rehearsal "to take out the improvements," and examples of how actors have gotten banal or broad in their interpretations. Part of the job of the cast and the stage manager is not simply to repeat what was found in the rehearsal period but to improve it within the form set by the director. It is not necessarily inevitable that all actors simply get worse and are wooed into bad habits by the audience. The audience is our teacher, too.

For me it is always there, always part of the performance, and it has been at different times all the things I have suggested. When I first started to act in New York I imagined Guthrie McClintic in the audience every night. I knew one day he would come back, I would see him, and my real career would begin.

That is exactly what happened. He came back to see Judith Anderson after a performance of *Medea* and I was there in my black make-up and he smiled and greeted me. The following year I was playing the Second Woman of the Chorus in the nationwide tour of *Medea* that he produced and directed. I was acting in a stock company when the telegram from his general manager, Stanley Gilkey, arrived. He asked if I were free to tour that year. I was so afraid that it might mean as the Serving Woman that I wired back and asked if it were for a speaking part. No more black make- 187 up, lovely words to say, and my first time to be directed by Guthrie. It was one of the happiest experiences of my life. Oddly, it set a pattern that was repeated in *Equus:* a long run, a re-creation of a successful first production, and my part essentially that of a witness.

But it was not until I was in *Equus* that I saw an actor stop a performance and talk to the audience. We were having a benefit and a bus with seventy people was late. They came trooping down the aisles after the play had been on at least ten minutes. Tony Hopkins stopped the play, asked the latecomers to find their seats quickly, suggested that we start with my entrance into the Doctor's office and we began again to a round of appreciative applause. Another time he had to stop the play because he suddenly became ill. He was ashen. I got up from my seat and led him off the stage. The stage manager explained to the audience that Mr. Hopkins's standby would continue the performance. They waited. Alan Mixon was called; he raced to the theatre and fifteen minutes later we began again with Alan acting with control and strength. One evening a woman became ill in the audience. We heard strange moans, a scuffle on the stairs to the balcony, the siren of an ambulance. All through it we continued the play. The audience remained attentive. The concentration was amazing. It shocked us to learn later that the woman had died in the ambulance. We questioned our roles in this sad event.

There were funny times, too. When I toured in *Medea* I did not know it was possible for a member of the audience to fall asleep and snore during a performance. I learned from Judith that there are ways of waking sleepers. Medea had a special sound — a cry — that ripped through the space between the stage and the house. She made the sound and
188   the snoring stopped.

By the time *Equus* opened on Broadway a generation of people who grew up eating and talking and lounging in front of television sets had started to come to the theatre. Our stage managers had a lot to do in order to teach theatre manners to people who had no idea they were distracting others by rattling cellophane, sticking gum under the stage seats, fanning themselves with programs and talking — not whispering — while the play was going on.

The stage manager — who had been in Los Angeles for a week helping with the opening of *Equus* there — watched the play from the audience when he returned. It was the first time he saw me as Dora from the front of the house. It is hard to explain how the approval of a stage manager may be as important to an actor as a review in the *New York Times*. He is your surrogate director, your link with the management and, in the case of *Equus,* the great friend of the company.

It is a job few can fill with grace. The constant corrections, the attempt to keep the rules, the need to be on management's side in many cases, makes it a position for a politician, a teacher and a benevolent dictator. Some of the great stage managers I have worked with, during my years with McClintic, for instance, were also good at lighting a play and managed touring companies with enormous tact and skill. I have toured the country twice — once with Judith Anderson and once with Katharine Cornell — and I know that the relationships in a touring company are even more intense than the ones I have been talking about here. There is a loneliness and a reliance on the friendships in the company that can lead to love affairs or feuds or nothingness. In a place where you have a home and family or friends to return to after the play it is not quite as difficult to keep your sense of values.

189

And yet there are train trips and dinners in restaurants and parties in hotel rooms that I remember with much pleasure. There was a freedom, a language, a sense of ritual in both those companies, that I adored.

Guthrie used to come to all our parties when we were on tour with *Medea*. He sat on the floor and told us stories of what was going on in the New York theatre. A fabulist, he would begin: "It's a curious thing . . ." and tell a tale that even if he had told it many times before continued to fill him with wonder and fascinated us.

I felt privileged in those days because he would take me to dinner on the night he arrived. We would go to the best restaurant in whatever city we were playing and I would share his curious wonderful memories. He told me about knowing Laurette Taylor, directing Ruth Gordon, about the writers he knew and of course about Kit. Sometimes while I was listening I would think, Ask me a question, ask me a question . . . What did I want him to ask me? What did I want to tell him? He knew everything about me that was of any interest. And he knew how much I loved being in the theatre. He did not need to ask.

I did not think then that I could ever feel apologetic about my own part in the theatre. Sadly — or happily — I felt that since I loved it so much and wanted nothing else but to contribute to it, I would do so in an important way.

Is what I am writing now, feeling now, an apology? For an actress's life? For my life? I do not want it to be that. Because in spite of the fact that the realness and humanness of my life seem separate now from those early dreams, the actual living of my life as an actress and as a person has been much richer, much more interesting than anything I imagined. The evidence is not where I can show it to myself or to a stranger but it is in me somewhere. It is the thing that keeps me alive.

News of the casting of the film of *Equus* began to appear in the newspapers.

"Don't you wish you were going to be in the movie?"

"No. Not really. I never expected to be —"

"But wouldn't it be thrilling to be in the *movie* . . ."

It is always a revelation to see how dramatic material is handled on film. I suppose if I had been considered for the movie I would have become excited about it. But it was clear from the first that the cast would be composed of English actors, and a fine group was assembled. For the part of Hesther they chose Eileen Atkins. I had met her during the first year of the run and liked her. After the film cast had been announced I saw her again and we talked about the part. It made a bond between us, made friendship easier. She described her interview for the role and it was so like many of mine it made me laugh. The same little injustices, the ridiculous social amenities that have nothing to do with whether you can act or not. She went to the wrong hotel to meet with the director, arrived late, could not remember the part clearly from having seen it in London over three years before and had no chance to read it. The nice thing was that they knew they wanted her and even the secretary's misintroducing her as "Dorothy Tutin" did not seem to matter.

People who are not in the theatre think actresses behave badly to each other and are jealous and cruel. I have had the opposite experience. It seems to me that we are all trying to help each other and feel free to call on each other as friends for such help. It is second nature to me to suggest another actress for a part I do not think I am right for. I am not saying we don't get angry when an actress we think has less talent gets a part, but we know how much individual taste weighs in decisions of casting. And if you ever want to hear actors be cruel about each other's work, set *them* to work casting. They start at the top with the famous "names" and demolish them all. But as soon as the star category has been exhausted a serious interest and insight comes to the surface and you will hear appreciation of the craft.

Actors are funny about names, too. Name-dropping seems to be a crime and yet we all do it. If an anecdote is told we want to be able to recognize the cast of characters, and if it is about a great actor or a famous one we enjoy it more. I know that a theatre story about students would not be interesting but if I could tell the same story with theatre names it would be listened to with delight. Picasso said, "What we have to do is *name* things. They have to be called by their names. I *name* an eye. I *name* a foot. I *name* my dog's head on my knees. I *name* my knees. *Naming* — that's all. That's enough." The artist names, the conversationalist name-drops.

I grew up hearing the music of wonderful names. When my father was an editor of the *Dial* magazine many writers and artists came to Henderson Place. Later they came to the apartment where I live now and I remember those meetings clearly. My father had a remarkable talent for friendship. His friends embraced us. Now all that remains are letters and post cards and a book of my father's reminiscences he left unfinished. But the idea of feeling comfortable with celebrated people was born early in me and I have never been self-conscious about it. I started my career in the theatre with extraordinary people and this happy condition has continued.

*

Shopping for food late at night, getting the early edition of the paper, walking along the avenues when the crowds are gone: the evening rituals connected with being in a long run.

The men who work at the Dover Delicatessen on East Fifty-seventh Street have known me most of my life. They are excellent at what they do and each is my friend in a different way. Meyer, avuncular, remembers me as a little girl. He loves the idea that I was connected with a big success. The proprietor calls me a "star" and introduces me to people who look blank and try to understand what on earth he means. The cashier is a young woman who reminds me of Judy Holliday.

I had fantasies of acting with Katharine Cornell and Judith Anderson. In 1946 when I saw Judy Holliday play the delicious ex–chorus girl Billie Dawn in *Born Yesterday* I had no such dream. Her world of theatre seemed so far away from mine. Her sweetness, unique timing and original wit belonged on a stage full of laughter.

On Broadway I had seen *The Man Who Came to Dinner*, *Life with Father*, *My Sister Eileen*, *The Voice of the Turtle* and *Harvey*, but until I saw *Born Yesterday*, and saw Judy/Billie fall in love with learning, I had never been moved by a modern comedy. I went to see it three times. I did not dream that I might be in a play by Garson Kanin. All that was in the future.

The chance to play with Judy came about because I was cast as Julie in *Showboat* at the Corning Summer Theatre in 1951 and to save money they were trying to use each actor in more than one play. Would I play in *Dream Girl* with Judy Holliday?

Once again I had the chance to see her in a comedy that had touching truths in it. It was there that Judy's brilliance 193 as an actress shone brightest. I thought there would be a time when she would play parts like Laurette Taylor's and would be considered not only a fine comedienne but a completely fulfilled artist. It was never to be.

The serio-comic was a part of her life offstage, too. She talked to you about anything that interested you or herself, made you laugh, made you think. She adored crossword puzzles and games and was the first person I knew to make a long-distance call to find out a word for the *New York Times* Sunday double crostic.

Judy's mother was with her. Once we were talking about child development, and Judy said, "I didn't talk for a *long* time. How old was I, Mom?"

"Three, four . . ."

"What was the first thing I said?"

"Please adjust the venetian blind."

I do not think of her as a sad creature just because she died young. There was something so vulnerable about Judy that while she lived you wanted to make life happier for her.

The living reminder of Judy at the Dover gives me an odd, sweet feeling.

The quietest moment of *Equus* is the scene where Alan and Jill, the stable girl, meet at night and take off their clothes so that they can make love in the warm straw. It is played in silence. The lights instead of dimming come up to a high mark and flood the stage. For the first ten months of the run every night a street musician took his place outside in order to be ready for the crowds when they left the theatre. He would play the same song from *Fiddler on the Roof:* "Sunrise, Sunset." When the musician decided to move to another location and I did not hear the faint, inappropriate tune, I found myself missing it.

He must have gone to a theatre where a more affluent audience assembled. We began to attract a younger crowd, mixed with many out-of-towners. The lady holding the donation can, forcing herself in front of the patrons and commanding them to give to her charity, was gone, too. In the alley — Shubert Alley — a street magician entertained. After the applause had stopped in the theatres you could go out the stage door to the street and hear *his* applause.

Shubert Alley is clean and wide and brightly lit. The crowds stay to watch the dancers come out of the stage door after *A Chorus Line*. The commuters cut through it to get to Grand Central. The actors and their companions use it on their way to Sardi's or the subway. The posters of plays and musicals on the walls are bright and free from graffiti. I think of walking through it before it was refurbished, before I had parts in plays. Wondering who owned the limousines that had special parking privileges. Hoping I might see a famous actor. I never did.

I love walking through the alley now.

I remember taking my daughter to Henderson Place and showing her the house where I grew up, describing my fear of the dark but somehow neglecting to tell her my feelings about the mirror. As we walked away she looked longingly at what I thought was the prettiest street in New York and asked, "How old were you when you lived in that alley?"

Many wonderful actors have the quality of childlikeness that never leaves them. Tony Hopkins's face in repose often looks like a sleepy child's. And he has a child's pleasure in friendships and jokes.

When he had to leave the company because of his phlebitis we missed him in the play and in the greenroom. We were told that he would be back with us on a certain Monday and did not expect to see him before that. On a Saturday afternoon as we gathered for coffee between the acts not one of us expected the visitor who seemed to be occupying Tony's usual place.

The man sitting there with one leg up on a chair in front of him was Richard Nixon! Without my glasses his features looked softer than they did in photographs but it was a sickening likeness. A split second later we were all screaming with laughter as Tony pulled off the lifelike rubber mask, rose to his feet and let us welcome him home.

Long after his return the rubber mask hung on a peg in the costume room, its features sadly sagging. A grim reminder of current history and our prankish star.

Hopkins could imitate other actors brilliantly. It was a shock and a surprise to me when Dexter urged him to do Dysart's part as Brando, as Burton, as Gielgud, as Humphrey Bogart, at the final rehearsal on the day we opened. A way of loosening tensions? A waste of a rehearsal? The naughty children laughed.

My early experiences with imitation were unfortunate. During the war, when Helen Parkhurst decided that the students at Dalton should learn what it would be like to be evacuated, she arranged for the high school to spend several months in barracks that were built in Buck's Rock, Connecticut. I liked the cramped rooms with their bunk beds, the easy intimacy with girls in other classes, seeing the faculty in ski pants, meeting for classes in dining rooms or under the trees. The emphasis was still on excellence in our classes and the social life was confined to drinking far too much Coca-Cola and staying up later than we were supposed to.

A festival — the story of America — was planned and we

all took part in writing it. We were passionate in those days. Perhaps that was my religion then. Someone got the idea that we should have a party after the performance. One of the skits would include imitations of the faculty. I was chosen to imitate Marion Dickerman.

This gentle gray-haired lady had a high-pitched voice and an accent not unlike Eleanor Roosevelt's. She had been the headmistress of the Todhunter School when Mrs. Roosevelt taught there. Todhunter had merged with Dalton in 1941 and several of the teachers and Miss Dickerman had joined the Dalton faculty.

Marion Dickerman pronounced knives, "knaves." Her manners were impeccable. When announcements were made at meals she would say softly, "Girls, do I hear knaves and forks?" We were polite. We did not giggle. But when I got up at the party and "did" Miss Dickerman there was laughter and I gloried in it. I did not realize how cruelly I must have hurt my target.

I was sent for by Madame Ernst, who had come from Todhunter, and was advised to go to Miss Dickerman's cottage and apologize. Suddenly I knew what I had done and that there was no one to take the blame. I could have refused to do the imitation, I could have made it less accurate.

I found her lying in bed. She said she had a cold but I thought what I had done had made her ill. I said I was sorry and that I would not do such a thoughtless thing again.

Four years later, when I was a senior at Dalton, the faculty did some takeoffs of the students. My Latin teacher, Lauralee Tuttle, "did" me. I knew then how Miss Dickerman had felt. The audience roared. I was fascinated and frightened. There was no question who the person she was acting was; I couldn't decide if I loved or hated her.

On the stage where I had played my favorite parts was

Lauralee Tuttle. Her hair combed straight back, which accented her cheekbones, dressed in a smock (as all the high school students were), talking earnestly and swiftly, making wide and forceful gestures. "I see life as a ladder. A tall ladder, and we must climb that ladder, we must reach the stars." *Per ardua ad astra*. Mrs. Tuttle. Me.

We cannot help a certain amount of mimicry in acting, not only of the actors we have admired but of the people who have influenced our lives. I have caught myself doing something exactly as my mother would do it without making a conscious decision to act that way.

Seeing wonderful acting can give you courage or frighten you. When I went to the Neighborhood Playhouse I saw almost every play in New York. Sometimes I *knew* that it was only a question of time before I took my place with those golden creatures bathed in the bright stage light, but other nights I walked home in fear. Did I belong with them? Could I command the attention of the audience? Most actors have the same double feeling on an opening night. I can do anything. I can do nothing. The value of a creative rehearsal period is that the positive side of one's nature wins the battle. For some actors this victory does not take place until the split second before they walk on the stage.

I have always wanted to get on, to begin the sharing of the work with the audience. In fact, at some rehearsals I long for a new eye and in a comedy for a new sound of laughter to renew my faith in the choices I have made.

A friend of mine who knows a lot about theatre and even more about people is writing his master's thesis on stage fright. He asked me if I had it. I told him I did not, I loved the challenge of the opening night. The fears came only when I was not prepared. It is part of the game of theatre that you cannot predict the audience's reaction.

But the longer I thought about his question the more sure I was that I had avoided answering it truthfully. I had not thought enough about the subject. Other people's nerves on opening nights make me jittery. I hate the silly things they say about "wishing they were somewhere else" and losing confidence in themselves and the play. I have heard all the stories of the people who get physically sick and the ones who are afraid they will forget their lines. But all those nerves have had their chance to plague the actor from the first reading of the script, through the interview with the producer/director/casting person, through the first rehearsal, the first run-through without books, the first time a stranger comes in and sees a rehearsal. By the time you have the technical rehearsals and the dress rehearsal you are ready for — you need — the audience to complete your work. Things go wrong, things that have worked do not work. More rehearsal, script adjustments are made and the problem gets solved. Or does not get solved, as Lynn Fontanne said, "and you wrestle with it every time you do the play." That is also the nature of our work. But I think it is the mark of a professional not to be silly about stage fright. To harness that energy into the performance. If I have stage fright, then I have to admit that I have life fright too. There is nothing challenging or thrilling or romantic I have encountered in my life — no matter how many times the experience has been repeated — that has not frightened me in some mysterious way. And if that thrill of fear were taken away I think the joy would be diminished, too.

After twenty-two months on Broadway, the talk of the theatre was that *Equus* would close on September 15, 1976.   199

Opening night, with a playwright's roses.

I found out that the run was planned until Thanksgiving. That Perkins was contracted until then, and just as he had to be paid while Burton played the Doctor, he would now be paid for another piece of time in which he did not have the opportunity to act. He had decided not to go on the tour.

What happened to make us lose those New York weeks? No one in the management said anything, but the word was that while the other producers and the company manager were in Los Angeles preparing for the triumphant opening there, Kermit somehow released the Plymouth Theatre to another producer. Too bad. Or would it work out for the best, as most *Equus* plans seemed to have done so far?

I called Juilliard to tell them I would be available to direct the first project for the incoming class. A commitment. And fighting to get through my thoughts was the dream of another play, another chance to work on my dream. To work on my life.

After I had played the mother for a week I went to Woolworth's near Bloomingdale's and had four pictures taken by a machine for fifty cents. I put them in an envelope and sent them to my daughter, who does not use any cosmetics. I had chosen two pictures and threw the others away. It was not the blondeness, it was the tenseness. I will have to work on that, too.

And I will have to work on the truth. I went to Woolworth's, took four pictures, looked at them, went home. Went back to Woolworth's and took four more, chose the two least discouraging images and mailed them. I underestimate my daughter. She is so *for* me even if what I do makes her laugh.

How does an actor handle stress and tension? We have to learn ways to relax in order to perform well. Why is it so difficult to do the same thing in our lives?

Much good work in the arts depends on physical strength. Energy. When you don't feel well you compensate in ways that make your work acceptable but less compelling.

I have had extraordinarily good health for most of my life but when I was in my early twenties I began to notice — gradually — that the simplest physical tasks became increasingly difficult. Because I had a reputation for not tiring I did not admit to being tired. It is hard to believe that I let this condition go unchecked for such a long time. At yearly checkups the doctors would give me one hundred percent good marks. But the discs in my neck and lower spine were wearing down and by the time I went to a specialist it was serious enough for a double operation to be suggested. It would fuse the discs in each place and in all probability stop the pain.

I went to see Dr. Lee Ramsay Straub at the Hospital for Special Surgery. He had been crippled by the very illness he treats. No one told me that instead of walking into a room this impressive, handsome man would roll down the hospital corridor in something that looked like a golf cart, ease himself onto a high leather chair and take my hand and talk to me like a father, friend, doctor, and earn my trust. He prescribed a back brace and a neck brace, using traction and a series of exercises to do every day "for the rest of your life."

I rehearsed, joined in the dance classes and played some of the performances in that brace. I wore the collar most of the day and every night and I became a prisoner of a traction set attached to my bed. The exercises became part of each morning's ritual. After a year I put away the collar and the brace.

Sitting on the wooden benches during the play presents a problem for even the youngest, strongest actors.

When St. Denis and Houseman created the curriculum for Juilliard they found a teacher of the Alexander Technique to work with the students on physical problems. Judith Leibowitz became my teacher for a short while, finding time between her classes to give me help in understanding the principles of F. Matthias Alexander. He had been a Shakespearean actor who suffered from vocal problems that threatened to end his career. He could find no medical help and detected that it was his misuse of his muscles and the faulty alignment of his neck and shoulders that was causing his loss of voice. In a slow, careful process of retraining, he broke away from the destructive patterns and habits of his earlier life and cured himself. Alexander worked for many years in London, and among his pupils were George Bernard Shaw and Aldous Huxley.

I had read Alexander's books, but as he himself says, it is almost impossible to follow his training without a guide. To approach a new way of using your body from moment to 202 moment in a way that will break the tensions that your life-long habits have established, is an enormous undertaking. It is a task that does not end, and a fine teacher can help you to free your will so that you can be in control of your body and therefore prevent tension.

After studying dancing and acting it was difficult not to "do" anything in my sessions with Judith. It was more difficult to give up the familiar ways of sitting and standing that "felt right." She showed me anatomical drawings and a skeleton to help me understand that the relationship of my head to my spinal column was causing me the constant pain I had been trying to live with.

She had the same quiet approach that Dr. Straub had. They taught me ways to avoid stress, to take care of my body and to find a kind of peace.

In the course of two years I worked with Billy Redfield on the radio dozens of times. One day he came to work carrying the reviews of *One Flew over the Cuckoo's Nest,* in which he had a good part. He was overjoyed at the film's success in the New York press. He gave me a note to take to Richard Burton. He had written a book, *Letters from an Actor.* The subject was the production of *Hamlet* that John Gielgud had directed starring Burton. Billy felt Burton was offended by the book and hoped the note would heal the breach. He told me to read it. He wrote Richard that he was sorry, that he loved him as much as it was possible for a man to love another man. I delivered the note. Richard read it and told me he did not have the faintest idea why Billy was troubled. It had not occurred to him to be bothered by the book. He smiled his dear smile and told me to reassure Billy. I am glad I had the chance to do so. Shortly thereafter the New York *Post* reported that at forty-nine — having been an actor for forty years — Billy was dead.

He told me such an "actor" thing: As I was exclaiming about the reviews of the Kesey film he said that a lot of his part had to be cut in order to give Jack Nicholson the spotlight. Otherwise it would have been he — Billy — who received the nomination for the Academy Award.

Those are the dreams we live on. And die with.

When Billy told me about his fears that his book had offended Richard I began to worry about the writing I was doing about *Equus*. In all my notebooks from the other plays there is little about the personal lives of the actors. In the short runs I never got to know the intrigues of the companies. When I was young I was so stagestruck that I could not bear to write an unkind thing about an actor or director I admired. For years I had the reputation of never saying anything negative. I kept quiet. It was easier. But when I began to teach and direct and to know my own mind I censored myself less often.

Reading about a theatre experience, you cannot help wondering what the backstage life was like. I believe it has nothing to do with what the audience sees on the stage. It does not matter if the rehearsals were fun or agony. But in looking at my work-life in the theatre I see how the private lives and opinions and behavior of my coworkers have influenced my life and thoughts and behavior, for good and bad.

Knowing more about my peers has not made me love them less. Knowing more about myself has made me able to look at my work more objectively in retrospect. There is no place for objectivity in rehearsal. The director must be the sole possessor of that attribute while the play is being discovered. But it is hard to be objective about *his* judgments.

The relationship between the director and the cast is as clearly a love-hate combination as is any professional situation. "The Boss" is the subject of greenroom gossip and speculation as long as the project exists.

Chekhov has Nina say, "It seems to me a play must have some love in it." So should a book that deals with the life of a play. But that quality of love that pervaded even the most difficult times in *Equus,* the fellowship we felt — the feeling of good fortune that we could do a play we had respect and love for — were the strongest things we shared. And when any person left the company we felt diminished.

At the end of July in 1976 Michael Higgins played his final performance as the father as sensitively and surely as he had all the others. We were moved and tried not to show him how much it meant to us to watch him act Frank Strang for the last time. We had champagne afterward, and I sat near him. Brent Peek, our stage manager, stood up and said, "I have a toast!" and looking at me, added, "And then there was *one!*"

I looked at Michael, the last of the original cast but me.

He leaned over and said gently, "If only we could own the people we love."

He expressed my feeling for him and for the perfect friendship actors can have for each other. The following Monday I had a rehearsal call with my old friend Page Johnson to run the father scenes and a new Dalton (Page's part) would be there to take his place. Our life went on. But our father was gone and we missed him.

13

The chemistry between actress and director is one of the key elements in rehearsal as well as performance. The strangest combination I have witnessed was Tallulah Bankhead and Tony Richardson. After the failure of *The Milk Train Doesn't Stop Here Any More* in March 1963, Tennessee Williams revised the script and David Merrick announced that he would present it on Broadway again early in 1964. It would star Tallulah Bankhead, for whom the part was written originally.

Tony Richardson had directed *Arturo Ui* (for which I also read) before turning his attention to the Williams play. I had read the Witch of Apri for the first production, but was not chosen. My theory of continuing to audition was working out. The reading for the part of Blackie, Mrs. Goforth's private secretary, took about five minutes. Richardson decided at once. I was given the script and a rehearsal call.

Everyone in the theatre has a Tallulah story to tell. She meant glamour and daring and toughness. I had never met her. When the telephone rang a few days before rehearsal

As Blackie, Mrs. Goforth's secretary, rehearsing *The Milk Train Doesn't Stop Here Anymore* with Tallulah Bankhead, Brooks Atkinson Theatre, 1964.

and the familiar voice purred my name I was sure it was some friend doing an imitation. "Who is this?"

"It's Tallulah Bankhead. Listen, dahling . . ." It really was good!

"Who *is* this?"

It *was* Tallulah inviting me to come across Fifty-seventh Street to help with her lines and to play some bridge. When I told her I would come she laughed happily; when I told her I did not play bridge she growled.

Her apartment was dominated by the Augustus John portrait in which she looked pale and thoughtful. The actual Tallulah dressed in tight slacks and a loose silk blouse was vivid and energetic, friendly and distracted. She would do anything rather than study her part. I saw the pattern of excuses developing. I had seen it before. The actor sets up a series of barriers between himself and the words and, when they are not learned, blames them.

Marie, her servant, provided a delicious dinner. Marie did everything for Tallulah. It was clear that dressing, washing her hair, doing simple, daily tasks was almost impossible for her because of a self-inflicted cigarette burn on her right hand. Unbandaged, with a freshly lit lipstick-stained cigarette constantly in it, the carefully nail-polished hand was constantly before my eyes. The burn did not heal and she wrapped a chiffon square around it when she was onstage. Part of my job as an actress was to protect that awful, helpless hand.

At dinner Tallulah told me, "I am a victim of bad publicity, darling. They say I'm a lesbian, a nymphomaniac, a dope fiend . . . When I was playing in Dennis one summer in *The Second Mrs. Tanqueray,* Tennessee brought me *The Battle of Angels.*"

"Why didn't you do it?"

"I told him, 'I think it's the most disgusting play I've ever read in my entire life.' Years went by and he rewrote it for Anna Magnani but she didn't play it —" She lit a cigarette.

"I saw Maureen Stapleton in it on Broadway."

"— and finally I saw Magnani in the movie and I said to Tennessee, 'I think it's disgraceful. They have absolutely ruined a bad play!'" She roared with laughter and tossed her famous mane of hair. "Now that's the sort of thing they should write about me. Not that I go around naked. My figure's not good enough to go around naked."

Several days later at noon the first reading of the play took place at her apartment. Tallulah was sitting in the middle of her white couch wearing lavender slacks and the light silk shirt. She looked stunning. Dolores, her little white dog, sat at her side. Each time the doorbell rang Dolores barked. As Tony Richardson was explaining his ideas about the script she barked. As he entered the room Tallulah demanded, "Give me a kiss; the first time I saw you, you gave me a kiss."

"I'll kiss you forever. You're marvelous . . . marvelous . . ." Tennessee's agent Audrey Wood, Reuben Ter-Arutunian, the designer, and Kermit Kegley, the stage manager, arrived. Tennessee was late. The dog barked so he was not able to slip in unnoticed. "You're not serving drinks, are you?" he asked twice. Both times Tallulah said no, so he sat and smoked until his neat dark blue suit was covered with ashes. He laughed at all the jokes, he chuckled through the serious scenes. It was his way of listening.

Tony said to the company: "I don't want to say much" — Dolores barked — "it's a play about death. The set will be formal, Kabuki-like, simple. In Mrs. Goforth's death we should all feel tragedy and suffering" — barks — "Fuck you!" — Dolores subsided — "They are all fighting against death" — barking again.

Tallulah: "I can hardly hear you, darling? What are you saying . . . ?"

On November 20 we started rehearsing at the Lunt-Fontanne Theatre. Tony asked the actors to write down the blocking "even if I change it a hundred times. It drives me mad when actors don't remember." I never saw a pencil in Tallulah's hand. The stage manager, or the young man who took care of her or I, wrote down the directions, which she seldom followed.

She never did learn the lines as they were written. She knew most of them and some of her cues but she rehearsed and played the long and difficult part of Mrs. Goforth with blind instinct, making the part so much Tallulah that her lack of preparation seemed to be part of the characterization. She loathed taking changes or cuts; they were hardest for her to learn. "Everything in this goddamned play he copied from me! I'm not going to cut it!" She would yell out the line as if to impress it on her own and everyone else's memory, and at the following rehearsal she would forget it, and the stage manager would put a light pencil line through it in his script. You never could tell.

When Tallulah was late or tired Tab Hunter and I would do our scenes for Tony Richardson. We rehearsed them more than any other part of the play because they were the only scenes without Mrs. Goforth, and it soon became clear that directing them was pleasanter for Tony. Tallulah and he did not share the same theatre background or vocabulary. They were out of each other's time.

Tallulah: "When shall I stagger?"
Tony: "Let it come from you, Miss Bankhead . . . from deep inside your gut . . ."

Tallulah: "How shall I read this, darling?"
Tony: "I prefer to hear what you feel, darling."
Tallulah: "You're a great help."

Tallulah: "This is the speech that everybody loathes . . ."
Tony: "It's my favorite speech in the play."
Tallulah: "It would be."

Tennessee's stage direction: *"Mrs. Goforth starts to cough. She covers her mouth with her hand and rushes, in a crouched position, toward the library."*
210   Tony: "Try to cover her coughing attack with laughter."

Tallulah: "I know this is a terrible thing to ask you, of all people — but how long would you like me to laugh? And how long would you like me to cough . . . ?"

Tony: "Five minutes of laughing and five minutes of coughing . . ."

Tallulah tried the exit two ways.

Tony: "That's not enough!"

Tallulah (getting down on all fours and crawling off the stage): "Enough?"

Tony: "No."

Tennessee Williams walks into the theatre and calls from the back row: "Oh, have you got the script out of your hands?"

Tallulah is not insensitive to Tony. She brazens it out at rehearsal but she says, "It's like working with someone with his hat on . . . his gloves on . . . in the house; I feel he wants to leave all the time." When she tries to explain something to Tony he mutters, "Yes . . . yes . . . right . . . yes . . . All right, let's go on. Stay at home tonight . . . rest . . . eat dinner . . . look after yourself and rest . . ." They do not hear each other.

Tallulah: "How shall I say this?"

Tony: "Any way you want."

Tallulah: "You're the director."

Tony: "Well, *invent.* You are the actress —"

Tallulah: "I signed the wrong contract. I'm sending you back to Oxford."

Tony: "Let's go from the bottom of page seventy-two . . ."

Tallulah: "What, darling?"

211

Tony: "How was dinner last night?"

Tallulah: "There's nothing about dinner here . . ."

Tony: "No, I mean, how was dinner last night?"

Tallulah: "You mean where she leaves . . . ?"

Tony (shouting): "No, not in the play, darling. I mean how was your dinner with Tennessee last night?"

Tallulah: "Oh! He was tight . . ."

One day Tennessee sits in front and watches for a while. "Am I bothering you, sweetheart?" he asks Tallulah.

"No. No one's ever bothering me . . . if they're helping me."

We were rehearsing the first scene of the second act. From the stage Tab's voice was saying, "We don't all live in the same world, you know, Mrs. Goforth, oh, we all see the same things — sea, sun, sky, human faces and inhuman faces, but . . . one person's sense of reality can be another person's sense of — Well, of madness! — Chaos! — and . . ." Tallulah didn't answer him. She cried out. Tony had interrupted to tell her that President Kennedy had been shot.

She was weeping. Tennessee came holding his Boston bull terrier and some brandy which he shared with Tallulah. We stopped rehearsal for ten minutes. Then Tab began again: "Madness! — Chaos . . ."

I took Tallulah home after the rehearsal. We talked about her father, Senator Bankhead, whom she adored, and Adlai Stevenson, whose voice comforted us on the taxi radio. She was shaken but surprisingly controlled. The following week was the most disciplined rehearsing for her. She had a vitamin B shot every day and although she was tired, she 212 knew her words pretty well.

One stunning, unforgettable rehearsal of the final scene in the first act made us think that the project would be magically transformed and that Tallulah was going to give a performance that would be remembered with her work in *The Little Foxes* and *The Skin of Our Teeth*. She took Tony's direction and used it with thrilling intensity and power.

She knew how good she was that day, yet she went to Tony and told him she could not do it his way. "It would kill me. I'm going to play it my own way."

"With that old Georgia charm?" I think he gave up on her then.

Tallulah could not sleep. In Wilmington the doctor came to her suite in the Hotel Du Pont and treated her hand and gave her sleeping tablets. They did no good. She would call my room at two or three in the morning. Her sleepy voice was deceptive. She was wide awake and expected me to come and talk to her. While we were in Wilmington I did, but when we moved on to Baltimore it was not as easy. It was the Christmas vacation at Dalton and my daughter was with me. Whatever time I had I wanted to be with her and I treasured my sleeping as well as my waking hours. It was difficult for Tallulah to understand, but eventually she started to ask me to come to her suite in the daytime when we were not rehearsing. Tony Richardson had flown back to England for the holidays and most of our days were free. Tallulah, who did not want to rehearse with him in Wilmington, was furious that he had deserted us.

On Christmas Eve Tallulah asked her secretary to buy presents for Katharine. She sent for us. My daughter's first glimpse of the fabled, wonderful Tallulah Bankhead was of a naked woman half covered with a sheet sitting in a hotel   213 bedroom smoking, coughing, laughing and talking.

"Do you believe in Santa Claus, darling?"

Katharine looked at me and then at Tallulah.

"No."

Tallulah gave me a reproving look. "Oh, my *God!* I did! I did, all through my childhood, and when I found out there was *no* Santa Claus" — her eyes filled with tears and she pushed her uncombed tawny hair back from her face — "it was the most terrible moment in my whole life — until I heard that Kennedy was shot." She wept. Katharine said nothing. Then Tallulah gave her a pretty red dress and white sweater. Katharine thanked her gravely and we went out to play in the snow.

"Upstaging" in the theatre is old-fashioned and rarely practiced anymore. Tallulah could not help it. In the scene with the Witch of Capri, played by Ruth Ford, these two grotesques have dinner on the terrace of Mrs. Goforth's villa. Part of the staging included Blackie — the secretary-of-all-work — bringing two chairs to the table. I always placed them evenly on either side of the round table but as the scene progressed they were moved. Not by me. At one rehearsal Tony asked one of the actresses, "Can you give her a look there?" and she replied, "I don't even know where she is!" So it was decided that the chairs should be placed "fifty-fifty," and he gave me a hard look. They played the scene that way at rehearsal but when we had audiences the actresses came to me — separately — and showed me where to place each chair. It became a bad patch for everyone involved in the scene and one day there was a dust-up about it. One of the actresses said, to end the tirade, "Fifty-fifty." The other replied, "I'm *tired* of fifty-fifty."

Tony decided to put a green light in the candle flames on the dinner table. One of the assistants said, "That's marvelous, like the witches in *Hamlet!*" We stifled our laughter, but it was funnier still when one of the leading actors asked us why we laughed.

It was fitting that Tallulah and Tony should have had their last quarrel about the curtain call. The sight of Tallulah pretending to be surprised when the audience applauded her exit so vociferously that she had to come back and bow to them again — worse still, her habit of bowing to the company and waving her chiffon scarf — offended him and he begged her to be simple. By the time we reached New York her false exit and subsequent performance was a small production and I was involved in it. This actress whom everyone thought of as self-centered was anxious for me to have more of a part in her choreography of the calls. Tony had gone back to England. Tallulah put me in the call with the stars and when her fans threw flowers at her she would bow deeply, pick them up and turn sweetly and hand them to me! "I've always staged my own calls, darling. It's part of the performance."

At supper after the play one evening she spoke admiringly of Tony's work. I wished he had been there to hear it. I knew she would not say the same things to his face. His direction of the play and of her performance had been imaginative and strong before they stopped communicating with each other. Then the changes in behavior in life and the theatre, and the gulf of years between the antagonists, prevented any kind of truce. A few days later the entire adventure was over. Tony's brilliant notes, Tennessee's mysterious responses, Tallulah's theatrical behavior, all seem like events 215 that took place many more than fourteen years ago.

And Tallulah's unforgettable, tired voice asking my opinion of Tony: "Tell me, darling, tell me the truth. Is he a genius?"

When the revival of *The Milk Train Doesn't Stop Here Any More* opened at the Brooks Atkinson, Ralph Roberts was getting settled in his dressing room. We were discussing the beautiful stage and costume designs of Aline Bernstein. She was an actor's daughter, a theatre creature and is remembered too as Esther Jack in Thomas Wolfe's *Web and the Rock*. She had encouraged me to be an actress. Ralph was organizing his few possessions. He took a miniature box of soap flakes out of a bag. I lost the thread of our conversation and laughed. It looked like the samples we used to send away for as children.

"Don't know how long we'll be here," he mused. Three days later we were gone.

14

In the course of my life and career no actor has had a greater influence on my appreciation of acting as an art, my love of going to the theatre and my belief that the profession is important and necessary than Laurence Olivier. From 1940, when I first saw him at the Fifty-first Street Theatre in his own production of *Romeo and Juliet,* there has hardly been a conversation among theatre people in which I have not heard his work discussed. Since that magical afternoon in May I have seen every play he has done in New York, all his films and television appearances. I have seen his influence in other actors' work and followed with interest his choice of plays as a director and producer. I suppose most actors have fantasized about working with Olivier, but I have never had any realistic thoughts about such an opportunity.

An irony of theatregoing in New York from the 1940s to the 1970s is that I have seen an English actor in more great roles than any American actor. Leaving aside the impact of Laurence Olivier as a film actor, I have seen him play twelve parts on the stage — some of them twice, four of them three times. Often the plays were selected, cast and directed by him as well; plays of Sophocles, Shakespeare, Sheridan, Shaw, Chekhov, Anouilh, and Osborne.

In May 1958 I was living in Hollywood and flew to New York to do a live television program. I saw Olivier in *The Entertainer* on the afternoon I had no rehearsal, and on the actual day of the show I had an engagement for lunch with Guthrie at Mercurio's. He telephoned in the morning and said, "I'm sorry, darling, we won't be able to have lunch alone. There will be a third person."

The television program was being rehearsed at the Century Theatre. I ran the few blocks to the restaurant and there was Guthrie. We told each other our news and a perfect English gentleman joined us. "Larry, this is Marian Seldes. Sit down, dear boy."

He had exquisite manners. It was he who ordered the wine; he wanted a special vintage for Guthrie. I had some wine too. It was the first time in my life that I had something to drink before I worked. I knew it would affect my performance and began to make allowances for it as I swallowed each delicious sip. I listened to Guthrie and Olivier talk and was struck for the first time that Guthrie was of a different generation and that Olivier deferred to him gently, approvingly. They talked of shared times when McClintic's production of *No Time for Comedy* was playing in New York, of Sneden's Landing, where the Oliviers had spent weekends when they were playing *Romeo and Juliet,* and Olivier joked with me about the theatres he had closed when he found out that I was working in a TV studio that had once housed the Old Vic productions of *Henry IV, Oedipus, The Critic* and *Uncle Vanya.* I told him that by not saying I had seen any of the performances I was able to accept invitations to see each of the plays three times. There was no way to express my gratitude for those great theatre

nights. I attempted to describe the impact of his performance in *The Entertainer*. "When did you see it?"

"At the matinee on Wednesday the twenty-sixth."

"Ah, that was a marvelous audience!" He was the first
actor I had heard praise an audience instead of saying, "Oh,
you didn't see it *that* night . . ." My father told me that
when he was a theatre critic most actors had that reaction of
mock or real horror to his attendance at their plays.

While they were having their coffee I had to go back to
rehearsal. I thought my knees would buckle when I stood to
say good-bye. The wine? I don't think so. The happiness.

Two years later I saw Olivier in Hollywood at a big
party. He had been shooting *Spartacus* and was utterly exhausted. He sat with Jean Simmons on a couch at one end
of a large richly appointed room and looked handsome
and — I thought — depressed. He spoke quietly and did
nothing to attract attention. He was the least theatrical person in the room.

In the next ten years I saw his films and his one appearance in New York as Becket in the Anouilh play and later as
King Henry when Anthony Quinn left the cast. I saw the
film of his *Othello*, followed his career as the director of the
National Theatre, and by the time I saw him again he had
been created Lord Olivier.

Tony Hopkins talked about him obsessively. Both he and
Dexter imitated him when they discussed him. But it became
hard to laugh when the troubling reports of Olivier's health
began to appear in the newspapers.

He said in interviews that he would do no more plays but
signed for a film, *Marathon Man*, part of which was to be
made in New York in September 1975.

It was over a year since the first rehearsal of *Equus*. Tony
Perkins was playing the Doctor and Tom Hulce, Alan. The   219

musicians' strike had begun to affect our houses; Broadway seemed quiet. *A Chorus Line,* which had made Shubert Alley a carnival, had shut down.

On September 18 we had a good brush-up rehearsal with John. On the evening of the twentieth Nick Russyan, who had been with us since the first day and taken over the stage management, told me that John expected me at Charlie's Restaurant after the performance. I wondered what it was about and did not consider that others might be there as well. I was not dressed for any kind of social evening; I had come to the theatre directly from Juilliard. I stifled a perverse impulse to say I could not make it and walked across the street, asked the owner of Charlie's where Mr. Dexter was sitting and he pointed to the large table at the back of the room. There was John and as I approached he rose, masking the other person at the table. It was the perfect English gentleman of 1958. His hair was white; he was thinner, his face more beautiful than I had ever seen it. The skin was clear and pink like a child's; his eyes were bright. On his right hand there was a small bandage shaped like a harness that held a square of gauze in place. The tips and knuckles of the fingers were startlingly red and sore. It was when he found he could not dial a telephone he realized how strength-sapping the muscular disorder was. He said he felt he was at about a quarter of his energy and would work in television and films, but no more theatre.

John said, "Marian plays the magistrate in *Equus.* She cries all the time. She has a love affair with the audience."

My daughter says I have a *look* that terrifies her. I gave John that look. At the same time I wondered what he meant by "cries all the time." Long after that evening I realized that at my most unhappy times with John I certainly was tearful at the theatre and it must have been reported to him.

220

I thought he was telling Olivier that I cried *on* the stage. The look worked. John was sweet the rest of the evening. I asked Olivier, "Is John as terrible to you as he is to us when you work at the National?"

"Oh, God, much worse!" and he rolled his eyes in a special way I have never seen anyone else do. Fascinating eyes which he uses the way other people use their hands when they talk. He illustrates with them. He was able to make the others at the table — we were joined by Roberta Maxwell, Tom Hulce (who was having trouble with his voice), another young actor, Mark Shannon, and John's friend Riggs O'Hara — shriek with laughter by shifting his glance. I think the others must have known there would be a party. I had never seen Roberta look prettier. The boys were wearing suits. (I remember that at Mercurio's I felt embarrassed because I was wearing bright red nail polish for my television part and thought it looked cheap.) I know now that my appearance was of no importance. The room felt warm, and Olivier let me help him out of his dark blue jacket. I wondered how he tied his tie with his bandaged hand. His shirt was buttoned at either wrist.

The young actors asked him about his films. He told them that when his children saw him play Heathcliff on television the year before they asked him why he dyed his hair! Roberta, who is Canadian, wanted to know how he worked on his accent for *The 49th Parallel.* He told her that he found someone to talk to. And that he studied his part in the film of Dreiser's *Sister Carrie* by talking to Spencer Tracy. "How lucky I was to have known him," he said, and the eyes were sad. For his role in *Marathon Man* he was working with a man on his German accent.

Drinks were ordered and reordered. If he must work the next day I wondered how he could stay there with us in the 221 hot, smoky restaurant. But he stayed. He talked with Tom about his voice; they discussed the problems of a long run in an emotional part. Colleagues.

It was getting late. I knew he had been at a party the night before; his comings and goings were reported in the papers. There was a picture of him dancing with the members of *A Chorus Line* that reminded me of his physical transformation as Archie Rice in *The Entertainer*. I said something about going home but he wanted to stay. I looked at John. We stayed and talked until the restaurant was empty.

When *Henry the Fifth* was released there was a cover story about Olivier in *Time* magazine. "They said my form of relaxation was to listen to phonograph records with a few friends. It was during the war. I used to go out with my friends and get potted!"

"I still have that interview," I said.

"So do I." He rolled his eyes and smiled. Around the table we leaned forward to hear him talk softly about Lillian Baylis and what she meant to the Old Vic, about Basil Dean — "No one ever talked back to him" — Gertrude Lawrence, William Wyler, Noel Coward — "I am very grateful to him; he started me reading books" — his fear of Jed Harris when he came to America to be in *The Green Bay Tree*. He told us that even then the problem of English actors coming here to play the good parts was infuriating the Americans and that they threatened to strike. "They had a perfect right."

More about films. When he was asked about *Spartacus* I reminded him of that time in Hollywood. "Were you unhappy?"

"I was very unhappy. It took five months . . . It wouldn't take that long now." And *Richard the Third*. I

222

told him they showed it at midnight at the Coronet Theatre so that all the working actors could see it before it opened. In the opening sequence when Olivier as Richard turns his profile — long nose, pointed chin, a wart or two, thick black hair hiding part of his face — the audience seemed to grasp the essence of his character and in a silence my husband whispered, "Marian! That's *you!*"

There was a long sequence between "Larry," as he asked her to call him, and Roberta about *Last Tango in Paris*. The subject under discussion was: Did Maria Schneider have her pants on in the first scene with Brando in the apartment — or didn't she?

He referred to Vivien Leigh, "my late wife," with enormous tenderness. We talked about their production of *Romeo and Juliet* and he described the morning after the opening. *Gone with the Wind* and *Wuthering Heights* were playing on Broadway. The ads for the play read: "Watch Them Kiss for the First Time!" The newspapers with the reviews were handed to him. He picked up an imaginary paper, turned it to the theatre page, found the review, looked at it, looked up, looked at it again closer — stunned — again, more closely, looked up. Stunned.

It was time to go. Tomorrow he would be working with "my leading man, Dustin Hoffman. Great mobility in the lower part of his face . . ." I wondered how he would get enough rest. He paid the check for all of us. Insisted.

It was raining. He was staying at the Blackstone. The others were all going downtown or to the West Side. I prayed that I could find a taxi quickly and a Checker cab drove up. We got in and on the ride uptown he talked about the McClintics and how important they had been to him. "When, exactly, did Kit die?"

"On the ninth of June, two years ago." That telephone   223 call I dreaded had come at eleven o'clock in the morning. Olivier closed his eyes.

The following night John came to the theatre. I thanked him for the evening. "You must have said 'Oh, God' a thousand times." Chastened, I turned to Tom Hulce. "Did I?" Tom said no. John asked, "Did he get home all right?"

"Oh, yes," I said. "I took him with me."

"And was he — ?"

"Perfect. A perfect gentleman."

15

Each Father's Day I call Oliver Hailey, out of loving habit. He asked me to go to a run-through for an off-Broadway company of *Father's Day* and I said I would. We laughed at how we always seem to choose what will not make money. He knew I had turned down, or to be more honest had not pursued, a chance to be in a TV Movie-of-the-Week to be shot in Hollywood during what turned out to be the penultimate month of *Equus* in New York. He thought it a wrong choice.

"You should get your ass out here!"

He thought I needed a TV name. I told him how much ·it meant to me to be in the play.

"I saw *Equus* at a preview here. How good your part is! The one sane voice in the play."

That made me happy. A good word for Hesther. He reported that Doris Cole Abrahams had expressed interest in his new play at the Mark Taper Forum for Broadway booking, but that he would have to recast it with stars. "Oh, Marian, why do I keep writing for the theatre if it's so full of pain?"

I answered that success — or being in a success — had meant more pain for me than all our times together. Even when he came to my hotel room in Providence and told me that Maureen Stapleton or Colleen Dewhurst would know how to play the part he had written for me.

"But I can say *anything* to you, Marian."

Yes. That was true. He helped me to give the performance his play demanded.

"I did not try to destroy you." No. He said he would send me the California reviews. Oliver had not wanted me to do *Equus* in the first place. The rehearsals conflicted with the schedule of a television version of *For the Use of the Hall.* He chastised me for choosing to do an English play. Now we made peace again. I told him I was writing about my experiences in a book.

"That's a marvelous idea. You can't write about a failure. People think it's sour grapes, but now you can say everything you want and it will be of help to us."

When Kermit Bloomgarden produced *The Wall* — Millard Lampell's dramatization of John Hersey's novel — in 1961, I started out in one part and changed to another during the run. Kermit was in charge of everything in those days, made all the decisions. No producer is always popular, but it was a touchier situation for Kermit with *Equus* because his health was failing and because the director had announced to the cast at the first rehearsal that he was against *all* management and rehearsals would stop the moment either of the producers walked into the theatre. An awkward moment.

He was at the theatre all the time as we struggled to keep *The Wall* running for its 176 performances. The company was fond of him and proud to be in the play.

226   I feel close to Kermit now. He calls me darling but it

means daughter. He knows how fond I am of his son, John, and what hopes I have for him as a new producer. But it has taken many years to achieve this closeness. I was one of hundreds of young actresses Jane Broder sent to Kermit for parts in his productions in the late 1940s. I read for him and Lillian Hellman for the revival of *The Children's Hour* with Patricia Neal, but it was not until there was a chance for me to be in *The Wall* that I began to feel at ease with him.

He let the directors and the stage managers control the auditions so that the actors were just aware of a figure sitting in the front of the house who greeted them with hello and said good-bye when they were dismissed. In his office he was direct and businesslike. *The Wall* was important to him. One of his proudest achievements had been the enthralling production of *The Diary of Anne Frank*. Now here was a chance to say something more about the incredible time in history so many of us had lived through in ignorance. My desire to be connected with the play made me freer at the reading. I returned Kermit's greeting and felt welcomed. I did not get the part I wanted most, Rachel, but the part I did get was a lovely one. I played Symka, the wife of Dolek Berson, played by George C. Scott. Later in the run when Yvonne Mitchell left the cast I replaced her as Rachel.

Having the chance to play two parts with George was fascinating. He is an unusually sensitive actor. You receive an entirely different set of vibrations from him the instant you bring him a new impulse, a look, a thought. What touched me most was his gentle worldliness, his humanity.

After I had played Rachel for a few performances he asked me to come to his room after the play. It was the same room in the same theatre where John Gielgud had offered me the part of Dounia. This time my face was black-

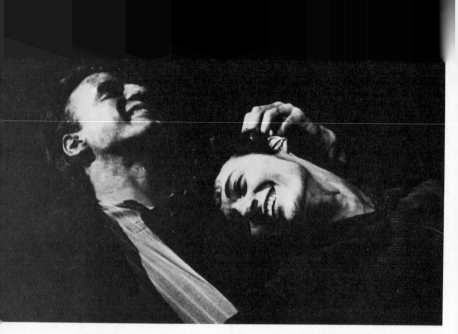

In the Warsaw Ghetto with George C. Scott. *The Wall,* Billy Rose Theatre, 1960.

ened again. The play ended in a bunker and my face was smudged with dirt from the artillery explosions. So was George's.

Dolek and Rachel have made love in that foul, cramped bunker, she for the first time in her life. The scene had been staged for George and Yvonne so that they were kneeling opposite each other and as they embraced the lights dimmed. George said, "What would you think if I just climbed on top of you?" It seemed the right thing to do in the circumstances. I smiled at him.

"Do you want to rehearse it or shall I just do it?"

"Let's —"

"Just do it then?"

I nodded.

At the evening performance as I reached forward to touch his face he half-rose, loomed over me, covered me and the next thing I knew the lights had come up for the next scene. We had moved together in the darkness and I was lying in his arms. We played the scene effortlessly and never spoke of the change in direction to each other or to anyone else.

I wanted to ask him a lot of questions about the rest of
The Wall but knew it would be wrong to do so. Even if I
had dared, there was no time. One evening George was no
longer a member of the company and his understudy finished our all-too-short run of that play. He disappeared into
his private hell of bars and lonely places. For several days no
one could find him. He never came back to our theatre but
his direction of the love scene remained in the play.

Now Kermit was much older and ill. One of his legs had
been amputated and during the first year of *Equus* he had
become increasingly frail. The large parties at his apartment
for the actors and members of all his productions ceased
and he did not come on matinee days to eat his corned beef
sandwich at the stage right prop table. His son, John,
started arriving on Saturdays and it was from him that we
learned Kermit was having chemotherapy. Howard Bay,
who designed *The Wall,* told me that Kermit had been asking his oldest friends to come and see him "to say good-
bye." Kermit's invaluable production assistant, Noel Gilmore, said Kermit would like a picture of me for his
study wall. I knew that room, and all the pictures in it, the
royalty of talent in the theatre. But the casual act of inscrib-
ing a photograph took on an eerie quality because I felt
Kermit would see it but I would not see him again.

Participating in the dramatization of *The Wall* defined
part of my life. While I was growing up in New York, going
to high school at Dalton, wanting to be an actress, the
events of this play were actually taking place. My knowledge of them was confined to the radio broadcasts my
parents listened to religiously every evening. I think of my

father as a teacher, but I know he did not teach me to relate reality to creative work. He expected that to happen in time. How many years before I understood what had happened to the Jews in Europe in a way that would allow me to share the guilt and the pain? Was it through the theatre I would grow toward some maturity? I think so. *The Wall* meant so much more than the opportunity to act. Because it did not succeed commercially we had to fight for its existence. Vera Stern, a woman of enormous public and private spirit, came to see it one evening when the closing notice was up and insisted to Millard Lampell it could have an audience if we were all willing to go out and find it. With Vera's guidance we did keep the play open. I met men and women who had escaped from concentration camps, whose families had died in them. I read many books, too many — it became an obsession. I resented the schoolgirl I had been without true knowledge of the event. I was grateful for the chance to be in a play that dealt with a modern tragedy in an uncompromising way.

16

When Richard Burton came into *Equus* for a twelve-week engagement he seemed as apprehensive as a young actor with his first important role. He looked ill the first few days of rehearsal and it was only through the discipline of the work that the colors of life came back to his face and his voice. Far beyond pleasing the public who wanted to love him was the task of proving to himself that he was the kind of actor he had dreamed he could be. He had his models — Olivier, Gielgud, Emlyn Williams — and referred to them often in humorous rueful anecdotes, the kind we tell when we hope the person we are talking about still knows we love and admire him.

Going to the theatre you are influenced in ways that are mysterious. In the same way you use life experiences in creating a part, you use theatre experiences in forming the kind of behavior you will use as a professonal actress. I have had extraordinary models. Perhaps that is why I often feel I have fallen so short of what I thought I could do. All they had done and more. But it is the nature of an actor to fight both ambition and a kind of love of failure all through his life.

Richard Burton is so famous that most of the stories he tells we have already heard or read. While he talks it is interesting to watch him. The private Richard? No, we do not see that except in the most intensely personal moments of his performance — which are breathtaking — otherwise he will be surrounded by friends, coworkers, hirelings. Carefully guarded, he cannot stop to share in the time-wasting pleasant give-and-take of a theatre company. He must do this play, plan his next two films — one of which will be *Equus* — and move on.

The people I saw outside the theatre wanted to know about his wife, Elizabeth Taylor. She came to see the play a few nights before Richard's official opening. It had to be planned as carefully as if she were a head of state because if she were seen in the audience before the lights dimmed the performance would be ruined. The audience would want to look at *her*. It was rehearsed where she would wait until a new cue for the lights to dim was put in, how she would get to her seat, surrounded by other people, how she would escape to Richard's dressing room between the acts and so on. It worked like a charm. And for the few moments she was with the actors she was incredibly generous and polite, and her beauty radiated in the darkness of the wings. That night was the only time Richard sat with us in the coffee room. I asked him if he were going to do the film of *Equus* and he said he was not sure, he had not read the shooting script. I felt that he would do it and wanted to do it but that the business advisers in his life were influencing his career choices now. I asked him about doing more plays and he told me that it was hard for him to run all his houses and pay all his bills if he worked in the theatre. I was sorry I asked. He was getting $10,000 a week for this engagement. It seemed to me that much money could pay for anything. It irritated me because I have had this same conversation with successful and rich actors before. They all need more money. They can't get it in the theatre. An exception was Marlon Brando. He told me in 1955 he did not want to make any more films, he wanted to be a chicken farmer.

When Richard started rehearsing there were items in the papers about a rift with Elizabeth. A few days before she came to New York, Richard and his friend Brook Williams went to the airport to meet Susan Hunt. She was a tall, fine-looking young Englishwoman. Brook told us she was his girl. They made a nice pair. She came to see the play. She had never seen Richard Burton on the stage before.

We read in the papers that she was Richard's girl.

Elizabeth Taylor did not come to the opening night. The "rehearsal" night was the only performance she saw. She left a lipstick scrawl on Richard's mirror: "You were fantastic love," which he never erased. Susan came to all the other performances and stayed in Richard's dressing room. It must have been a difficult time for both of them but they managed it smoothly. Sometimes Richard looked exhausted and drained of energy, but he did not miss a performance and the audiences adored him.

After his best performance (the night of the Actors' Fund benefit), I was invited to a party with him and Susan. The other guests were friends of Richard's from other companies, the closest being George Rose, who had played the Gravedigger with him in *Hamlet* eleven years before. Richard drank lots of wine and talked and talked. He told all the old stories again. He invoked his father and his stepfather. I   233 could see that Susan had heard them, too.

It was late. There was a big gray limousine waiting outside to take them home. We persuaded Richard to get in it at three o'clock in the morning. He was telling us about his father and his stepfather again and reciting bits of poetry. He kept apologizing for drinking so much wine. A young actress and George Rose got into the car. I stood on the street waiting for Susan. Richard came over to me and held me and said all the things you want to hear about yourself as an actress. It seemed to take too long. I was sure Susan was waiting but did not want to move away. Then it became important to. Richard had forgotten who I was or where we were and he tightened his embrace.

Silence.

"Richard?"

It was Susan's voice. I pulled away. We got into the car and we drove toward the Village, where the young actress lived. Richard and Susan were tense with each other. The car stopped and Richard got out to see the girl into the hallway of her building. The minutes went by. Too long. He did not return. George and I chatted frantically. Susan waited. She called, "Richard!" Finally George went to look for him. We rode in silence to George's house and he got out and said good-night. All evening Richard had been saying that George was the greater actor and should be playing star parts. George had been protesting that he was indeed a character actor and played just what he expected to. Several months later he won the Tony Award for the best performance in a musical as Alfred Doolittle in the revival of *My Fair Lady*. He is genuinely fond of Richard. But he was tired and distressed about the young girl. He made his good-byes brief. The limousine glided uptown. Susan scolded Richard for being rude to her. "I'm bored," he groaned. "I'm *bored.*" They got out at the Lombardy. The driver took me to where I live, a block away; he heard everything I heard. I remembered this when I read the entire story of the adventure with the young actress in a column someone showed me at the theatre three weeks later.

17

Holidays, birthdays, anniversaries, deaths and births were all recognized at the Plymouth by announcements on the callboard. At Christmas, presents were exchanged after the secret drawing of names from a hat. Later we figured out whose wit, or lack of it, was responsible for the gift received under the tree.

In August of both my *Equus* years Eric Harrison provided a birthday cake and extravagant presents, all in shades of lavender and purple — my favorite colors — purchased for me on his yearly vacation in England.

Each birthday I played Dora — first filling in for Frances, then as my own part. Not knowing it was a date of any special interest to me, John Dexter stood near me in the wings for a few moments.

"Would you like to be in *The Merchant*, Seldes? I won't be upset if you think the part is too small. Would you *mind* acting with Zero Mostel?"

It was time for the play to begin, no chance to answer. Brent gave me the cue to take my place on the stage. Two slow steps toward that place and a stinging slap on my behind! What? Birthday? Stage manager gone berserk? No, it was John Dexter.

How I loathed that moment at birthday parties — my own and other children's — when the child was slapped for the number of years he had lived, with one to grow on. I could not understand why the adults permitted the hated ritual. I had not thought of it in forty years. But dear John jolted my senses from past to present with a flick of his wrist.

After the performance John was warm and relaxed. There had been some difficulty talking with him about casting in the past. He once had a plan to take a company on tour with two plays, *Pygmalion* and *The Importance of Being Earnest,* and had offered me Mrs. Higgins and Miss Prism. I did not want to play either part enough to leave New York and my teaching. He implied that I was not much of an actress. I countered by explaining that I would have many years in the future to play those parts but I did not want to give up either Hesther or Dora in *Equus* for the parts in Shaw and Wilde. Part of the reason was that when I was in my twenties, I had played Eliza Doolittle and Gwendolyn Fairfax in summer stock. And when I thought about leaving *Equus,* it was to play a *new* part, in a *new* play. And in the meantime I was content.

John wasn't able to raise enough money to launch his touring company, but it is his plan to establish a company of actors in America.

I wondered what I could possibly play in Dexter's production of Arnold Wesker's version of *The Merchant of Venice.* The days of playing either Portia or Jessica were far behind me.

I read Arnold Wesker's *Merchant* in my dressing room   237 between performances. The coffee from Eric's greenroom was fresh and hot and he brought me some delicious food from home.

To have a copy of a play in script form and to read and see it for yourself is an important event for an actor. It forces you to rely on your own judgment and it gives you the pleasure of making your own discoveries. All the other Wesker plays I had read in English paperback editions or in *Plays and Players,* the only theatre magazine that fills the gap left by the demise of the glamorous *Stage* and the informative *Theatre Arts* of my childhood. Dexter had directed all of Wesker's plays in England at the Royal Court Theatre and Jocelyn Herbert had designed them. The team would be together for *The Merchant.*

The part John chose for me was an invention of Wesker's: a sister for Shylock, a small but a strong part and not like anything else I have played in New York. It would mean the chance to work with John on a play he had not staged before and I would be reunited with Roberta Maxwell, who was to play Portia.

On the opening night of *Equus* Roberta had given me a small book. On the flyleaf she wrote: "This has been the high point of my life." The inside pages were a calendar of days and each week was preceded by a quotation from a Shakespeare play. I jotted *Equus* notes on every page. One entry reads: "RM [Roberta] to see play for first time since leaving last year. Says 'I think actors and actresses must be gods and goddesses.'"

We had played together in *The Three Sisters,* in which Olga and Natasha have a brief, searing scene. In *Equus* we exchanged a look as she walked toward the imaginary shop where Alan worked. In *The Merchant* we would not exchange a word.

238

Roberta is disciplined, instinctive and gifted. Her performance in *Ashes* by David Rudkin was remarkable. Shaken by it, I decided to write her a note rather than visit backstage. The following morning at nine o'clock I had a part on the radio show "Mystery Theatre." Roberta was there before I was. Knowing her, having seen her and been devastated by her acting so short a time before, I had felt unable to express my praise. She won an Obie for her performance.

Brent arranged for me to have a mimeographed copy of *The Merchant*. He was going to stage-manage the play and Eric was to be wardrobe master. Everett McGill — who played the Horseman when *Equus* opened — would be Lorenzo. John Tyrell, who played one of the original horses, Trooper, would be with us, too. It would be a year before rehearsals began. Zero Mostel had to finish his engagement in the revival of *Fiddler on the Roof* and John had to plan the new season at the Metropolitan Opera, where he is artistic director.

On August 21, 1976, Richard Burton married Susan Hunt. It was reported on the front page of the *News* and the *Post* in New York and hidden away in the *Times*. A world event but a private one for us.

On this same afternoon Kermit drove down to the Plymouth in an air-conditioned limousine and parked near the stage door hoping to see Tony Perkins and Peter Shaffer, who was at the theatre to talk with Tony. As he came out of the stage door Kermit hailed him and Shaffer made a rude gesture and walked on. When Perkins came out Kermit called to him. Tony ignored him and walked away.

Inside the theatre a good house had applauded and bravoed the play the man in the car had produced.

Shortly after the play opened I was on an interview pro-   239 gram for cable TV with Peter Shaffer and Kermit. In answer to a question, I said it was necessary to expect certain kinds of humiliation as a worker in the theatre, that I knew most actors at one time or another have felt this. I turned to Kermit and asked him if he agreed.

"Humiliation? No, never. *Never.*"

Rumors that this successful, moneymaking play would close in several weeks were whispered backstage. No one seemed to know why *Equus* had lost its lease on the Plymouth and we were going to be given two weeks' notice.

More rumors: that we would close for some time and reopen at another theatre. The Lyceum, where we had our first rehearsals? The Ethel Barrymore, where I played in *The Chalk Garden* and *A Gift of Time?* The Martin Beck, which housed *That Lady* and *A Delicate Balance?* More theatres were mentioned. Too large, too small, not available. We were all experts. We knew nothing.

In two weeks I would leave the dressing room where I had stayed for nearly two years. I took home my books and possessions on Saturday night so that on closing night the leaving would be simple. "Last Weeks," the ads kept reminding me. One day when I arrived for the matinee I heard Hesther's words being rehearsed by a new Hesther for the touring *Equus*. Friends asked, "What next?" I planned to return to Juilliard in the fall as usual, but that was not the answer theatre people want or expect. "Another play" was the only healthy reply. In the last three days I had been told about *The Merchant,* that the Bloomgarden office wanted to talk to me about their next production, *Poor Murderer* by Pavel Kohout, and John Guare had asked me not to sign for anything until I had talked to him about his new play. And I had had a television inquiry. Oliver Hailey wrote me a post card asking when the play would close. Could I come out to California now and *act*? He meant in *Mary Hartman, Mary Hartman,* on which he was now the script consultant. Frances Sternhagen's agent called to say that if I would do commercials he could get me a "mountain of money." I did not want that. I wanted a wonderful part in a wonderful play.

On Monday, August 9, I heard my name called. Max Allentuck was looking for me. I met him in the corridor under the stage and joked, "Are you going to give me my notice?"

Instead of smiling his eyes filled with tears.

"Marian, this is a tragedy. This play shouldn't close."

I tried to reassure him. I believed we would survive.

Backstage I had a cup of coffee with Billy McDonough. He was our sound man for *Equus* and had been with us since the beginning. He and I were the only original members of the company left. Billy's vacations or short leaves to do other jobs were infrequent but I felt them. His wife was a Rockette. He had told me about the strike at Radio City and the possibility of that enormous important theatre shutting down. We remembered the weeks of the musicians' strike that closed the theatres in September 1975. Broadway — the theatre district — was hurt terribly by those weeks of dark marquees and empty auditoriums. Some shows never recovered. Even though *Equus* had a few minutes of music on tape, composed by Cy Coleman, we had been allowed to remain open. Billy told me that he had known for three days that it was a sure plan we would move. He had to order the equipment. But as yet there was no formal announcement. The other actors asked me if I knew anything. I told them what Max had said and Billy's statement. I longed for Doris or Max to call the company 241 together and tell us as a group. If Kermit were strong enough that was what he would have done. Perhaps not; gossip said he was against the move.

Tony was as much in the dark as the rest of us. What would shape our lives for the next few days? Weeks? Months?

We needed information, facts.

In the days after we got our notice the feeling in the company changed. As so often happens, the management had become the enemy. The fact that Doris had to be introduced to several members of the company the night she told us of the closing made us embarrassed for her. It was felt that the loss of the Plymouth while we were still showing a profit was inexcusable. But the excuses were to go on long after we had closed.

Max said, "There is still a gleam of hope."

On Saturday, August 14, as we were leaving we read on the callboard a note from Brent saying that there had been difficulty in locating a theatre. Near it was a note from the management saying that "closing weeks" would be announced soon so if we had house seat orders please submit them at once. Our ray of hope was dimmed.

A message on the loudspeaker asked the cast to assemble after the play. Doris Cole Abrahams and Max Allentuck — he had been Kermit's general manager for as long as I could remember — stood before us and said there was a *possibility* we could reopen at the Helen Hayes Theatre with the same cast if we were all willing. Except for one actor who had a previous commitment, we were all free to continue. Max said we should discuss it. But we were impatient, we

242   wanted to say yes as a company and for the manage-

ment to hear it. Tony was sitting in a corner where costumes were hanging, his face hidden. Someone said how much it meant that *he* would continue. We all knew that without a star the move would not be made. We barely saw his smile of pleasure as he acknowledged our appreciation of his value. Doris added, "Tony has been wonderful." Did either of them remember, even for a moment, those sad days when he was asked to step out of the play? I admired his self-control and his knowledge that it was useless to look for logic or fairness in our profession. We have to find our logic and reason in the plays and the playing and be strong enough to outlive the pettiness and unpredictability of the marketplace areas of our careers. Tony had a brush-up session with Dexter and went back to work as Dr. Dysart.

Gossip Along the Rialto: Peter Shaffer was upset about the play closing in New York when it was making a profit; he was going to sue Kermit Bloomgarden. We also heard that Kermit's health had deteriorated to the point where he could not be expected to live more than a few weeks. We no longer saw John, who used to brighten our Saturdays. Was that because his father was so ill, because he had to manage the business now? Would he take it over?

After months of not seeing — and missing — Peter Shaffer, months of rumors about his feeling about the play ("He can't look at it. The performance isn't what it should be"), about his reaction to a possible move ("Shaffer won't take a cut in royalties so the move will be exorbitant"), about his work on the film ("It's taking up all his time"), suddenly on the stairway there he was. It was our last Wednesday evening at the Plymouth. He watched the first act and accompanied by two friends went to see Tony Perkins. They were about to go into the dressing room when the woman recognized me. It was my Dalton classmate Helen Frankenthaler. Her eyes were wet; she was smiling and frowning simultaneously. This was the first time she had seen *Equus* and instead of talking about it we just embraced and laughed at the good fortune that had brought us together. We were chattering like schoolgirls but it was time for her to go in and see Tony. Her escort was an English friend of Peter's, the art critic John Russell. A few minutes later we were on our way to Sardi's for supper. Peter, the host, looked rested and young after a short visit to Nantucket. That is where he had met Helen a year before. New friends. And John? They had gone to school together in England. Four school chums then, drinking white wine, eating salmon, all talking together and having a lovely time.

I told Peter what a relief it was to see him. The rumors were disquieting. He was aware of it all and felt that he must appear to be an ogre. He was trying to get the play moved. Several lawyers were now mixed up in the transaction and it had become extremely complex. I told him of the simple sweet meeting of the actors where we raised our hands and said we would go on.

"At Equity?" he asked.

"No, at the theatre. We were still in our costumes after a performance —" Peter tried to explain some of the confusion about our closing to Helen and John. It sounded childish to them. They kept asking "Why?" Peter had no answers either.

The final matinee was exciting. Friends of mine who had not seen the play since Burton's first performance watched from stage seats. They felt that in general the performance was fine and were amazed by the size (sold out) and reaction (bravos, standing, and applauding) of the audience, so many of whom were young. They felt they were watching a healthy play and it was hard to convince them that in three days this company would close.

The following evening I got to the theatre earlier than usual. It had been raining and the city was cool and clean. The lobby was empty except for Max Allentuck, who needed to talk. He was utterly spent, having dealt all day with the lawyers Peter mentioned. He was concerned about getting the actors their new contracts before we closed and the Labor Day weekend began. I said I needed no piece of paper to insure my connection with the play and thought the others would feel the same. Saturday was his wife's birthday. He wanted to be in East Hampton with her. I thought of that long hot trip on the train. If only he could leave in the cool of the evening and his problems could be taken away for a weekend. He kept repeating the dilemma of the contracts. He did not hear what I said. Why should he? It was foolish. The contracts must be made up and signed. That is the way business is done.

The last Saturday at the Plymouth was the first Saturday in September. The streets were empty, but the theatre was crowded at the matinee and sold out with standees at the evening performance. We were told that Peter and John and Doris were there, but no one in the company saw them before or after the performance. It was not as different from another Saturday as it might have been. By now half the company had contracts for the Helen Hayes reopening. More would have been signed, but Max ran out of contract forms and Equity was closed for the Labor Day holiday. Our good-nights were quite casual. Berry Perkins had given Tony a turquoise and silver belt buckle of the *Equus* logo 245 and he displayed it happily as we said good-bye. Our costumes would go to the cleaners and be delivered to the Helen Hayes.

Our company had played 787 performances at the Plymouth. Fourteen were previews. Two were benefits for the Actors' Fund of America. From the moment we knew about the move to the Hayes the question of how long we would run *there* was asked. The doom-eager predicted a short stay based on previous resurrections of plays. The optimists said Christmas, at the least.

As I cut through the park between the new skyscrapers at Forty-fifth Street near Sixth Avenue I saw the white horse that had been painted on the wall of a remaining old building. Under it the letters: YANKEE THE HORSE FROM 46TH STREET. Yankee was heading toward the Helen Hayes. The year-old graffiti was still legible:

> *With my feet on the street*
> *I'll go the distance to my dream*
> *Look out for them cracks in the sidewalk,*
> *kiddo!*

I said it over on the walk home and thought of Peter's last words to me. His new descriptive word for me was "runic," but this was more mysterious than I could invent; in the lobby as we said good-bye he had given me a gentle look and said, "Mine is another voyage."

There was a story in the New York *Post* about John and Kermit Bloomgarden on September 7, 1976, with a photograph taken almost two years before on the *Equus* set. John
246 was being questioned about his upcoming production of

Poor Murderer and said that there was still strength in *Equus*. Under the interview was a news item headed . . . AND SPEAKING OF EQUUS," which contained the first news of our definite reopening at the Helen Hayes Theatre. The following day there was an article in *Variety* reporting that after our 777 performances (they did not count previews or benefits), *Equus* would end its run on September 11 at the Plymouth and that we "might" reopen at the Hayes. There followed the most logical explanation for our recent history:

When Richard Burton took over the starring role last spring it appeared likely that the stimulated attendance would drop below the breaking level after his limited appearance ended. So the producers booked road dates in cities the regular touring edition had not played. Firm contracts were signed.

With Anthony Perkins returning, however, business declined only moderately, and the show has continued to earn a substantial operating profit. Receipts have consistently topped $70,000 a week over the normally slow summer period, so *Equus* remains a prospect to run indefinitely on Broadway . . .

The Bible of show business told us what we longed to hear.

A new set was constructed, new masks produced, the company reassembled and we were at home in our new theatre.

October, November, December. My last three months in *Equus*.

Wynn Handman scheduled rehearsals at his American Place Theatre for a workshop production of *Isadora Duncan Sleeps with the Russian Navy* by Jeff Wanschel around my teaching and performing schedules. For nearly three weeks we rehearsed a few hours each day. We gave three 247 performances after the *Equus* curtain fell and two on my free day. Wynn decided to put it on for a limited run in February and it was arranged for me to play my last performance of *Equus* on January 2 and start rerehearsing *Isadora* on January 4.

Eric knew that I would leave to play *Isadora* and I told Max and Brent, but I asked them not to tell the other actors until the beginning of December.

Between performances on Wednesdays and Saturdays Tony saved his voice and did not speak. At dinner if he was with someone he would write on a pad, then return to his dressing room and rest. I knocked on his door several times just before the half-hour call. I heard a whistle. I went in. He was sitting on his couch looking alert and calm. "Tony, I promised you I'd tell you if I was going to leave the play —" His eyes widened. He whistled. "And now I know that in a month I'll leave to do *Isadora* and I wanted to —" Another understanding whistle. I looked at him. He whistled. There were to be no words. A loving look, another whistle, a hug and I went across the theatre to my dressing room. I didn't hear his voice until he spoke the first lines of the play.

I left *Equus* to play the part of Isadora. A month later I was a member of the audience watching Alec McCowen play Dysart.

Here was the chance to see the actor who created the part — and with whom I had expected to work when I first knew I had the part of Hesther.

The completely familiar words sounded fresh. The movement of the character in the enclosed stage space had the quality of a brilliant prisoner — caged, aware of his prison, but no longer fighting to get free until the final moments of the play when McCowen's passion broke down the "walls" of the theatre, the play, the time and place we were sharing. He transformed the end of the play into a personal desperate cry of pain and triumph. I was stunned. Before I could pull myself out of the play and go backstage to thank him I sat still for a long time. I thought of Walter Pater's description: "Life consists in action, plays are imitations of those actions, and when they are fine plays they contain what Aristotle called 'the element of the wonderful — and the irrational, on which the wonderful depends.' "

18

It was in my father's study at Strawberry Hill that I discovered *My Life* by Isadora Duncan and read it continuously during the summer months of 1942. It repelled and fascinated me. I knew little about other dancers' or actresses' lives then and was appalled by the rejection and hardship that plagued Isadora. I could not understand how she could love so many different men. At twelve I believed that each woman and each man who found each other remained faithful always. Her passages about childbirth decided me never to have children. But the mythic beauty of her artistic life appealed to me in a secret and exciting way. The blue-green binding of *My Life* is faded now, the dust jacket has been folded inside the book with Dorothy Parker's review and a carbon copy of a note to my father from Uncle George saying that although he did indeed go to Isadora with an offer from the Chicago *Tribune* to print her memoirs in the paper for $5000, the *Tribune* had nothing to do with the "blackmail" she mentions in her letters to Irma Duncan when she had refused to continue dictating her experiences.

My father talked about her. So did the pianist

George Copeland, who used to accompany her in her New York recitals. I loved to listen to him reminisce and play the piano and reminisce again. I collected pictures and articles about Isadora and added to the dream-plan of my life that I would act in a play about her.

We feel that we have known and talked with the great characters in fiction. They become part of our lives and we discuss them with the people we care about. It is the same with the extraordinary artists of the theatre. When I was growing up I heard the names of Caruso, Pavlova, Duse, Isadora Duncan. My father had literally carried a spear on the stage with Sarah Bernhardt when he was at Harvard. One of his first jobs was as music critic on the Philadelphia *Evening Ledger*. He had seen and written about most of the wonderful characters that were part of his daily conversation. Dos and Scott and Zelda and Bunny and Cummings and Marianne were familiar sounds. Because he was an editor of the *Dial* magazine he had met James Joyce and Pablo Picasso. My opening night presents to the actors who played Dysart were reprints of a silver point etching Picasso gave my father as a wedding present: a centaur ravishing a woman — Nessus and Dejanira; a copy of it hangs in my room as I write. The original probably haunts my brother's children as it haunted me when I was young.

Isadora — known everywhere and forever by that one name — combines the living passion of a more than real, larger than dreamed-of life and the fascination of a being created not by parents but by an artist. It was almost as if she had created herself, made up her life as she went along, carelessly, dramatically, thrillingly. A too-short life filled with pain and delight.

When I met Wynn Handman on a rainy evening on Sixth Avenue as he was leaving rehearsal and I was running to

As Isadora Duncan at the American Place Theatre, 1977.

play *Equus* he told me that he was planning to do a play about Isadora. "I'll do it," I said as I hurried away.

I hoped it would be a serious play, an important play. But I took the chance that it would be fascinating just because of its subject. By serious and important I mean a play that shows the audience a full life, so that they remember the characters as complete and complex human beings. Actors want to play the great roles because they know that having fulfilled what Shakespeare or Chekhov or Shaw wrote they will have brought a whole being into existence. More often the actor and the audience are allowed only a glimpse of another life.

That turned out to be the case with Jeff Wanschel's play. Isadora was glimpsed through the eyes of the other characters. He chose a frame for his play of a writer and a producer quarreling about a film based on her life. Luckily, most of Isadora's words were taken from her writings and many of her dances were included in the search for her elusive spirit. Part of her existed for a short while as the play ran its course and all of her lived in me for those few weeks.

Isadora wanted the world to be free and to express that freedom in beautiful movement. Before her ghastly accidental death at forty-eight, most of her ambition and beauty were gone.

When Uncle George saw her in her studio in Nice in 1927, he said she took the cover off the piano, draped it around her and "except for that awful fat and gin-bloated face began dancing like her 1910 self . . . She was still a great artist." But his most vivid memory of her was three years earlier in Berlin. He said he never wrote about it because it seemed too cruel but thought it might someday be part of a play. While I was rereading everything I could find about her in 1976 George reminded me of the incident:

In 1924 at the time Isadora was at the Central Hotel near the Friedrichstrasse Bahnhof in Berlin, deserted by everyone, a German musical comedy company imported a show called *Little Jesse James*. There were the usual American chorus girls of that time, blondes, beautiful in the magazine cover sense, and available. One of the leading journalists of the time, Lincoln Eyre of the *World*, 'dated' them all.

"Someone — probably a rich German or American with a magnificent apartment in Berlin — threw a big party for Isadora Duncan, inviting everyone who knew her, and the press, and the six little Jesse James girls.

"By the time we arrived Isadora had had too much as usual, and was stretched out on a couch. We tried to cheer her up, the six American chorus girls who knew nothing of classical dancing or of ballet joining in a dance — an American musical comedy dance — around the couch where the half-drunken Isadora lay with glazed eyes — each kicking   253 up her legs and singing a chorus from their last American show . . ."

In *Isadora Duncan Sleeps with the Russian Navy*, Jeff Wanschel wrote a scene at a party where Isadora flirts with other men and enrages her husband, Paris Singer. In her stupor she falls to the floor and the others leave in embarrassment. Dorothy Parker said that Isadora's glamour came from "her great, torn, bewildered, foolhardy soul." We see glimpses of that sort of glamour still in the celebrated people in the public eye today. But it is harder to find the greatness.

After a long rehearsal the ageless, aging, beautiful Martha Graham, exquisitely costumed, coifed and made up, came into a room crowded with friends celebrating a birthday. It was December 1977.

In her light, querulous voice she mourned the lack of wonder in the theatre today, marveled at the ever-surprising experience of her own creativity and spellbound me with her descriptions of Sarah Bernhardt and Eleanora Duse.

Martha's eyes move — rove — then focus. She sees herself watching Sarah, who having survived the amputation of her leg was lying against a prop tree and dressed in her *L'Aiglon* costume reciting the great speech on the battlefield of Wagram.

"Her voice was — golden." I thought of my father, who had no desire at all to be on the stage, standing on that stage in Boston in 1916, hearing that voice. I showed Martha how Robert Edmond Jones acted Sarah's *Phèdre* for me. I dared to be as free as he had been. Martha beamed her smile. "And Duse? Did he see Duse?"

"He talked about her hands . . ."

"When I was in the Follies, not the Ziegfeld Follies! — John Murray Anderson's — I went to see Duse. I went by myself. It was the play where she pleads for the life of her child . . . and the child grows up to be a *monster*. Duse was sitting in a chair, listening to a report of her son's wickedness and — I can never forget what she did." Martha was silent. She placed one hand at her throat, was still for a long moment, then slowly dropped her hand into her lap. Acceptance, grief, understanding. Another moment, she repeated the gesture.

It is possible to sit with Martha and not talk. She is interested in almost any subject, but I have found that to wait for her to speak is to be rewarded.

"I did not know what was going to happen at the studio today. I had an idea, worked on the idea — and then — as always — the idea overtook me. I found myself doing, being forced to do, things that surprised and astonished me."

I remembered standing before her as a student, and later at rehearsals of *Mendicants of Evening,* and *seeing* the idea take possession of her.

In her class we learned much more than the physical vocabulary of modern dance, of Graham technique. They were master classes in acting. She asked us to memorize speeches from classic plays and would use the words as music. Speaking songs. The men invented extraordinarily original things with the Queen Mab speech. In pairs we played out the first meeting of Romeo and Juliet, no two alike, each pair learning to love the talent of the others. The Greek plays we prepared for her scrutiny became as immediate and real as the modern texts we were using in our acting classes. Martha was to us, as she has been to thousands of students, a guide and an inspiration. The class was to some extent afraid of her, too. Not only of her temper (which I never saw), but of her greatness, which was simply *there*. What impressed me most about studying with her was her gentleness and her utter concentration on the work to be done. She was as articulate in speech as in movement.

After a class she sent for me. I went to the tiny dressing room she used to change into her stylish street clothes.

"Sit down, Marian. I have something to say to you." She took my hand. I thought of all the things I had done awkwardly in class. I hated myself for misusing the precious hour. Before I could apologize she said, "*You* are the only person who can destroy your talent." And sent me away.

I kept getting angrier and stupider in Martha's class that day because I would not take a moment to examine what was wrong. I have seen myself — and others — go through hours of rehearsal simply compounding the tension and rage they feel and wasting the time of everyone else because of a mood, a whim. It is easier to recognize than to deal with, but it is lucky if you diagnose this illness early and learn its symptoms because when it is recurrent, habitual, it is fatal to a career.

All actors have that weakness. Of recognizing the sense of failure and in some way welcoming it and holding on to it. It is unprofessional to indulge those feelings, but tempting. Surely someone will come and rescue us and tell us we really are good and talented.

No one will come. We have our bad days, and we have to pay for them. What is difficult to realize is that the director or producer may be going through some sort of crisis and that is why the whole feeling of the rehearsal is strained. Actors tend to believe the director is father and friend and God. We put off as long as we can the recognition of his humanity.

In a few moments Martha returned to her original theme — the loss of what is special and astonishing on our stages. I did not want to tell her what she already knew.

That she had represented just such glories to me from the first dance concert I had seen her give. At sixteen, the male-female relationships in Martha's work astonished me. The sexuality of her dancers, and more particularly of her choreography, was more explicit than anything the later decades permitted theatre and film audiences to view. The myths, tragedies, comedies, of Martha's theatre were not ahead of their time but like their creator, timeless.

Martha — delicate and strong — endures. I have seen her during some of the most difficult stages of her life and career. She did not let the fates defeat her as Isadore did. Martha's glamour is armored with character and disciplined will.

My neighbor on the eighth floor asked me what I was doing. "I'm working on a program by Paul Shyre of Janet Flanner's *Paris Journals.*" He was interested and I could tell he thought it an odd switch from Isadora Duncan, whom he had seen me play a few months before.

"When you played Isadora, you were Isadora!"

"Oh, thank you."

"I mean *here,* in the building, coming in and out of the elevator."

He was right, I suppose. I had felt freer then, dressed more casually, had more confidence about daily living. Would working on Janet Flanner's precise and brilliant reportage change me, too?

It gave me another kind of pleasure, not the delicious freedom of Isadora's world but the precisely observed world that Janet Flanner knew and wrote about in the *New Yorker* from 1925 to 1939. Janet dedicated *Paris Journals* to her editor, William Shawn. What a joy it must have been for him to edit Flanner. From the way Janet talks you know the real editor is there inside her brain. What we hear and read is the essence of her perceptions.

While we were working on the script the fiftieth anniversary of Lindbergh's flight was celebrated, an article about one of Colette's novels was in the Sunday *Times,* and a program of Isadora's dances was being rehearsed at the Riverside Church. It did not seem like the past when I rehearsed in front of Janet. The life she described became part of my life.

What drew Paul Shyre to Janet's work for the stage was her wit. All he asked me for when he directed the reading was to include Janet's laughter. Once during the performance I heard Janet laugh when no one else did. I promised Paul that if we ever went ahead with the project I would "get" Janet's laugh for him.

19

The process of self-examination started again. It was time to face the negotiations for the contract for *The Merchant*. The management must attempt to prove that they were doing me a favor to have me in the play, that it would be fair to both parties if I started my work in this new play at the precise salary I took at the start of *Equus*. My part in *The Merchant* was a much smaller one than Hesther and the production was "heavier." All costs — cast, sets, costumes, running the play — were much higher.

I talked with my agent, Lionel Larner, and we agreed the *Equus* starting salary was never fair for any of the supporting actors. Each of us suggested another figure. Mine was fair. His was outrageous. His job was to get me the best "deal" possible. I would not have paid myself the salary he asked for. But he had to do that in order for the management to meet the figure I had chosen. They did.

The reason was that John Dexter had "seen" me in the part for many months and he was willing to stand behind his early decision. I felt that this was so, and if it wasn't, I was willing to take the consequences. What I would miss by not being in the play had nothing to do with money. I would miss being part of a collaboration — author Wesker and director Dexter — that was responsible for exciting and important theatre, and I would miss the chance to work with a nonesuch: Zero Mostel.

Yes, it crossed my mind that it might be a difficult time for me. The fact that the part was not a major one might make me restless. But that was something I would have to deal with. If my philosophy was that an actor should work at acting, it would be wrong to avoid this opportunity because I felt there was not enough for me to do. The child that stays alive in every actor's heart made me feel that not only would this be a fascinating time but that it might lead to another part that would make more demands on me.

And if my relationship with John were not a happy one on this play? I had learned from my life in the theatre and from the *Equus* experience in particular that my "happiness" was not what is important in a theatrical venture. The wholeness of the experience, the relationships with all the others connected with it, were what mattered. What remains. The difficult times in *Equus* have left no bitterness at all. They were like the lessons I struggled with in school before I mastered them.

During the early rehearsals of *The Merchant* Arnold Wesker asked me to write a piece for an English magazine about working with him in the play. My notebook was already full of discoveries, the work was exciting and there was much to tell.

I thought that the most interesting personality for the article would be Zero, but the playwright and the director consumed my attention. To be in the theatre with Zero was 260 fun. He had the compulsion to play games, tell jokes like a schoolboy. It was necessary to be in a receptive mood for his high jinks and most of us were most of the time. His good friend Sam Levene was playing Tubal and was a dour sidekick for him. Howard Rodney, his dresser, was constantly near him, ready to do any errand and to be the butt of all his jokes.

At the first reading it was clear that the jokes were simply time-fillers. Zero had studied his lines and was prepared to draw on his own life's learning for the complicated part Arnold had written. Zero loved Jewish history, his family, painting and architecture. He responded to the scholar in Wesker's Shylock as strongly as the humor. He was as serious about the part as his costar, the distinguished Sir John Clements, who had the title role.

The play was long; the early run-throughs took three hours. John told us that there would be drastic cuts but that

With Zero Mostel on the first day of rehearsing *The Merchant,* New York, 1977.

we would not take them until the play was ready. Surgery too early would destroy Arnold's structure.

"Shape the phrasing, like music. To quote my late employer" — Olivier at the National Theatre of Great Britain — "audiences don't *listen* anymore, they have been spoiled by television and stereophonic sound. You have to make them listen. Find Arnold Wesker's rhythms. They are *his,* not Shakespeare's."

Several of the actors read sonnets before rehearsals. Zero made outrageous comments about them. Sir John critiqued them. There was a good deal of joshing about American versus British acting, but underneath it Zero was firm in his belief that sound and speech were secondary to true acting impulses.

Dexter told the company to go to the Metropolitan Museum and look at the Titians. "Find yourself there; choose something from a painting that you can use in the play. Remember the broadness of the clothes when you move."

A model of the elaborate set and the luxurious costume designs were available to us at all times. Once again John was working in a controlled space; our moves were specific but we were given the freedom to adapt and change them within the limits of the other actors' needs and the boundaries of the white tapes that marked the stage floor.

The weeks in New York included private times with Arnold discussing our parts, costume fittings, a dinner party in a restaurant that Zero gave the company and a party in the Village that Arnold's wife, Dusty, arranged for us. In the restaurant we overate. All but Zero. Our host drank seltzer. He had lost fifty pounds on a special liquid protein diet and he did not cheat.

As rehearsals progressed John's notes urged us to control and drive the play. "You have an opportunity with *The*

Merchant to open the doors for other American actors. There is no reason that you cannot do classic theatre in this country. You can clear the way for others if you do this play properly. Remember the sounds are of 1563, not 1977." Then John stressed his major theme: "I know the story; tell me the ideas."

John's face became alive with his passion for perfection. "Oh, love the words, for Christ's sake, love them! This is a play of ideas and words. In the last twenty years we have had the theatre of behavior — your Tennessee Williams is an exception, a poet, yes — in this play there is such variety! They are all articulate, brilliant people. They know what they want to say. Think fast, not while you are speaking. It would be wonderful to do *The Merchant of Venice* with this company, too. You'd all do it better because of your work on this play."

I found a copy of the variorum and reveled in the many interpretations of the play through the years. If John were to do *The Merchant of Venice* there would be no part for me. But I do have a memory of doing the play.

The eighth grade always did Shakespeare in what was called the Green Room on the seventh floor at Dalton. It was directed by an exquisite papery Englishwoman, Dora Mabel Downes. She taught us the play and directed it with the same dryness and wit she taught her classes in composition and grammar. She had been Tim's teacher, too, and loved him.

I hoped to play Portia but the obvious choice for that part was beautiful Allegra Fuller. I played Shylock. My mother and father came to see the single performance given at midday in the Green Room.

My father's single comment: "Don't be a flycatcher."

I did not know precisely what he meant but I was sure it   263 was not a good review. The reactions, the minute details of my work in the trial scene — could they have been distracting? Yes, An important lesson.

In four days we would be on our way to Philadelphia. There was to be a run-through for the producers — members of the Shubert organization. The only other guest would be Zero's wife, Kate. It was at this particular rehearsal that we saw what Zero was going to do with the part. It had a kind of innocence and thrilling inventiveness that completely justified the risk of casting such an eccentric actor in a classically oriented play.

The next two days of rehearsal were spent with Arnold as John worked on the technical problems at the Forrest Theatre. We sat comfortably and ran the scenes, asked questions. Zero was impatient, Sir John indulgent. We were anxious to add costumes, make-up, and most important of all an audience to our work. John had cautioned us: "There is no reality in this play — only *truth*. Do not confuse them. The set isn't real, you are not 'real' people. You are actors playing parts."

At lunch in Sardi's with Arnold we talked about the article. "Shall I write it before we come into New York? Must it include the opening night reaction?"

"It's up to you. How do you feel about it?"

"I'd rather deal with my feeling about the play before the critics do. By the time the magazine is printed anyone interested in the first night reaction will have heard about it." Was I trying to avoid the problem of dealing with possible failure? The play as a piece of writing existed as an entity. How well we produced it would be written about at length by others. I wanted to confine myself to the work. The work

Arnold did on the script, what the actors brought to it, and John's concepts as a director.

A handsome couple came into the restaurant. I had my Sardi's vision problem. I knew I recognized them . . . and yet.

It was Richard and Susan Burton.

His work in the film of *Equus* completed, he was flirting with the idea of doing another play. Shakespeare. With John Dexter directing. I hoped he would.

This was the first time I had seen Richard socially since the party he gave the *Equus* company the night he played his final performance. He was completely at ease, his manners delightful, and the personality that makes him a star was there. Softened, not dulled, by proximity. Susan was glowing. They wished me luck with *The Merchant*.

Wesker's reason for writing the play was the feeling that Shylock would cry out "Thank God!" when he was released from the bond, that he would abhor the reality of gaining his pound of flesh. The play tells the story of the Merchant and Shylock from Shylock's point of view. Their friendship is the basis for the bond, not their enmity.

Zero in rehearsal: He always wore a hat, a dark blue beret with a toy bird pinned askew on one side. His trousers were too large for him. He asked Eric Harrison to have his street clothes taken in at the same time his Shylock costumes were being made.

He moved lightly, with agility. The ghastly accident that crippled him when he was hit by a bus in 1960 did not seem to have affected his mobility. Occasionally he would rest one leg on a stool or chair.

He watched every scene. Made suggestions, laughed, did imitations in the wings. Younger actors sat exhausted, read newspapers, drank coffee. Zero observed.

At the Minskoff studios where our rehearsals started he showed me his dressing room. "Come in. Sit down." He opened a celery tonic, offered me one, put the twist-cap on his nose and kept it stuck there as he regaled me with double-entendre jokes. When the five-minute break was over I went back to work. Strolling into the rehearsal he queried, "Do you fool around?"

In a scene that was eventually cut, Zero had to rage against the complacency of a young Venetian. In rehearsal he grabbed a goblet and threw it on the floor. Tiny shards of broken glass bounced into the air near our faces. John warned him not to do it as there was no way to clean the stage between scenes in performance. At the next re-hearsal Zero, carried away, broke the glass again. The scene took possession of him.

He worked on his part obsessively; watchful, wary, guarding his acting moments as an animal guards its young.

Other actors had warned me that he would be selfish. In the scene we shared he was outrageously generous. In ac-tors' language, he "gave" me the scene. He encouraged and praised me. Zero the actor was the Zero I wanted to be with.

It was evident that Zero wanted the cuts put into the play before we left for Philadelphia. I had heard so much about how powerful he was that it surprised me his demands were not met.

Yet John deferred to Zero, Sam Levene and Sir John Clements. He was polite, thoughtful and supportive of them. He made occasional witticisms at the expense of some of the younger actors but was never heartless or cruel. They were impatient to rehearse, to act, to receive his direction. Zero accepted most of John's notes instantaneously and incorporated them into his part. The notes he did not agree with he seldom questioned. He simply ignored them. There was no friction.

Knowing Zero meant responding to his outrageous, meaningless flirtations. At the Russian Tea Room, on the street, backstage in his dressing room. "An overgrown schoolboy," Wesker's Shylock called himself, and a man in love with learning. Zero loved to teach. I was longing to share more serious times with him and felt sure I would when we were in Philadelphia.

He had a gift for odd phrases. He called John "the Rocky Mountain goat of directors." His dialogue with Sam Levene was scatological.

A limousine took him everywhere. In Philadelphia, on September 2, after what my notes remind me was "an amazingly smooth first preview after a grueling afternoon full of mistakes," Zero called to Julie Garfield and me to get in the car and took us back to the hotel. Julie and I were going to have coffee and discuss her feelings about playing Jessica. "Bring me some seltzer —" I thought he was joking. Howard Rodney kept seltzer, celery tonic, available for him everywhere. I was surprised there was none in the car.

At one in the morning on September 3 an unfamiliar voice on the hotel telephone:

"Where is my seltzer?"

"Zero?"

"What are you doing?"

I was half-asleep. We had a matinee the next day and a   267 note session before then. My bones were aching. "I've gone to bed."

"Why don't you come up here?"

"Oh, no, Zero —"

"I'm in twenty-one nineteen —"

"Zero, it's too late."

"Ah . . . just for a little while."

I got out of it. He hung up. Had I been rude? Was he lonely? Was he going to call Julie, too? I could not believe he wanted to see me. He wanted — an audience.

The Merchant ran well over three hours during its first and only preview in Philadelphia. It was nearly that long at our final rehearsal in New York. A few cuts were made and Arnold was sure that a half hour would be gone from the play. He expected the actors to pick up the pace. They did, but at our next rehearsal only ten minutes were gone.

In a long, serious script like *The Merchant*, ideas, concepts, ideologies, are discussed. Themes echo, reappear. Arguments are begun, dropped, and begun again. To tear apart that design and rearrange it while preserving the original shape and motivation of the play was the task before author and director. John told the company, "Actors are wonderful at suggesting cuts — for *other* actors' parts." He asked them to accept any cuts without comment. "Later on, if you can think of a better cut, we will listen and consider a substitution." Sam Levene could not refrain from grumbling when his longest speech was cut from the trial scene. "I might as well phone it in." John did not react to the remark.

The first preview had to be treated like a rehearsal with an audience. We were all drained of energy at the brief note session on the following day. We sat in a circle below the stage of the Forrest, sweltering in the September heat. Zero had his wig on, combed carefully around the yarmulke that now replaced the beret above his huge, smiling face. Partly costumed, we gathered around John. He thanked us for last night's work, gave a few typically incisive, usable notes and dismissed us. The dressing rooms at this recently refurbished theatre were not connected to the stage, so most of the cast dressed in the same space where we had our notes and coffee under the stage.

Eric had strung curtains to give us privacy. There were mirrors and long tables and costume hooks for our magnificent clothes made of velvets and brocades that burdened the hangers and our bones. I guessed mine weighed over twenty pounds. The Venetian senators' and the Doge's costume —a work of art — weighed much more. I hesitated before dressing. A few more relatively cool minutes. Time for the fifteen-minute call. Arnold suggested we have some kind of a cast party after the evening performance. "We need to be together; we're a family." I said I would help him arrange it. Zero went to his dressing room, followed by Howard, to have a celery tonic. He gave me a wink.

The steady, low roar of the matinee audience on the intercom was interrupted by Brent's voice, but it did not say the familiar words. In fact, he did not seem to be talking to us over the loudspeaker. He began, "Ladies and gentlemen," which is how he addressed the company, but it sounded unusually formal. The voice continued: "We are terribly sorry, but due to Mr. Mostel's illness this afternoon's performance has been canceled." The audience fell silent.

Brent hurried backstage to explain that Zero was on his way to Jefferson Hospital. He had suddenly felt faint and terribly sick. A doctor was with him. We were asked to come back to the theatre for a rehearsal in place of the evening performance.

Outside the theatre Michael Higgins — who was playing at the Playhouse in the Park in *Equus* — waited to talk to me. He had no matinee and had bought a ticket. Like the rest of the audience he felt stunned and disappointed.

Zero stayed in the hospital for a day, went back to the Barclay for a day, returned to the hospital. We were told it was not serious, his electrocardiograph was good, all tests were good . . .

For four days John rehearsed the company with Zero's understudy, Joseph Leon, reading the part. A great deal of his attention was on the scene changes and staging. He expected Zero back for rehearsal on September 9. Encouraging reports were issued from his hospital room. The company sent notes and flowers. Sam Levene went to see him every day.

My friendship with Sam deepened in the following week. He talked to me about Zero, about his own career, about mine. Walking home from the long technical rehearsals, his doom-slanted opinions of the play made me laugh.

On the day before Zero was expected to be released, Sam took him some art books.

We were rehearsing, were dismissed for dinner, came back and took our places for the courtroom scene.

John stopped the rehearsal. He asked us to sit down on the stage.

"Zero is dead."

No one remembers what else he said. He talked in his deepest, most reassuring voice. He motioned for me and I went to him. "Go and find Sam." I obeyed. Sam was in the alley outside the stage door. We embraced. Sam had been in the room with Zero when he died. We stood in the alley and

Sam, wet-eyed but in control, told me what had happened:

Zero had sent Howard to Shore's restaurant, where most of the company dined that night, to find out how we were and to bring some food back to the hospital. Sam went to see Zero during the dinner break, gave him the art books and got the expected reaction: "I don't want to read anything serious." Sam offered to get him a copy of *Hustler*. Zero laughed and said it might arouse him. As they laughed together discussing the various nurses in attendance Zero said, "I feel dizzy — you better call a nurse." He reached out for the bell and pitched forward out of the bed. Sam thought he might strike his head on the night table and pulled it away. He tried to break Zero's fall but was unable to. He was lying on the floor when the nurses and doctor arrived to help him. They did everything they could as swiftly as possible. They performed surgery and inserted a pacemaker, but to no avail. They kept trying — for several hours — but he did not regain consciousness. His heart never beat again.

The questions that cannot be answered were asked. The empty, helpless, inadequate efforts to explain to oneself, to each other, what this loss meant — to Zero's family, to all those who loved him, and to this play. It was repeated that Zero would have wanted the play to continue. But that night was it seemly to project the possibility of this production with another Shylock?

In Sir John Clement's suite at the Barclay a group of us stayed together drinking wine and making telephone calls. The news of Zero's death had been announced on radio and television. The operator at the Barclay put through all *Merchant* calls to Sir John's number. On another extension he called his wife, the extraordinary comedienne Kay Ham-mond, to tell her of the event. Arnold called his wife. Julie Garfield called her mother. Repeating and repeating the unbelievable, the unacceptable truth.

At midnight the group broke up. Arnold, shattered, talked of Kate Mostel. All his plans were fragmented. We finished the wine and went to the elevators. "Well, Marian — we had our party."

I went to my room and, without planning to, packed everything in my suitcases, locked my typewriter, looked over some notes I had written the night before and went to bed.

The following day we met at the Forrest and John told the company we would go ahead with the production. Sam was going to leave; it was not possible for him to stay in Philadelphia any longer. We said good-bye tenderly. Perhaps we would work together in another play . . .

John and I walked up and down Walnut Street discussing possible recasting. What hurt John almost more than losing Zero as Shylock was the dissolution of their future plans. They had discussed Falstaff and Galileo and other major roles. John was as anxious to foster Zero's talent as he was those of the less experienced actors whose talent he respected. He wanted to create a theatre in which the actor could express himself through great playwriting. For a while we walked in silence, neither of us wanting to go back to the empty, sad forrest.

The Shuberts would decide on Sunday if we were to continue rehearsing on the set in Philadelphia or return to New York. The hotel list for our Washington engagement was on the callboard: "Please sign up at once!"

The technical crew received Xeroxed form letters stating that due to the death of the star, their employment was suspended . . .

I did not go back to the hotel. I packed my theatre things

in Eric's box; I had my manuscript and a copy of *The Merchant* with me. Eric went to his hotel, got his luggage and we bought tickets for the 7:45 P.M. Amtrak for New York . . .

Perhaps we would be called back for rehearsal on Monday. It did not matter, I wanted to get away. Some of the actors stayed and I made arrangements for my bags to be brought back to New York with them.

Three days later the company met in New York in a rehearsal studio. John announced to the newspapers that Joseph Leon would take over the part of Shylock and as soon as the gentlemen of the press had gone he would start rehearsing.

What does "protected" mean? When Arnold Wesker wrote his piece about the tryout of *The Merchant* in Philadelphia he described himself as "a protected playwright." Before the article could be set up in type the actor whom he envisaged in the part, whose fame had made the extravagant production plan feasible, whose career might well have grown into a new area of important action — Zero Mostel — had died.

The loss of Zero altered forever the fate of *The Merchant*. The expectation of the audiences to come, the dreams of the creative team connected with the play from its inception, the atmosphere in the surrounding air — all were changed.

Everyone worked hard, tried too hard, perhaps. There were times when it appeared we would succeed in spite of the great blow. My notes for the two weeks of rerehearsing in New York and five weeks of playing at the Kennedy Center in Washington contain many optimistic, positive reactions.

273

Without shame I wrote of my pleasure in working happily and closely with John, of my joy as the scenes I played grew in reality and power, as my relationship with Arnold deepened. I had a sense of this play working and other plays to come in which we would reunite.

I could not have endured those weeks without hope, however feathery.

Joe Leon, too, must have existed in somewhat the same sort of protective dream. He worked tirelessly. The part was not cut down as we had expected; he had pages and pages to learn. John coached, cajoled, insulted, praised him. The company cheered him on. The audience loved him.

As always when a part has to be learned swiftly, compromises are made. The natural, true rhythms of the language are sacrificed for expediency. The same thing happened with Burton learning Dysart. He knew the lines, just as Joe knew Shylock's, but not *perfectly*.

After several weeks of playing Dysart, Richard wrote a letter to the company and posted it on the callboard. It was a humorous apology to those whom he had not yet "royally screwed up" onstage. He wondered if those who had been through "the fire of his disorientation" might suggest ways for him to "majestically screw up" the actors who had not as yet been affected. "You have all saved me at one time or other from beating off the flutter of angel's wings — I thank you all deeply . . ."

Nothing Richard did in *Equus* upset me because of the unique relationship of our characters — the trust, the love — and the echo of that relationship in our work.

One night as I returned to my place after a scene with Richard, he simply turned toward the front of the house and sang the lovely English madrigal, "There is a lady sweet and kind." Then he left the seventeenth century and went back to the text. Was it fair? Was it funny? No one seemed to care. He had changed *our* earth and sky and had beguiled us.

John asked Peter Shaffer to come to Washington. He saw a performance of *The Merchant* and talked to John and Arnold the following day. Not that evening. John had planned a small party for the actors in *The Merchant* who had played in *Equus* as well. Arnold joined us for a while, but John made it clear that this was to be an *Equus* night. Champagne, sandwiches, talk and laughter. The problems of our present play were put aside for an evening as we became increasingly merry, then outrageous.

John and Peter urged each other to tell stories of their early working times in England. Did John lock Peter in a dark room with a dog during the tryout of *Black Comedy* to force him to face certain problems of the nonseeing characters in that play? Was John as hopeless an actor as he described himself? What was true or even partly true did not matter. The release of laughter healed us and warmed us. With the subtlest cues from John I was suddenly, for the first time in years, back to my imitations as I acted out for Peter the trials and crazinesses of our weeks with Wesker's *Merchant*.

The champagne, the laughter, the energy released and shared, made the evening memorable.

Three days later, on October 2, 1977, a somewhat more formal party was given for *Equus* in New York. It was held at Charlie O's in Rockefeller Center where six months before the party to celebrate the thousandth performance had taken place. At that point the New York company had made $4,111,502. The first national tour with Brian Bedford had made $3,326,320, and a second company headed by Douglas Campbell and later Ken Howard had made $1,842,099. Now the play was closing in New York and the film was about to open.

The room was crowded. The cast, the replacements, the understudies, the crew, the production staff — all were represented. Kermit was eulogized, but John Dexter was not mentioned. Peter spoke feelingly about his play: "I wrote this play for myself and somewhere along the journey found that others were interested in it." So many memories fought for focus in my head — the sound of Peter's words and the power of John's staging always merging into one moment, one vision, one idea.

As I was leaving I thanked Doris and she asked me to wait. She brought out a package from Cartier for me to take to John in Washington. I told her I would be happy to deliver it and did so. With her message: "Tell him Cartier isn't open on Sunday . . . I got it some time ago."

It was an ornate antique magnifying glass. John opened it in my dressing room, improvised several obscene gestures with it. We talked about the party and then we talked about *The Merchant.*

"Had you any idea how good your part was when you took it?"

"Had you any idea how good it was when you offered it to me?"

"I *knew* the scene would work . . ." But he added, "You are . . ." He told me what I wanted to hear and instead of encouraging him I tried to stop him. Even with John the sense of not being all that I want to be overwhelmed me. He talked about my contribution as a teacher, too. Safer ground. "And, if when you were young, what you could have done with Jessica."

276   Dreams.

The next day, reality. John's next project: *King Lear,* with Richard Burton. As casually as he had offered me Shylock's sister, Rivka, he offered me Lear's daughter Goneril. Less casually, I accepted.

Then back to talking of *Merchant* problems. The cuts. The producers say they will not open the play in New York if a half hour is not cut. The cuts so far have *not* shortened the running time. Must John risk his friendship with Arnold to get the play in shape?

I knew the play must be cut, but my loyalty to the text made me disapprove of others' tampering with it. I knew John's staging could not overcome the overlong sections of text without a company of genius actors to fulfill his tasks. The actors needed more help and time and there was not enough of either.

The Merchant made me a divided person.

Arnold flew to England. John went to New York to stage *Rigoletto* for the Metropolitan. Then five more rehearsals and seven more performances before the first New York preview.

John to Joe Leon: "Your apprenticeship is over. You are now in the big leagues! You can't let anything slip by you. Every time you decorate a word with your hand you should be doing it with your voice." He included the company: "Shape. Phrase. Speak. You have to have hair-trigger minds. If I seem fierce it is only because I am angry at myself for having to be away."

The play had been criticized for being unclear. "*You* must make it clear. You won't get words like these for many a season. Show me the shapes of the ideas. I don't care if *you* believe in the character or the scene. It is your job to make *me* believe it."

The company rehearsed that day with energy and passion.   277

The performance went well. The play was ten minutes shorter. The Shuberts came and were pleased. My last note in Washington: "Company morale is wonderful. A feeling that the play will live."

I flew to New York with Roberta. At La Guardia she got on a plane to Toronto; her father was ill. She would miss the Monday line rehearsal. If all went well her father would be strong enough to come to the opening night at the Plymouth Theatre.

At the previews, the audience response was appreciative. Hopes rose again. The cuts put in a week before in Washington had been absorbed. The playing time was two hours and fifteen minutes. Friends came backstage and prophesied success.

My *Equus* dressing room was mine again. It was exactly the same. Arnold came in after the final preview.

"Unhappy?"

"No. Not really." But he looked sad.

"What is it? The play has never gone as well. Is it that —"

"— it will be good for the actors."

"— but not for your play?"

"Yes."

After five performances on Broadway *The Merchant* closed. One day it will have an ensemble, a company, that has faith in it and it will live again. The experience in New York production was costly in every way: life, money, time, relationships.

Roberta, looking solemn and radiantly lovely in her Portia costume, said good-bye. "I wouldn't have missed any of it. Would you, Marian?"

278   "No. Not *any*. Not even the worst times. Is it the same

for you?" Her look mixed happiness and disappointment in a way that wrenched my feelings.

"Yes. It is the same."

My theatre life began with an illusion — a figure moving in a mirror that caught my eye and mind and heart because it seemed more interesting than the actual person being reflected.

My theatre work has been to translate illusion into reality. First for myself and eventually for the audience. In acting and teaching it has been to discover the actor's problem and to attempt to solve it, to free the imagination so that a group of people — including an audience — is free to exist really in an illusory world.

The theatre did not attract me as a mecca of glamour, money or fame but as a place to work at what I loved.

As a child I believed that if you worked hard and well you would succeed. I have learned that this is not always true and no longer expect it to be. And yet . . .

If as Max Beerbohm assured us failure is more interesting than success, I will not have to apologize for the lack of descriptions of gala opening nights, batches of ecstatic reviews, references to glamorous liaisons in my working life. The years I have written about — four decades in the New York theatre — were rich ones in terms of accomplishment. I was fortunate to be connected with some of the most gifted artists who illuminated those years with their dazzling talents.

I did not comprehend my mother when she told me not to expect happiness. I did not want to hear her prophecy: "Oh, you can work for it, pursue it — yes — but don't expect it." I looked for happiness in others' lives. In the novels and biographies in my father's study. In my friends, my teachers and later on in my colleagues. Then toward the end of a performance of *The Trojan Women* at school I heard Cassandra's words: "*Oh, world of men, what is your happiness? A painted show. Comes sorrow and the touch, a wet sponge, blots the painting out. And this moves pity, sadder still than death.*"

How many years of living does it take us to face the Cassandra truth about our lives? Theatres fill up year after year with people searching for answers to the great questions about living and dying. They find in Billie Dawn and Willy Loman and Blanche DuBois, in Oedipus and Hamlet and Saint Joan, the beautiful uniqueness of each human being.

We go to the theatre to find moments that are perfect beyond dreaming — even if they are a part of someone else's life — knowing that in that place of wonder we will be able to relate all that happens to an imaginary character (showgirl, salesman, southern belle, king, prince, saint) to our own humanness.

Katharsis: thus the Greeks called the state of mind produced by the spectacle of tragedy, the stillness of heart in which compassion and fear have been dissolved, the purification of the soul which springs from having grasped a deeper meaning in things; which creates a grave and new preparedness for acts of duty and the acceptance of fate; which breaks the *hybris* as it was seen to be broken in the tragedy; which liberates from the violent passions of life and leads the soul to peace.

I found this in J. Huizinga's *In The Shadow of Tomorrow*, a book my father urged me to read in the last conversation I had with him.

His final gift, for which I have never been able to thank him.

And Then

When *The Bright Lights* was published, it had no formal dedication other than a sentence of Gertrude Stein's that is still on the fly leaf. I wish that I had been courageous enough to dedicate this book to my father. He died before I began to be published and the next book I wrote, a novel, I dedicated to my daughter.

Readers asked me why I had not written more about my family in this book. My family is in my fiction, where I have used them shamelessly to tell my stories. But *The Bright Lights* was to be a book about my discoveries of theatre living. Seven years have passed since I started to write it and now I must choose what to add, not what to rearrange or change.

I am writing in a new room. The building on East 57th Street where I lived for so long will be torn down to make way for a modern money-making structure. A small group of tenents banded together to try to save it at the same time the members of the theatre community were fighting to save their favorite Broadway theatres.

The Helen Hayes Theatre, The Morosco, have gone. The Plymouth, where *Equus* began, has had a happier fate. 281

When its auditorium embraced the *Nicholas Nickleby* cast, I was able to cross the street from the Music Box and see long sections of that marvelous marathon. A company of actors transforming a space I knew so well into a complete and wonderful Dickensian world.

The theatre has suffered great losses. Tennessee Williams is dead. And the beautiful Lynn Fontanne. On the July night of her death we planned to dedicate the performance of *Richard III* to her memory. The large cast gathered in Central Park, the audience too. But it rained, dispersing us all, and the rain poured down for those hours on an empty stage. For Williams the tributes—starting with Jessica Tandy's heartrendering performance of a scene from *A Streetcar Named Desire* at his memorial—will continue. Each revival of his plays will be an acknowledgment of his talent and our loss.

My move to the West Side has brought me nearer my work. Juilliard is a short walk, the theatres a longer one; and on the way there is a pool. I now swim every day, and on my way home from swimming or working, the markets and fruit stands are open. I have, at last, cultivated a real interest in shopping for and preparing food.

The health and strength of my life go into my work. I say to my students: "Take care of yourselves." They will find out that while their work seems to summon all their energies, life will ask for more. The heart breaks and is mended, the mind sleeps and wakes, the days and nights demand all that we have to give. Take care, there is always more to learn, to use, to share. That is the mixture that makes a theatre life into a real one.

Early in February in 1978, the city of Boston was covered in snow. There was no electricity, no traffic, no sounds. There is a silence in the theatre filled with expectation. The audience and the actors are still. It can last a moment but seem to last an eternity. When the silence is broken, the stillness jarred, a connection is made that is as strong as the clasp of a hand, as startling as a shout of joy. Nothing shattered the silence of the snow. This must have been how the Common looked before our time. This was the way daylight broke and night came to Beacon Street. Here was peace within the heart of a city, and in the center of this silence I pencilled in the final corrections of the galleys of my first book.

Ira Levin's *Deathtrap* opened after a seamless dress rehearsal and played eleven performances before the snow began. Monday Tuesday Wednesday Thursday were white days. At night my hotel room was lit by candles, the electric typewriter sat unused on the desk. By telephone I reached Jonathan Galassi in New York. I wanted his eye but had only his ear. As editor, he had guided me with care and insight from our first meeting at the Algonquin Hotel two years before. Now from another hotel in another city I sought his judgment. The last time we had been able to meet was between *Deathtrap* rehearsals in New York. He had told me we needed several hours. Where to meet? Sardi's. It was a Tuesday afternoon and Vincent gave us a table upstairs. I had coffee, Jonathan nothing. We worked and the waiters waited.

At length the snow blackened and melted. The noises of the city returned, the theatre reopened. *Deathtrap* completed its tryout and went to Broadway where it played for five years.

At one time the working title of this book was *A Long Run*. I was in *Equus* and the phenomenon of coming to the theatre week after week, month after month, and then year after year, was important and worth noting. Then came *The Merchant*. It closed in the week it opened. Then *Deathtrap*. I stayed with it from its first to final performance. As the cast changed I had the opportunity of working with a large group of splendid 283 professionals, and playing Myra Bruhl for so long gave me more than pleasure, it gave me confidence and security.

I had never been to London. Less than two months after the play closed, I was on the Queen Elizabeth II. I wanted to sail there on a great ship and this one had been refurbished after the Falkland Islands conflict. It was a thirteen-deck-high floating city, larger than three playing fields of Eton.

I prepared for my trip by studying maps and books, by asking questions, making lists. On the ship I read Boswell's *London Journal* every day and kept a journal of my own.

We arrived on Bank Holiday. Another quiet city. I sat in the front seat of a double-decker bus and toured streets and avenues that I had glimpsed in the twilight the night before. The buildings I had stared at from the speeding car from Southampton at dusk were now gleaming in the sun. I made a new list and followed it to Hampstead to visit Keat's house. I walked through his rooms—all of them—and the place was holy. Until I heard a harsh voice address, not me, but a young boy: "Come *on!* Pick up your feet and look at the relics." No one ordered me to do anything. I was free to stare, to glance, to examine everything in the city. I never got tired. I went to Dr. Johnson's house. I was the only visitor. I touched his table, his chair. At Dickens's house I saw the desk where he wrote *Nicholas Nickleby.* Once again I was quite alone. The only time I encountered a crowd was at the Tower of London. I stood in line for a time, went in, roamed through that chamber of horrors but did not stay to see the jewels. The place oppressed me. Would I have stayed longer and studied more if I had even the vaguest premonition that a year later I would be playing Queen Margaret? In Central Park our Tower was an imaginary one, existing in the wings of the stage. I had a real one in my actor's eye.

284   In London I saw sixteen plays: three by Shakespeare,

one by Coward, two by young women, two musicals based on American themes, a Chekhov, an Ibsen, three comedies, and five plays dealing with man's hunger to live life more fully. I knew that when I came home I would be asked which I thought was best. I had no answer. Part of the miracle of this first trip so late in my life was the wondrous feeling of seeing theatre for the first time, of not having to have an opinion, of simply becoming part of each performance as I had when I was a child and went to plays with my parents. London restored an innocence to my head and heart.

I walked through Gray's Inn, where my father and uncle lived in 1916. I stood outside what was once their window. On my list were all the places they had lived. It was too far to go to Penzance or Land's End in Cornwall. But I did see Land's End—and Cornwall and the sweetness of the country-side—in the Tate and The National Gallery and every other museum that was open during my less-than-two-week stay. I bought hundreds of postcards and look at them now. How odd to have seen at last the actual paintings that I have loved in reproductions and to buy small reproductions of them, to remind me once again.

Nothing prepared me for the impact of the Elgin Marbles. In the vast room they hang suspended in time and space, yet it is possible to move close to touch them. There was only one frieze I could not get near, because I could not bear to cross the gaze of a man who sat before it. He was alone in the room, staring at the horses in a procession at the Panathenaic festival. I looked at him and he became the character and all the actors who had played Dr. Martin Dysart in *Equus*. He did not move; he did not seem to blink. He became part of my memory of the marbles.

I was visiting friends in the country the day Ingrid Bergman died. My friends were her friends and mourned her not only 285 as a screen star but a stage actress. The following day, walking past Sir Thomas More's Chapel, past the house where Henry James died, to the western end of Chelsea, I saw the house where she lived. Outside her private door huddled a group of fans and photographers waiting for something more to happen to remind them of her. One more picture, one more memory of her, to tell their friends about. I walked on to Cheyne Gardens, past flats where Chopin played, where Tennyson came to call, where Rossetti had his studio. Rossetti had a wombat and a bull and peacocks in his garden. Later, the leases for these flats contained a clause stating there were to be none of these birds about. Rossetti's peacocks screamed in the night.

On my last day, outside of Westminster Abbey, I saw a badly crippled man coming toward me and knew he was going to speak. He said I had a smiling face, I told him I loved his city. He looked at me intently but it did not seem that he was going to speak again. I walked on and then I heard him call. I moved quickly so that he would not have so far to walk.

"Do you pray?" he said.

"Sometimes."

"Will you pray for me? On Monday I get m'legs amputated."

I tried not to gasp. "I'll pray for you," I said. "What's your name?"

"Mark."

"I'm Marian."

"Don't forget, then. Monday." At exactly the same moment we grabbed each other's shoulders in an awkward, very strong embrace.

Boswell said that he was going to put down all sorts of little incidents in his London diary. Samuel Johnson told him: "There is nothing too little for so little a creature as man. It is by studying little things that we attain the great knowledge of having as little misery and as much happiness as possible."

After thirteen days I flew home. The Juilliard year began and so did my search for a new play. Interviews. Auditions. For every bright encounter with theatre professionals, there have been others so time-wasting and sad they do not merit recording. I tried to get the rights to a play in London and my search led me to tea with a fascinating literary agent, to talks with theatre managers and directors. It was exhilarating even though I did not succeed. But so often we have to read what is basically trash, be interviewed by fools and bear the embarrassment of pretending that the exercise is worthwhile. We have to learn how to behave in the circumstances.

When *Medea* had just opened and Florence Reed was enjoying her greatest success since *The Shanghai Gesture,* we used to meet and have tea at her home in the Windsor Hotel. She was crazy about Richard Boone, and so this great star entertained the spear carrier and the serving-woman. Miss Reed had a rumbling laugh and laughed often. She dressed in rich fabrics and wore gold jewelry as if her cue to enter the stage were about to be given.

Once, costumed that way, her bracelets gleaming and her dark eyes outlined in kohl, I saw her in the waiting room of the East Coast Twentieth Century Fox studio. The tiled walls and carpets were gaudy with color, a perfect setting for this most theatrical os actresses. For over an hour she sat while actors with little or no experience were called to the receptionist's desk. I blushed when I heard my name. Instead of giving my résumé, I explained who Miss Reed was and an impersonal voice assured me that the "Shanghai woman" would be called next.

I do not know if Florence Reed made a screen test for *The Robe.* When it was released years later, she was not in it and 287 neither was I.

She taught me how to behave in a waiting room.

Ira Levin's twisting, brilliantly funny, frightening mystery play lasted long enough for my name to be placed above the title. Jeffrey Richards who handled the press relations when I played Isadora Duncan was now with *Deathtrap.* He saw to it that I was interviewed thoughout the run. He called me Star. Before a matinee he told me that Alfred DeLiagre, our distinguished producer, was coming to my dressing room. Jeffrey stood aside, Delly came in and sat down, took an envelope out of his pocket and gave it to me. It was the proof of a press release dated September 23, 1981, and it said (I am quoting) A STAR IS BORN.

Where is my father? Where is Katharine Cornell? What real meaning did this piece of paper have? Jeffrey was laughing with pleasure and kept repeating, "The first time! The first time!" I did not have the heart to interrupt and say it was the *third* time. The first was when I played Rachel in *The Wall,* the second, during the brief run of *Before You Go.* But now it was to be there (after a lapse of many weeks and a move to the Biltmore Theatre, where a new sign had to be painted) above the name of a *hit.* I do not think an actor's name belongs above a playwright's unless that actor can bring the audience to the theatre. My name brings *me* to the theatre. One thousand eighty-nine times for the dazzling *Deathtrap.*

In many interviews I've been asked why I stayed in the play for so long. The simplest, most honest, answer would have been to present a list of the people connected with it. Ira, who was truly faithful to his play—I wonder how many performances of it he saw? More than most directors or authors. The stage managers who rehearsed the standbys, and the understudies who all eventually appeared on stage. The original director, Robert Moore, whose taste and timing are infallible and whose pattern we followed and trusted, and the actors: John Wood, Victor Garber, Marian Winters, Richard Woods, Stacy Keach, Patrick Horgan, John Cullum, Robert Reed, Farley Granger, Darren Kelly, Elizabeth Parrish, Willliam LeMassena. The audience saw us in a setting designed by William Ritman that was so inviting we were often asked where to find such curtains, chairs, and above all, the massive partner's desk.

If the *Equus* family was close, imagine how strong the emotional ties were in this company. The gentle, wise woman who took care of our costumes, Marianna Torres, read the pages of my novel as I finished typing them in my dressing room/ workroom. The title was *Grown Up Games.* Even after it was published as *Time Together,* Marianna called it "Games."

The crew, the ushers, the staff in the box office loved having the play in the Music Box. The theatre, which was built by Irving Berlin, had a true family connection for me. When we were young, my brother and I, visiting the Berlins in Livingstone Manor was the highpoint of the summer. And when my parents were young their friendship with Ellin and Irving had the glow of the 1920s the way people want to remember that era. After Ellin saw a matinee, she took me home in her luxurious car and talked of Gilbert and Amanda. Her voice saying their names made them come alive.

One morning I found a note in my letter box at Juilliard from Elizabeth McGovern describing a play she had read, urging me to read it. *Painting Churches* by Tina Howe. I read it and loved it and craved the part of Fanny Church. I was chosen and played it with Donald Moffat and Frances Conroy for The Second Stage in a five-week run at a small theatre on 42nd Street, in February 1982. Another family. A small one. Three intensely complicated characters. Tina's family became mine and will again. After the joy of playing Shakespeare with   289

Kevin Kline—a strong, virile and witty Richard III—I am planning to meet with the two actors who will become the Churches in a new production. Donald and Frances are already at work on other projects. George Martin will be the father and Elizabeth McGovern, who is famous for her work in *Ordinary People* and *Ragtime* but dear to me as a student playing Iras in *Antony and Cleopatra,* will be the daughter. Our rehearsals have been postponed for two weeks because Carole Rothman, the director who made the play live in its first incarnation, has just had her first child. The son that was with her during rehearsals last year will wait for her at home now while she orchestrates the play T. E. Kalem said in *Time* magazine "is Chekhovian in tone—with the same edgy surface of false hilarity, the same unutterable sadness beneath it, and the indomitable valor beneath both."

I study my part—all of it—every morning before the rest of the day begins.

It is August 23, 1983. Thinking about this part of my book, walking home from swimming early in the morning, I saw a neightbor across the street. He looked at me but did not seem to see me or the traffic. When we met on the sidewalk he said, "I was *dreaming* there."

I dream while I swim and while I cook. Both activities are nearly silent. I hear the voices of the bathers in the locker room. I put on my plain suit and goggles and cap and an anonymous thin human fish goes into the water, swims, dreams, comes out, returns to the real world and sees a neighbor on the street. In the kitchen, there is immense concentration. Follow the recipe, dare to adapt it to my taste, time it, serve it, eat it—and dream again. The next meal, the next swim, the next play, the next book.